USE
ENOUGH
GUN

ROBERT RUARK
On Hunting Big Game

USE
ENOUGH
GUN

WITH DRAWINGS BY THE AUTHOR
EDITED BY STUART ROSE

The New American Library

First Printing

Published by The New American Library of World Literature, Inc.
1301 Avenue of the Americas, New York, New York 10019
Published simultaneously in Canada by General Publishing Company, Ltd.

Library of Congress Catalog Card Number: 66–28647

Printed in the United States of America

CONTENTS

LIST OF ILLUSTRATIONS

facing page 160

INTRODUCTION:
The Bwana
by Eva Monley

JAMBO LITTLE MEM . . . . 5 A.M. and another safari day . . . . hot coffee over a low fire, snowcapped Kilimanjaro—the Northern Frontier Plains—dry arid Mozambique—the same greeting wherever, whenever . . .

It was worth flying in for from every corner of the earth, from Jordan where we were making *Lawrence of Arabia* to Nairobi, Kenya, or from Hawaii where it was *In Harms Way* to Beira Mozambique.

Robert Ruark, or "The Bwana ' as he was called, was always there, waving at the airport, couldn't get into hunting clothes fast enough, out of town soon enough . . . the first campfire with all the real talk—sunsets and sunrises—tents or grass-roofed mudhuts—with the old elephant gun or the new .244.

There is something very special about going on safari. It's hot coffee or chilled red wine at the crack of dawn, it's riding in a Land Rover or Toyota hunting car and getting hot, dusty, and incredibly dirty, it's space space space to stretch your eyes, it's warm gin and cold guineafowl for lunch and a sleep under the nearest tree, it's miles and miles of tracking an elephant that turns out to have only one tusk, it's the good feeling of watching a perfect shot kill a trophy, the yell of "PIGS" and leaving a sable to hunt a pig, it's wounding something and following it no matter for how long to finish it off, it's staggering home to the campfire at sunset for that first unbelievably marvelous scotch on the rocks, it's the luxurious slow relaxing of all muscles and the slow start of the stories, it's the shower under a bucket with a chain, it's the quick martini before a hot delicious dinner of Tommy steak or broiled sandgrouse accompanied by good warm red or sparkling white wine, and then, finally, it's the last scotch with the last story over the dying fire and then to bed full of that warm, happy, secure feeling that there is always tomorrow.

But most important, it's the person you are with, and Bob Ruark, always the *bwana,* was the most perfect hunting companion in the world. He made me absolutely and completely aware of every minute of each and every day and made all of them worthwhile. His enthusiasm was fierce enough to be catching, so that I would sit numb and wet and cold for hours to finally watch him shoot a leopard in the rain, or help him whoop with pig-fever joy tearing across the bush over, under, and through everything to chase a magnificently betoothed warthog. Then there was always the good talk whether of books written or books yet to write, the last film script or the next column, the pure excitement of words words words—the complete understanding of long silences and the bragging over a "No. 1 good shoot" and the grim misery over wounding something.

His gift of sharing experiences made the good things better and the bad things less bad.

Safari isn't all guns. The no-hunting days are an important part of it all. The pure luxury of *not* being awakened at 5 A.M., of *not* having to climb into khakis, but easing into brilliantly colored kikois, late breakfast, and time to listen to the news. A lovely chance for a girl to be all girl and wash her hair and even have a home manicure. The bwana would sit and beat out his columns with two fingers, ready at any moment to stop and argue about anything interesting I might be reading in a three-week-old *Time* magazine. Pink gin time was way before noon and scotch time way before sunset. Somehow these occasional days became as important as the real hunting-hunting days, and one that stands out particularly in my memory was in Camp Ruark in Mozambique when after all the hair and sweater washing and a considerable amount of pink gin there was still time and sunlight, and the *bwana* decided to paint us onto the walls of our white-washed mudhut. He tried with his finger, then fingers, next a stick and finally, some guineafowl feathers— it was hilarious! I stood and made a shadow figure and he outlined me, then he stood and I outlined him, and then he worked for hours filling us in with scarlet roof paint. I am told by Baron von Alvensleben that we are still there.

I guess also still there is Wally Johnson our most favorite white hunter, who with his trackers, gunbearers, skinners, cook and campstaff formed an efficient team that took us to any place at any time to shoot any thing. He is a round, red-faced balding little man, indefatigable during the days of driving, tracking, or competing with the bwana at target shooting, indefatigable during the nights of story telling of the early Rhodesias, Mozambique, and South Africa.

All of these things are *safari* and all of these things combine to make the magic that is safari and that draws you back and back again.

EVA MONLEY, the daughter of English settlers and a Kenyan by birth, was a longtime friend of Ruark's and often his companion on safari. She is a movie director and wrote this appreciation of Robert Ruark as *"Bwana"* while on location in Louisiana.

The Editor

USE
ENOUGH
GUN

PART ONE

THE
GIFT
OF A
GUN

THE OLD MAN knows pretty near close to everything. And mostly he ain't painful with it. What I mean is that he went to Africa once when he was a kid, and he shot a tiger or two out in India, or so he says, and he was in a whole mess of wars here and yonder. But he can still tell you why the quail sleep at night in a tight circle or why the turkeys always fly uphill.

The Old Man ain't much to look at on the hoof. He's got big ears that flap out and a scrubby mustache with light yellow tobacco stains on it. He smokes a crook-stem pipe and he shoots an old pump gun that looks about as battered as he does. His pants wrinkle and he spits pretty straight in the way people used to spit when most grown men chewed Apple tobacco.

The thing I like best about the Old Man is that he's willing to talk about what he knows, and he never talks down to a kid, which is me, who wants to know things. When you are as old as the Old Man, you know a lot of things that you forgot you ever knew, because they've been a part of you so long. You forget that a young'un hasn't had as hard a start on the world as you did, and you don't bother to spread the information around. You forget that other people might be curious about what you already knew and forgot.

Like the other day when we called the dogs and the Old Man and I went out into the woods to see if there were any quail around. Turned out there were some quail around. Pete, who is the pointer, whirled around like he was crazy, and then he stuck his tail straight up in the air and settled down in a corner of the peafield as if he planned to spend the winter.

"I ain't shooting much these days," the Old Man said. "You'd better do it for me. Take my gun, and walk in past Pete now. Walk gentle, kick up the birds without making the dog nervous, and let's us see can you get one bird. Don't worry about the second bird. Just concentrate on the first one. You got to kill the first one before you can shoot the second one. It's what we call a rule of thumb. Suppose you try it to see if it works."

I walked in past Pete, and the birds came up like rockets on the Fourth, and I did what most people do at first. I shot at all of them, all at the same time. I fired both barrels and nothing dropped. At all.

I looked at the Old Man, and he looked back at me, kind of sorrowful. He shook his head, reached for his pipe, and made a great to-do about tamping down the tobacco and lighting it with a kitchen match.

"Son," he said. "I missed a lot of birds in my time, and will miss some more if I shoot at enough of them. But there is one thing I know that you might as well learn now. Nobody can kill the whole covey—not even if they shoot the birds on the ground running down a row in a cornfield. You got to shoot them one at a time."

The Old Man said we ought to give the dogs a little more time, because the birds wouldn't be moving as singles the very moment they hit and they left most of their body scent up in the air, anyhow; so why didn't we sit while he smoked his pipe and then we would go put up the singles. The Old Man said he didn't know what I would be when I grew up, and didn't care a lot, but he said I might as well learn to respect quail, if only for practice in the respect of people.

This little bobwhite, the Old Man told me, was a gentleman, and you had to approach him as gentleman to gentleman. You had to cherish him and look after him and make him very important in his own right, because there weren't many of him around and he was worthy of respectful shooting. The way you handled quail sort of kicked back on you.

Figure it this way, the Old Man said. A covey of quail is a member of your family. You treat it right, and it stays there with you for all the years you live. It works in and around your garden, and it eats the bugs and it whistles every evening and cheers you up. It keeps your dogs happy, because they've got something to play with; and when you shoot it you shoot it just so many, and then you don't shoot it any more that year, because you got to leave some seed birds to breed you a new covey for next year. There ain't nothing as nice as taking the gun down off the hook and calling up the dogs and going out to look for a covey of quail you got a real good chance to find, the Old Man said. The little fellow doesn't weigh but about five ounces, but every ounce of him is pure class. He's smart as a whip, and every time you go up against him you're proving something about yourself.

I never knew a man that hunted quail that didn't come out of it a little politer by comparison, the Old Man said. Associating with gentlemen can't hurt you. If you intend to hunt quail, you have to keep remembering things—like, well, like you can't shoot rabbits in front of the dog, or you'll take his mind off the quail.

And then you have to worry about the dogs some, too. A dog that won't backstand a point—"honor it" is the word—a dog that won't concede to another dog is a useless dog, and you might as well shoot him. One of the troubles with the world is that everybody is crowding and pushing and shoving, and if your dog hasn't got any manners he hasn't got any real right to be a dog.

The same way with a dog that chases rabbits. If he's a hound, let him go chase rabbits. But a setter dog or a pointer dog hasn't got any right to indulge himself in chasing rabbits. It is what the people in Washington call a nonessential luxury. A dog or a man has got to do what he has got to do to earn his keep, and he has got to do it right.

The Old Man smiled and sucked at his pipe. "I mind well a little setter bitch named Lou," he said. "Belonged to an old friend of mine named Joe Hesketh. She was about as dumb a bitch as ever I saw in the field. But she was loyal. She was real loyal. She was a backstanding kind of bitch.

"Joe's real bird-finding dog was a big old Gordon setter who was as black as your hat. He was named Jet. He looked like a charred stump when he pointed a bird. He was as stanch as a stump and as black as a stump. So Lou spent her whole life pointing stumps. You would walk through the broom grass in the savannas, and there was poor old Lou, froze solid on a burnt stump. There wasn't much Lou could do except backstand, but that was the backstandingest bitch I ever saw. She made a career out of it and never got to hate it. Her eyes failed her finally, and she got killed. She backstood a fireplug in the middle of a busy street, and she wouldn't break her point for an automobile that was coming along in a hurry."

The Old Man smiled some more, in the gentle, evil way he had, and made a new essay for himself.

"Fellow can learn a lot about living from watching dogs," he said. "Like about snakes and terrapins. The best bird dog in the world will point a terrapin, and he will point a snake. But he won't back off from a terrapin. He will point a snake and walk backward away from it. This is what the dog would call a public service. But when a good bird dog points a rabbit, he cocks his ears peculiar and looks over his shoulder at you with a real guilty look, like he was stealing an apple from the fruitstand, and you know he expects a licking. He knows. He knows it just as he knows it when he gets himself all roused up and runs through a covey of birds. Or when he hard-mouths a dead bird when he knows it's wrong. Never underestimate a dog. If he's got sense enough to be bred from a family with a nose and a sense of decency, any mistake you let him make is *your* fault."

The Old Man said that he had kind of gotten off the subject of quail, which is a way he has of explaining that even an old man can get wrought up, and then he came back to the original subject. He said that any man with brains would never change a covey of quail from the original acre that they loved to live in.

The quail is a member of the family, the Old Man said again. He expects to get fed, like any other member of the family. So you plant him some field peas or some ground peas or some lespedeza or something, and you leave it there for him to eat. You plant it close to a place he can fly to hide in. A bobwhite is pretty well set in his habits. He will walk off from where he roosted, but he likes to fly home. It is a damned shame, the Old Man said, that the human race wouldn't take a tip from this.

But there is a stupid thing about quail like there is about people, the Old Man said. He won't let well enough alone. He starts a war and puts himself out of business just like we do, which is why we have wars and famines and even game laws, which I am basically in favor of, because they keep people and birds careful. If you don't lay the law of sound economics on a quail bird, he will start fights in the family and inbreed himself, and eventually he will kill himself off. The cock birds fight and the hen birds cannibalize the eggs, and all of a sudden where you had birds there ain't any.

This is no good for anybody, including the birds, the bugs, and you. Not to mention the dogs. So you shoot 'em down to a reasonable minimum each year. Let's say there is a covey of twenty. You shoot 'em down to half. The foxes will get some and wild tame-cats will get some more, and of the two clutches they try to hatch that year the weather will get one. But if you cherish 'em enough and don't get greedy, you can keep them in the back yard forever.

Just before I met your grandmother, the Old Man said, I dug into a place down South and I was interested in dogs. I lived there thirty years, and I trained all the dogs that I owned on the same covey of birds in the same back yard. While I trained the dogs I trained some young'uns, too.

This used to be called *laissez faire* by the French. I trained the birds to stay close to the house. I trained the dogs to be polite to the birds in the nesting season. I trained the children to be polite to the dogs while the dogs were being polite to the birds. I never shot over these birds more than three times a year, and I never shot more than three out of the covey at once. And I never shot the covey down to less than 50 per cent. And I planted the food for them all the time, the Old Man said. They were guests in the house, so to speak.

There's a lot I could tell you about birds, the Old Man said, but I find I'm talking too much lately. If you can remember to take your time and never shoot at the whole covey, if you can remember to keep them fed right, and if you can remember to make your dogs respect the birds—well, hell, the Old Man said, what I just delivered was a sermon about respect. I can say that it will cover most situations, whether it's bobwhite, dogs, or people.

"This ain't a very expensive gun," the Old Man said. "It's not a handmade gun, and it hasn't got any fancy engraving on it. But it'll shoot where you hold her, and if you hold her true she'll kill what you're aiming at. Some day when you go to work and get rich, you can take a trip to England and buy yourself a pair of matched doubles, or you can get a special job built in this country with a lot of gold bird dogs on it. But for you to learn to shoot with, this is all the gun you need right now."

It was maybe the most beautiful gun a boy ever had, especially if he was only eight years old at the time and the Old Man had decided he could be trusted with a dangerous firearm. A little 20-gauge, it was only a twenty-dollar gun, but twenty dollars was a lot of money in those days and you could buy an awful lot with it.

The Old Man stuffed his pipe and stuck it under his mustache, and sort of cocked his big stick-out ears at me, like a setter dog looking at a rabbit he ain't supposed to recognize socially.

(26)

Use Enough Gun

"In a minute," he said, "I aim to whistle up the dogs and let you use this thing the best way you can. But before we get out to the woods I want to tell you one thing: you have got my reputation in your hands right now. Your mother thinks I'm a damned old idiot to give a shirt-tail boy a gun that is just about as tall as the boy is. I told her I'd be personally responsible for you and the gun and the way you use it. I told her that any time a boy is ready to learn about guns is the time he's ready, no matter how young he is, and you can't start too young to learn how to be careful. What you got in your hands is a dangerous weapon. It can kill you, or kill me, or kill a dog. You always got to remember that when the gun is loaded it makes a potential killer out of the man that's handling it. Don't you ever forget it."

I said I wouldn't forget it. I never did forget it.

The Old Man put on his hat and whistled for Frank and Sandy. We walked out back of the house where the tame covey was. It was a nice November day, with the sun warm and the breeze not too stiff, and still some gold and red left in the leaves. We came to a fence, a low barbed-wire fence, and I climbed it, holding the gun high up with one hand and gripping the fence post with the other. I was halfway over when the barbed wire sort of caught in the crotch of my pants and the Old Man hollered.

"Whoa!" the Old Man said. "Now, ain't you a silly sight, stuck on a bob-wire fence with a gun waving around in the breeze and one foot in the air and the other foot on a piece of limber wire?"

"I guess I am, at that," I said.

"I'm going to be pretty naggy at you for a while," the Old Man said. "When you do it wrong, I'm going to call you. I know you haven't loaded the gun yet, and that no matter what happens nobody is going to get shot because you decide to climb a fence with a gun in your hand. But if you make a habit of it, someday you'll climb one with the loads in the gun and your foot'll slip and the trigger'll catch in the bob-wire and the gun'll go off and shoot you or me or somebody else, and then it'll be too late to be sorry.

"There's a lot of fences around woods and fields," he said. "You'll be crossing fences for the rest of your life. You might as well start now to do it right. When you climb a fence, you lay the gun on the ground, under the fence, with the safety on, ten foot away from where you intend to cross the fence. You got the muzzle sticking in the opposite direction from where you're going. After you've crossed the fence you go back and pick up the gun, and look at it to see if the safety is still on. You make a habit of this, too. It don't cost nothing to look once in a while and see if the safety's on."

We walked on for a spell until we hit the corner of the corn-field. Old Sandy, the lemon-and-white setter, was sailing around with his nose in the air, taking the outside edge, and Frank, who was pretty old and slow, was making some serious game with his nose on the ground. In a minute Sandy got a message and went off at a dead gallop. He pulled up in full stride and froze by a clump of gallberry bushes. Frank picked up a little speed on the trail and headed up to Sandy. He raised his head once and saw Sandy on the point and stood him stiff and pretty. Maybe you've seen prettier pictures. I haven't.

"Can I really shoot it now?" I said.

"Load her up," the Old Man said. "Then walk in, and when the birds get up pick out one and shoot him."

I loaded and walked up to the dogs and slipped off the safety catch. It made a little click that you could hardly hear. But the Old Man heard it.

"Whoa," he said. "Give me the gun."

I was mystified and my feelings were hurt, because it was *my* gun. The Old Man had given it to me, and now he was taking it away from me. He switched his pipe to the outboard corner of his mustache and walked in behind the dogs. He wasn't looking at the ground where the birds were. He was looking straight ahead of him, with the gun held across his body at a 45-degree angle. The birds got up, and the Old Man jumped the gun up. As it came up his thumb flicked the safety off and the gun came smooth up under his chin and he seemed to fire the second it got

Use Enough Gun

there. About twenty-five yards out a bird dropped in a shower of feathers.

"Fetch," the Old Man said, unloading the other shell.

"Why'd you take the gun away from me?" I yelled. I was mad as a wet hen. "Dammit, it's my gun. It ain't your gun."

"You ain't old enough to cuss yet," the Old Man said. "Cussing is a prerogative for adults. You got to earn the right to cuss, like you got to earn the right to do most things. Cussing is for emphasis. When every other word is a swear word it just gets to be dull and don't mean anything any more. I'll tell you why I took the gun away from you. You'll never forget it, will you?"

"You bet I won't forget it," I said, still mad and about to cry.

"I told you I was going to nag you some, if only to satisfy your mother. This is part of the course. You'll never walk into a covey of birds or anything else any more without remembering the day I took your new gun away from you."

"I don't even know why you took it," I said. "What'd I do wrong then?"

"Safety catch," he said. "No reason in the world for a man to go blundering around with the catch off his gun. You don't know the birds are going to get up where the dog says they are. Maybe they're running on you. So the dog breaks point and you stumble along behind him and fall in a hole or trip over a rock and the gun goes off—blooey."

"You got to take it off some time if you're planning to shoot something," I said.

"Habit is a wonderful thing," the Old Man said. "It's just as easy to form good ones as it is to make bad ones. Once they're made, they stick. There's no earthly use of slipping the safety off a gun until you're figuring to shoot it. There's plenty of time to slip it off while she's coming to your shoulder after the birds are up. Shooting a shotgun is all reflexes, anyhow.

"The way you shoot it is simply this: You carry her across your body, pointing away from the man you're shooting with. You look straight ahead. When the birds get up, you look at a bird. Then your reflexes work. The gun comes up under your eye, and while it's coming up, your thumb slips the safety and your finger goes to the trigger, and when your eye's on the bird and your finger's on the trigger the gun just goes off and the bird drops. It is every bit as simple as that if you start at it right. Try it a few times and snap her dry at a pine cone or something."

I threw the gun up and snapped. The gun went off with a horrid roar and scared me so bad I dropped it on the ground.

"Uh huh," the Old Man said sarcastically. "I thought you might have enough savvy to check the breech and see if she was loaded before you dry-fired her. If you had, you'd have seen that I slipped that shell back when you weren't looking. You mighta shot me or one of the dogs, just taking things for granted."

That ended the first lesson. I'm a lot older now, of course, but I never forgot the Old Man taking the gun away and then palming that shell and slipping it back in the gun to teach me caution. All the words in the world wouldn't have equaled the object lesson he taught me just by those two or three things. And he said another thing as we went back to the house: "The older you get, the carefuller you'll be. When you're as old as I am, you'll be so scared of a firearm that every young man you know will call you a damned old maid. But damned old maids don't shoot the heads off their friends in duck blinds or fire blind into a bush where a deer walked in and then go pick up their best buddy with a hole in his chest."

We went back to the house and up to the Old Man's room. He stirred up the fire and reached into a closet and brought out a bottle of old corn liquor. He poured himself half a glassful and sipped at it. He smacked his lips.

"Long as we're on the subject," he said, "when you get bigger, I suppose you'll start to smoke and drink this stuff. Most people do. You might remember that nobody ever got hurt with a gun if he saved his drinking for the fireside after the day's hunt was over, with the guns cleaned and in a rack or in a case. I notice you ain't broken your gun yet, let alone clean it, and it's standing in a corner for a child to get ahold of or a dog to knock over. I suggest you clean her now. That way you know there aren't any shells left in her. That way she don't rust. And since you have to break her to clean her, you might as well put her in her case."

Maybe you think the Old Man was cranky, because I did then, but I don't any more. I've seen just about everything happen with a gun. One fellow I know used to stand like Dan'l Boone with his hands crossed on the muzzle of his shotgun, and one day something mysterious happened and the gun went off and now he hasn't got any hands any more, which makes it inconvenient for him.

I've seen drunks messing with "unloaded" guns and the guns go off in the house, sobering everybody up. An automatic went crazy on me in a duck blind one day and fired every shot in its magazine. Habit had the gun pointed away from the other fellow, or I'd of shot his head off with a gun that was leaping like a crazy fire hose. I saw a man shoot his foot nearly off with a rifle he thought he'd ejected all the cartridges out of. I saw another man on a deer hunt fire into a bush a buck went into and make a widow out of his best friend's wife.

The Old Man nagged at me and hacked at me for about three years. One time I forgot and climbed a fence with a loaded gun, and he took a stick to me.

"You ain't too big to be beat," he said, "if you ain't adult enough to remember what I told you about guns and fences. This'll hurt your feelings, even if it don't hurt your hide."

When I was eleven, the Old Man stole my little 20-gauge from me. He grinned sort of evilly and announced that he was an Indian giver in the best and strongest sense. I was puzzled, but not very, because the Old Man was a curious cuss and a kind of devious mover. I went back to my bedroom later, and on the bed was a 16-gauge double with a leather case that had my name on it. There were engravings of quail and dogs in silver on the sides and my name on the silver butt plate.

The Old Man was taking a drink for his nervous stomach when I busted into his room with the new gun clutched in my hands. He grinned over the glass.

"That there's your graduation .present," he said. "It's been three years since we started this business, and you ain't shot me, you, or the dogs. I figured it's safe to turn you loose now. But I'll take that one away from you if you get too big for your britches and start waving it around careless."

I'm big enough to cuss now, and I've seen a lot of silly damned fools misusing guns and scaring the daylights out of careful people. But they never had the Old Man for a tutor. Some people ain't as lucky as other people.

PART TWO

THE
FIRST
SAFARI

T H E *implementation of dreams rarely follows the script, but the endings sometimes turn out surprisingly well. I got into the seafaring business, and later the writing trade, and then into the war business, and then again into the writing trade. I never got rich or famous, but I got action. And I never stopped dreaming of lions.*

"For no reason at all, save a boyish dream and a twenty-year itch, I suddenly rigged my own safari to Kenya and Tanganyika. It was mine. Nobody sent me. I was paying for it myself. Nobody goes along but my wife and the white hunter and a company of African 'boys.' I refused to share the trip with anybody else, even though I had offers of plenty of company.

"There is not much personal adventure left in this world —not many boyhood dreams that lose nothing, but rather gain, by fulfillment. So I combined two dreams in one; I was on a safari and I was going to write about it."

The seafaring business happened after he graduated from college in 1935. He got the job because he'd fought the ship's first mate to a standstill. He was the only college man on board, so they called him "the Duke." By the time he signed off in Norfolk, Virginia, six months later, it was "the Iron Duke." He started in Washington as a copy boy and graduated to writing sports columns for the Washington Daily News. *By August '42 he was in the Navy. "I got in it as soon as I could when it started and got out as soon as I could when it ended." In between, there was a Liberty ship in the North Atlantic and the Mediterranean, a fast transport in the Pacific, and six months in Australia "surrounded by lovely Australian women, lovely Australian beer, and lovely Australian race horses."*

In 1945, aged 30, he was back writing columns. The first column, on "Women's Clothes," he wrote for Scripps-Howard, won him notoriety and a syndicate contract. In 1947 his first novel, Grenadine Etching, *an outrageous Southern-type historical spoof, was a success. During the next four years, he published three more books: two of them non-fiction, based on the columns, and another novel,* Grenadine's Spawn.

Then in 1951 he put together his private safari and took off with his wife, Virginia, for Africa. One of the results, in due course, was Horn of the Hunter, *an account of the Ruarks on safari.*

"A man and a gun and a star and a beast are still ponderable in a world of imponderables. The essence of the simple ponderable is man's potential ability to slay a lion."

I T W A S very late the first day out of Nairobi when Harry turned the jeep off the dim track he was following through the high, dusty grass and veered her in toward a black jaggedness of trees. The moon was rising high over a forlorn hill and it had begun to turn nasty cold. The jeep bumped and lurched and stalled once. She wasn't really a jeep, but a kind of glorified jeep that the British call a Land Rover. We had named her Jessica, figuring that to be a nice name for a jeep, and Jessica, by temperament, seemed considerably more jeep than rover.

In the glare of Jessica's headlights the trees profiled more clearly now. Harry flicked the searchlight upward and said: "Lots of dead stuff. And water, too, down in that *donga*. I expect we'd best camp here. *Memsaab* stiff and sore?"

The *memsaab* said with considerable feeling that she was about as goddamned stiff and as goddamned sore as a girl figured to get after riding from 8 A.M. over no roads in a goddamned jungle until past 9 P.M. Harry made a little deprecatory cluck at the profanity and suggested that he had a priceless bottle of scotch someone in Nairobi had given him, which would make a

(37)

world of difference to anybody. He turned to Chabani, the Wa-Kikuyu car boy.

"*Na kuja* lorry?" he asked.

"*Ndio*," Chabani said.

"*Wapi pombe?*" Harry asked.

"*Hapa*," Chabani said. "*Kariba*."

The black boy handed Harry the bottle of scotch. "*Magi kwa bwana*," he told the black boy, who crawled out of the jeep, and bled two cupfuls of water—now cold from condensation—from the tied canvas bags of water that were lashed to the steel uprights that supported Jessica's canvas top. The dust and little wiggly things settled in the water. The scotch burnt through the water going down. It stayed warm when it got down, lighting a tiny little furnace in the stomach.

"Painkiller," Harry said. "Cures everything. We'll make a nice *campi* here soon's the lorry comes up."

We could see the lorry, overloaded and grotesque with a dozen black boys making silhouettes from the tarpaulin-lashed top, lumbering and complaining and wallowing along. She had stuck herself like a contrary cow twice that day already. We watched her lights leave the track and turn in toward us. All of a sudden her lights pointed upward and her black shape lurched and stopped.

"Oh, Christ," Harry said. "Pig hole. You two wait here with the bottle and one of the water bags. I'll send Chabani back with some camp chairs and have him do up a fire while we wrestle the old girl out of her troubles."

He said something swiftly in Swahili to Chabani, who began to untie the dead Tommy ram from the spare tire on Jessica's bonnet, where it had been lashed down a couple of hours before when Harry shot it just at dusk. Chabani dumped it on the ground and took a *panga*, a big, curved, sawbacked knife, out of the back seat and dropped it on the ground by the dead Thomson gazelle. Then he tortured out the heavy, square green wooden chop box and put two canvas cushions from Jessica's hard front seat on it. He pointed to the chop box, smiled cheerlessly, and said: "Sit." Then he took the *panga* and disppeared into the grove of flat-topped thorn acacias. We could hear him breaking dried branches. Harry climbed back into the jeep and drove off to check on the lorry's sad condition.

Jinny looked at me with a very small, pinched face. She was wearing my trench coat and looked very small, although she is not small, and very miserable, although she does not have the face for misery. I poured her another drink into the gay red plastic cups and took one myself off the top of the bottle of Harry's whisky. It didn't taste any nastier.

I looked down at the dead Tommy, at the hole in his shoulder, centered exactly on the point and traversing all the way through him where Harry had shot him with the little Mannlicher. I was glad I had no license for Kenya and that it would be two more days before I would be allowed to shoot in Tanganyika. I wanted to see more of it first.

Harry had shot the Tommy ram swiftly and competently. We had not seen much game that day. Just on dusk we passed a few wildebeest and an odd zebra or two and began to see the Thomson gazelles in groups of a dozen. They were beautiful and dainty with their sharp, straight black horns curving a little at the tip, and the black bars on the gold hides just over the white stomach hair. We came along at dusk into a large herd of a hundred or more and Harry stopped the jeep suddenly.

"*Toa bundouki,* Chabani," he said. "*Kidogo.*" He turned half apologetically, like a schoolboy asking for permission to leave the room. "If you don't mind," he said, "I think I'll just nip out and shoot one of those Tommies for the boys' supper. They've been lying around town for a month and they're fair starved for red meat."

He got out and held the door open. "Care to come with me?"

I followed him, clumsily imitating the half crouch he used and after half a hundred yards he stopped and held one hand downward, palm toward me. I stopped, and he crouched on his hams, both feet planted firmly in the short, crisp dry grass. The Tommies were moving off, not spooked but suspicious and shy, at least two hundred yards away. I could barely make out the flashes of buff against the Tommy-colored background. Only a little white blur caused by the flicking of their tails caught my city eyes. I wondered how a man could say definitely he was going to shoot anything and know to himself that he meant it and could produce it.

Harry was aiming swiftly at one of them—I couldn't tell which—and as soon as the gun came up to his left eye he seemed to fire. The little gun made an unconscionable amount of noise, and you could hear the bullet hit like a wet boxing glove on a sand bag.

"*Piga,*" Selby said to himself. "*Kufa.*" He turned to me. "He'll be dead just over there. I saw his tail stop when he took off. Always tell by the tail on Tommy. When it stops that circular motion, he's dead and just doesn't know it. Got this one through the shoulder."

We walked over to where the Tommies had been, and after about three hundred yards Harry pointed. "There," he said. I couldn't see anything.

"We'll just wait a bit until the lorry comes up. I usually have one of the Mohammedans in the Rover to make the religious thing, but Chabani is Ky-uke and no Moslem. We'll just let one of the boys leap off the lorry and do a *hallal*—cut its throat—so everything will be nice and legal."

The lorry came alongside, and one of the men, one with a white fez, leaped off and took a knife out of a sheath. "*Pandi hi,*" Harry said, pointing. The boy raced off with long bounds and bent over something. He touched at it hesitantly with his knife, stood up straight, spread his hands, and made a little shrug.

"Too bad," Harry said. "It's too dead to be *hallaled.* They're not supposed to cut the throat unless it's a wee little bit alive, or the *hallal* doesn't count with Allah or Mohammed or whoever's watching. Pity. About half my boys are Mohammedans, especially the Wakambas. Moslemism is very popular with the Wakambas these days. Gives them great style. Not that they know what the hell the priest is saying half the time when they go to the *mousquetina*. Oh well. Let's go and collect the dinner. He ought to be tender. I chose a young buck."

The Tommy was lying dead. He looked clean and very fresh and sweet-smelling and seemed undisturbed by the small bullet, which had taken him on the shoulder and gone all the way through.

"He'll be fine," Harry said. "Pity about the Moslems, though. I shouldn't be at all surprised if there's not some finger-crossing and a few broken articles of faith tonight. Those boys get ravenous for meat when they're lying around town between safaris. When we get into real game country and start bringing in masses of meat they'll all have the bellyache for a week. They eat up to twelve pounds of meat a day, you know. *Each.* All that rich meat is pure hell on the tummy after it's been used to a diet of nothing but mealie porridge. Here, Chabani," he said as the jeep drove up, Chabani proud and show-offish as he drove alongside the new *memsaab*. "*Hapa.*" Chabani got out, produced a coil of rope off the bumper, and heaved the Tommy onto the hood, where he lashed it to the tire. It bled a little into the circle of the wheel. It was the first dead thing I had seen in Africa, and I began to wonder, with considerable nervousness, if I would be up to the task of feeding fifteen people who considered ten pounds of meat per diem, per each, a bare necessity of living. I knew what I could do with a shotgun. I did not know what I could do with all the fancy rifles I had, owing to never having shot any sort of rifle at anything but a target at the Campfire Club.

I was still wondering as we sat on the chop box, drinking whisky and water and waiting for Harry to come back with the lorry. Chabani had dropped an armload of dried, dead limbs and twigs a few feet away from the dead Tommy ram. He came over, asked me for a match, and then scuffed a handful of the dried grass from between his big flat feet in their tattered tan tennis shoes. He lit the handful of grass with a match, blowing on it carefully, and then started to feed it twigs, one by one, each no bigger than a kitchen match. His little blaze caught, and he fed it more twigs, gnarled ones this time, as big as a baby's wrist. The fire danced and reached up for more food. In a very few minutes he was feeding it logs as thick as his thigh, and in a very few more he was dragging logs so big he couldn't lift them but only snake them through the grasses. When he had manufactured a blaze as high as his head and as long as the lorry, he flourished a flat shovel from somewhere and robbed his blaze of a heaping shovelful of coals. These he took to a point fifty yards away and built himself a fresh fire from a heap of dead wood he had evidently gathered and left there. When it was crackling he came back, picked up the *panga,* and began to scythe about him in the clumps of high grasses that accented the trampled-down terrain. He grinned foolishly in the firelight.

Jinny and I had said nothing. She got up, shivered once, and picked up the tails of my trench coat, spreading her legs and subjecting the back of her stiff, shiny new khaki-panted bottom to the fire, as women have always done. She smiled for the first time since late afternoon.

"This is rather nice," she said. "I think I could use another drink, though." She held out her red cup and I dribbled a few more ounces of Harry's precious scotch into it. "I don't seem to miss the ice," she said, "which is possibly just as well. I wonder how long before they'll get that bloody truck out of the whateverkindof hole it's in."

"You've been three days in East Africa, Osa Johnson," I said. "If you've picked up 'bloody' already, you may as well say 'lorry' too. 'Bloody truck' sounds like an unpleasant physical disability."

"We've named this dirty little backbreaker, this jeep thing of ours, already," Jinny said. "If you call a jeep 'Jessica,' what do you think you should call a lorry who is going to live with you for the rest of your life?"

The scotch had achieved a definite command post in my stomach, and the fire was beautifully warm and crackly noisy by now.

"Well," I said, "if a ship is a she and a truck is a she, too, and if this ungainly slut is a lorry, there is only one name for her. Annie. Annie Lorry. Nice, what? Bonnie Annie Laurie, who is in the process of laying herself down to dee."

"Jesus," Jinny said. "Alone in the wilds of darkest whatever with a strange Englishman, fifteen blackamoors who possibly eat white ladies underdone, and a husband who makes scotch-type puns. Annie Lorry, yet. I *like* it," she said with the charming consistency for which wives, the world around, are noted. "I wonder how fares it with Annie. She should have cancer of the differential."

"Not well," I said. "Here come the children of Israel bearing their chattels."

Harry was striding along at the head of his porters, carrying a rolled-up something, which proved later to be the toilet tent, on his back. The boys strung out behind him, loaded with other tents and odd, lumpy-looking packages and angular poles.

"Bloody thing's bedded down for the night," he said. "We'll dig her out after dinner. All the boys are starved, and I imagine you are. Also, they've all got dreadful hangovers, as have I. City life is not good for country boys, black *or* white. We'll set up the sleepers and turn old Ali loose at the cook fire for a little *chacula* and have a drink or so first to keep off the fevers and would the *memsaab* like a bath?"

The *memsaab* muttered that as long as she was going to die anyhow, she would rather die drunk and dirty.

"She'll doubtless grow to love it," Harry said. "Well, cheers, chums. Wonderful stuff, isn't it? Tastes so nasty and feels so good."

One of the blacks came and took the dead Tommy away. Another set up a portable table and unflexed three campchairs— canvas and comfortable. We set the bottle on the table. Harry excused himself and drifted away to supervise the erection of the tents. We weren't making an extensive camp—no mess tent, no tents for the boys, no tent for Harry. Just a tent for the *bwana wa safari*, which suddenly was me, and for the *memsaab wa safari*, which suddenly was Virginia. A hyena chittered across the *donga*. I didn't know it was a *donga* then—a dry river bed with just a trickle of water to one side. The hyena squealed, roared, growled, and then laughed in that maniac's mirthless hysteria which nobody has ever put down on paper correctly.

"My God," Jinny said, "what was that, a lion?"

"No," Harry said, sliding suddenly out of the darkness. "That was a hyena. The lion is over that way," with a sweep of his arm. "If you wait a second you can hear him. It's a cross between a cough and the first mutter of a summer thunderstorm. Now. Hear him? We call it *ngruma*, wonderful word for 'roar'— *ngruma*."

"No," Jinny said. "I don't hear him and I don't want to hear him."

There was a sudden crashing cacophony of assorted noises from the trees. It was a hoot and a squeal and a chuckle and a yell and a yip and a yap and a growl and a roar and a whistle and a clash of cymbals. We just looked at Harry.

"Birds," he said. "Baboons. Monkeys. Bugs. And away up the *donga*, one leopard. Also, there's lots of fairly fresh rhino sign down by the little river. Unpleasant beast, the rhino. Apt to come blundering into camp. Can't see very well. Knew a bloke once got up to go to the sanitary tent and when he stuck his head out to go back to bed there was this big rhino cow grazing between him and his sleeping tent. Stayed in the latrine all night. Most uncomfortable."

"My God," Jinny said.

"Looks like about time for a little *chacula*," Harry said. "You hungry?"

"Starved," I said.

"Famished," Jinny said.

"We'll be having a bit of the Tommy," Harry said. "A touch fresh for my taste, but if we don't get our bit tonight the boys'll have it gone by tomorrow. And it's a young one. Shouldn't be bad. Old Ali—he's the cook—is a ruddy wonder with game. Juma! Jum*aaaa*! he yelled. *"Lette chacula!"*

"Ndio, bwana," came back from the cook fire. A white-robed

wraith in a white fez, followed by another banshee in white, writhed up from the smaller grove of acacias. They cleared the table of bottle and glasses and reset it rapidly with china plates and condiments. *"Soupi,"* the head boy, Juma, said. I could recognize him now. He had a happy, evil sort of face, with a pencil-sized hole in his ear lobe that the fire shone through and an impudently cheerful look about him, owing undoubtedly to an Irish kind of snub nose. His color was very light, about gabardine. Juma was a Coast Swahili. He spoke and wrote Arabic Swahili—Coastal Swahili, impeccably grammatic, and unlike the crude pidgin Swahili the Wakambas and Kikuyus and Nandis spoke.

"Very important fellow, old Juma," Harry said. "Got hell's own amount of influence with the boys. Priest of sorts. Threatens 'em with Allah's vengeance and lends 'em money at God knows what interest rate betimes. Between praying and usury he keeps 'em on the jump."

Juma and the other man fetched tureens of soup, undoubtedly Campbell's. The bread was toasted and hot. The butter in its green plastic dish was fresh and sweet. The Tommy chops came smoking from the fire, and they looked and smelled wonderful.

"Fancy a beer?" Harry asked. "We've got a couple of bottles in the water bag. Kaluku!" He spoke sharply to the other white-robe. *"Lette beer-i kwa bwana!"* Kaluku bobbed his head and swished his skirts off after the beer. It was barely cool and very pleasant, rather like Australian beer in its heavy body. It was beer that never saw a ball game.

"Local product," Harry said. "Called 'Tusker.' Bloody awful, I think. I love that Danish Pilsen they have at the Norfolk, myself. But this can taste awfully good—well, say a month hence."

"I ain't knockin' it now," I said. "Pass the Tommy."

Considering that this particular Thomson gazelle had been dancing on the village green about four hours ago, possibly contemplating matrimony, he was great. He was not so tough as tender, and he tasted unlike any game I had ever eaten. No rankness, no gaminess, no stringiness. He was succulent and unfat and I had three helpings of him.

Juma, the head boy, came and swept away the dishes. He went back to the cook fire and returned with a smoking frypan.

"What's this?" Virginia asked.

"Dessert," Harry said. *"Crêpes suzette.* Old Ali always makes 'em first night out. Instills any amount of faith in the clients. Good?"

"Saints preserve us," Virginia said. "Wonderful. How does he do it on an open fire?"

"I don't know," Harry said. "I've had him for years. He can cook anything. Uses a biscuit tin for an oven. Tell me what you want and old Ali will produce it."

"If we eat like this on the first night out in a temporary camp," Virginia said, "God help my figure after two months of Ali's fine Swahilian hand with the skillet. I'm about to bust."

Juma and Kaluku came and cleared away the table. Juma fetched coffee, and I remembered a bottle of brandy I had stuck into the back of Jessica. We sat there facing the fire, listening to the night noises, the hyenas, the birds I did not know the name of, the leopard coughing somewhere up the creek, the bugs swooping and zooming but not biting. The moon had climbed steeply into the sky, and you could see the little hills plainly under it, like a long caravan of camels suddenly stopped and still to wait beside a well.

It was cold—not bitter, not quite frosty, but chilly-dew cold— and the fire was warm and wonderful. I was tired and I was full and the coffee was strong and black and the brandy slid down smoothly. I started to think about just how far I was from New York and newspaper syndicates and telephones and telegraphs and the 21 Club and income taxes and subways and elevators and then I sat up with a startled feeling inside. I am a hunter, I said to myself. I must be a hunter or I wouldn't be here in the deep end of nowhere with a city-slicker wife and fifteen strange black boys and a young punk with no beard, practically, who says he is a white hunter. Looking at the fire and listening to the noises, I ran my mind back about what brought me here and wrote a little mental essay for myself as I sat and sipped the brandy.

The hunter's horn sounds early for some, I thought, later for others. For some unfortunates, prisoned by city sidewalks and sentenced to a cement jungle more horrifying than anything to be found in Tanganyika, the horn of the hunter never winds at all. But deep in the guts of most men is buried the involuntary response to the hunter's horn, a prickle of the nape hairs, an acceleration of the pulse, an atavistic memory of his fathers, who killed first with stone, and then with club, and then with spear, and then with bow, and then with gun, and finally with formulae. How meek the man is of no importance; somewhere in the pigeon chest of the clerk is still the vestigial remnant of the hunter's heart; somewhere in his nostrils the half-forgotten smell of blood. There is no man with such impoverishment of imagination that at some time he has not wondered how he would handle himself if a lion broke loose from a zoo and he were forced to face him without the protection of bars or handy, climbable trees.

Man has found it exceedingly difficult lately to decipher the weird incantations and ceremonies which surround the provision of meat and shelter for his spawn. He is mystified by the cabalistic signs of the economist. He does not understand billions of dollars in relationship to him and his. Parity baffles him; the administration of ceilings and floors and controls and excises and supports does not satisfy his meat urge or his aesthetic response to the chase, when the hunter's horn of necessity rouses him.

But he can understand a lion, because a lion is life in its simplest form, beautiful, menacing, dangerous, and attractive to his ego. A lion has always been the symbol of challenge, the prototype of personal hazard. You get the lion or the lion gets you.

The fire was beginning to shake into solid glowing coals now, and some of the night noises had stilled others, and new ones had commenced. The boys had finally succeeded in dragging

Annie Lorry out of her sloven nest in the pig hole, and she was moored alongside the sleeping tent. Harry had stretched a length of canvas as a dew cloth from her topmost rigging to the jeep and had set up his cot under the canvas. I yawned. Virginia yawned. Harry yawned. Harry got up.

"Time for bed, I expect," he said. *"Nataka lala.* We'll up at dawn. Two more hard days' drive yet to come. Sleep well."

I T S T A R T E D out to be a funny trip. It had to be funny, funny peculiar, that is, because the kind friend who had been giving all the good advice either through malice or stupidity completely misled me on the time to go: He said June was great. I was in Nairobi a little less than an hour before I found out that June was not great. June was ungreat. June was lousy. June was not the time to do anything, because of a simple truth. Rains make grass, and animals stay up in the hills where the grass is short and the carnivores can't hide in it, and when the miles and miles of bloody Africa are a bloody sea of six-foot grass, there are no bloody animals to shoot at or take pictures of or even to look at. They burn the grass in July to get it short again, and the decent hunting starts in August. My fine friend, the expert, sends me over in June, when the prairies are wet and all the game is either hidden out in the hills or still working on the water holes in the reserves. Some friend, my expert friend. Ten thousand bucks' worth of former acquaintance.

But we got it stuck together with all the guns and the cameras and the money and the tickets and the farewell lunch at the numerical place, as Eddie Condon calls the 21 Club. The lunch was reasonably Homeric.

Use Enough Gun

Now in Kenya, a stone's toss across the border of Tanganyika, I woke up. A few mosquitoes buzzed dispiritedly about the net. Away off somewhere the lion coughed and complained. I contemplated the high cost of lions as I lay on an inflated chilly rubber mattress in a strange land. (The cost of lions is considerable.)

It had been such a swift transition from New York to a lion in your lap. Philip Wylie, I believe it was, once wrote that when you travel by plane you leave a little of your soul behind. I figured in my semi-sleep that a part of my soul was somewhere between Rome and Asmara, which is in Eritrea and which might stay right there in Eritrea for all of me. Or maybe it was just now trying to check into the second-worst hotel in Addis Ababa, since the Ras Hotel, naturally, would be off limits to souls that were traveling behind their corporeal headquarters. It is not lulling to think of souls when you are only half asleep in strange terrain.

A baboon barked somewhere down the *donga* and followed it with an outraged squawk. A little later the leopard which had outraged him sawed at the foot of the tree, from which the *nugu* undoubtedly was swaying from a limber branch. "Bastard," the baboon said. "Spotted, evil, ugly bastard." The leopard replied: "Just wait, *nugu*. I'll have indigestion over you yet."

So we'd been met by Donald Ker at the Nairobi airport, and he had twinkled his chipmunk's cheerful grin at us and said something like:

"I say, I *am* dreadfully sorry that your man Selby—your hunter, you know—isn't here to greet you, but the Game Department just called and said a rogue rhino's raising vast amounts of trouble with the natives outside of town and so we've sent old Harry off to reprove it. Minds me of the early days when the department used to call me or Syd for us to come to the airport to shoot the wildebeest off it so the ruddy planes could land. We've cleared your bits now, so we might nip off to the Norfolk and have a spot of lunch before they close the dining room."

(49)

In retrospect I am a great admirer of Donald Ker, a small man who looks no more like a professional hunter than he looks like Blackbeard the Pirate. But Donald Ker killed his first elephant before his voice solved its adolescent squeak, and his first safari consisted of a can of beans, a gun, a bullet, and a blanket. He is one half of Ker and Downey Safaris, Ltd., and if you wish to book him you had better write a letter stating your plans some five years ahead of the moment.

"You know," Donald said over a martini on the Norfolk veranda, "there's a popular suspicion going the rounds that all professional hunters are nine feet high and drink petrol cocktails neat. I claim I disprove the point. I put myself through elementary school shooting elephants on holiday. I was smaller then than now. And that, chum, was never yesterday. Shall we push along to old Ahamed's and get you and the *memsaab* suitably clothed for tomorrow's exodus?"

"Jesus," said I, "tomorrow?"

"I rather like to get the safaris in and get them out," Donald said, twinkling his teeth. "And we do have to see to the boots and jackets and things."

When your heart's in the highlands and your soul is lost, maybe still sequestered in the Nouvelle Eve in Paris, you go to the local Indian in Nairobi. He measures you. You go to the next local Indian—the bootmaking one—and *he* measures you, and of a sudden you have completed an outfitting that would take you six weeks to perform in the United States. In Nairobi no suit is so fancy it can't be delivered in a day. No boots are so special they can't be rendered unto the owner by tomorrow's noon. Under Donald's hand I was finished with the flannel pajamas, finished with the drill bush jackets, finished with the mosquito boots and the crepe-soled half boots before cocktail time.

It is a long, long way, although short in miles, from the modern civilization of Nairobi's Norfolk Hotel to where we aimed in Tanganyika, because you have to go through little places named Narok and Loliondo and across a big plain named Serengeti. After you leave the Naivasha area there aren't any roads much, only tracks through grass and winding over and around mountains, and when you start across the Serengeti there is only a double-barreled peak to steer you sixty miles, and unless the day is clear you can't see the peak. You drive the hunting car by guess and by God. The weary old lorry labors behind you and now and again you pause to wait for her to catch up, the boys gray-faced with the dust and clinging to the tarpaulined top like a flock of baboons on a rocky *kopje*.

After rescuing that tin tragedy of a truck from the muddy misery of Tanganyika's trails a few dozen times; after Mama had surfeited herself with photographs of the old Masai herdsmen we met; after a short call on the district officer in Loliondo, we pushed through a herd of spotted Masai cattle and rolled down a rocky hill and landed into the vast plain that is Serengeti. It is a plain now, sere dusty grass for as far as you can see. It was a lake once, a lake beneath the lip of mountains. It is some sixty miles straight across it and there is no road. There is no track. There is not much water and few trees and only a small, bitter alkali lake and a few damp patches of grass with treacherous soft cotton soil to stick you and, when it is dry, violent dust. And violent sun.

"This bloke I mention," Harry was saying, "was one of the few real crackpots I've been forced to entertain on safari. He was an Englishman, and he thought he was Tarzan of the Apes. He wanted to sleep in trees. He ran around naked all the time. I couldn't keep him from bathing in the streams, and the crocodiles were eyeing him appreciatively. He——My aunt! Look yonder. What a lovely lion."

I do not believe there are many more impressive sights than a city man's first glimpse at a live maned lion loose on a plain in strange country, sinister and far from home. This old boy was a movie lion. He had a luxuriant mane and tufts on his elbows and he was right smack in the middle of a bare prairie. Him and his lady. She took off in a swinging lope. The old boy stopped cold and turned to inspect us with a cynical yellow eye. Harry swung Jessica past him at about three feet.

(51)

"Jambo, Bwana Simba," he said. The lion grunted and scowled and began to move off. Jinny unlimbered the camera and stood up in the jeep. I placed both palms on her behind and braced her against the windscreen so she could take pictures. The lion, heavy-maned and very full in the paunch, swung off after his old lady. Then he stopped again, and Harry tooled the jeep to within six feet and halted it. The lion looked at us. We looked at the lion.

I know they will all tell you that so long as you stay in the car you are completely safe, but it is of small comfort on your first live lion. You keep wondering if maybe you won't find an individualist who dislikes automobiles someday and suddenly find him in your lap. (I met a lady lion later who did not like jeeps, nor the people in them. She charged it three times, and the last time her jaws snapped a touch closer to my trousers than I like to remember. She remembered her hatred months later and charged another car. And then another month after that. She is going to surprise some camera tourist one of these days by removing his face from his Rolleiflex.)

A lion, loose, and six feet away, with no bars in front of him, is bigger than the lion you remembered from the zoo. His teeth are longer. He is scrubbier, perhaps, but loses no dignity and no ferocity. I was not displeased when he sauntered off. Neither was Jinny. She had not yawned back when the lion yawned at her. She was not bored.

"He's just off a kill," Harry said. "Look at his belly. Full of zebra. No trouble from this type. Let's herd him off after his bride and proceed. We'll see another dozen or so before dusk. Yah!" he said, and slapped the door of the Land Rover. "Shoo! Scat! Begone!"

The lion sneered, curling his lip and grunting. He got up and humped away, his shoulder blades moving angularly under the loose hide. Harry put on a burst of speed and we chased him a few hundred yards, the lion looking sarcastically over his shoulder as if to say, Christ, more tourists out to play. He stopped one more time, faced us, opened his mouth, and roared. It wasn't a very serious roar, but it seemed rather loud to me. Harry

Use Enough Gun

very serious roar, but it seemed rather loud to me. Harry swerved the jeep and we bade him good-by.

"Lovely beasts, lions, you know," Harry said. "Live and let live. Not the king of the jungle, though. Never makes the effort. Elephant. He's the king. Buffalo the prince, and the leopard is the knave. The lion is a gentleman—a lazy old gentleman. Makes Mama do all the work. He stands upwind and lets his scent drift down to some poor *punda* or other and roars once in a while to amuse himself. The old lady, betimes, has sneaked around downwind from the zebras and they gradually work toward her. She makes two jumps and lands on the zebra's back. She hooks her feet into his stern and takes a mouth hold on his neck. Then she reaches around with her arm and grabs him by the nose, and crack! *Chacula.* Dinner. The old boy saunters up and they dine. Then they sleep. Then they dine again. Then they sleep some more. And then Mother bestirs herself and goes to market once again. Be nice being a lion on a reserve. Nothing to do but eat and sleep and pose for pictures and fight with your sons when they've got big enough."

I will never, possibly, forget that first day on the Serengeti. We saw fourteen lions—one pride of five drinking peaceably and serenely at a water hole with half a hundred Grant and Thomson gazelles, only a few feet away from each other, and each animal serenely aware that nobody was going to eat anybody else. As we got off the plain and into bush we began to see giraffes and ostriches, and the antelopes thickened into herds of several hundred. The first stirrings of the semi-annual game migration were beginning, and the flocks of wildebeest, shaggy and high-humped like American bison, were beginning to move, along with their friends and companions, the zebras. We saw bands of five and ten thousand, and coursed them briefly in the car. At one cutoff we paused for a few unforgettable moments while some five thousand zebras thundered past our bow, their hoofs thunderous even on the grassy plain, and the dust boiling behind them like the wake of an armored column in North Africa. And now the grass was high, towering over the windshield

(53)

of the jeep and pelting our faces with sharp grains from the heavy seed heads. Hundreds of coveys of tiny quail sprayed up from under Jessica's hood. The seed heads got into her grille, and every so often we had to stop and clear them out of her front.

"Bloody Rover smells like a bloody bakeshop," Harry said. "Grass. Nine miles high everywhere. Too much rain this year. Too much water on the plains. Too much water in the hills—anywhere the grass is short and the cats can't crawl unseen. I've high hopes, though, for where we're headed. It's freak country, a little strip about fifteen miles long by five wide, and the grass is never high there. I don't know why. Unless I'm off my reckoning, we'll find game in that area. We'll find the game in any area that's legal and isn't covered with a forest of this bloody grass. Let's stop for a bite of lunch and one of those delicious martinis you're always talking about."

We went down through a poison-green patch of grass that covered a wet spot, with Kidogo, the gunbearer, testing the terrain with his horny feet ahead of us, and trundled up to a high knoll where a patch of mangy acacias gave a grudging shade. Harry's curly black hair was whitened and stiffened by dust. Jinny's blond crop under the bandanna and the Stetson was blonder. There was dust in my whiskers and dust in my mouth and dust in the water bag and dust in the plastic glasses and dust in the gin, which made a very nice hot martini if you like them hot. I like them hot.

Chabani and Kidogo got the chop box out of Jessica's back seat and spread the front-seat cushions around under the trees. We had a couple martinis apiece and then we had a bottle of Tusker lager and some remnants of the cold Tommy and a can of cold spaghetti and bread and butter and pickles. The tsetses fed on us sparingly as we ate. A few hundred yards away a herd of wildebeest stared stupidly at us. The sun filtered through the acacia tops and we sweated and the insects' bites itched and our eyes were red and I still decided that I was a happy man, with two months ahead of me and nothing to do except look at the game and maybe shoot a little of it and not answer any telephones.

"When we get off this bloody reserve we'll have to shoot a big piece of meat pretty quick," Harry said. "It's been a hard three days for the boys, and they'll be ravenous and eat too much and I'll have to dose them all for the bellyache. Sooner we get them fed and over being sick, the better. I hope we can shoot something big like an eland. They love the fresh meat and the fat and they make *biltong* out of what's left and they make shoulder straps for their wives out of the hide."

"What sort of shoulder straps?" Jinny asked. "What do they use them for?"

"Oh, for carrying wood," Harry said. "The wives, I mean. They can carry more wood for their husbands with good comfortable shoulder straps. The wives are very happy when their husbands bring them the eland shoulder straps. Shows the men are thinking of their happiness and welfare."

"Men," Jinny said, finishing her beer. "Where is the ladies' room?"

"Try over there behind that tree," Harry said. "Mind the snakes."

Virginia walked off, and I had to laugh a little. She was wearing dust-stained khaki pants and ankle boots, a belted bush jacket with empty cartridge loops in the front, and a saucy double-brimmed terai over a gypsy bandanna. What she wore couldn't have cost twenty bucks, if you forget the Abercrombie and Fitch boots, and this was the girl who used to play the Stork-21 Club circuit in New York. If she had her mink with her in those days she was worth twenty thousand bucks on the hoof, and she wouldn't have thought of walking three blocks if there was a doorman handy and a taxicab to hail. She always needed a quarter to go to the little girls' room, and now here is a raw stranger, Harry, directing her to the nearest bush and telling her to mind the snakes. This, the girl who wore a Hattie Carnegie frock and a rhinestone hat to ride a camel after a slightly wet evening on the town in Cairo. . . .

"What are you snickering about?" Harry asked.

"Nothing much," I said. "I was just thinking about a dame who is afraid to walk the dogs in Central Park, who is afraid to spend the night alone in a Fifth Avenue penthouse, who spends God knows how much money on girl lunches and at the hairdresser and on her clothes, who would rather be naked than unminked, who wouldn't ride a bus or a subway to save her life, all of a sudden lost out in the African bush with twenty bucks' worth of Indian-made shoddy on her back, fifteen strange cannibals and a strange East African guide, riding in a jeep, looking at lions at close range, weighing a good ten pounds more from dust alone, drinking a hot martini, and going to the john behind a tree while a rank stranger tells her to mind no snakes take a chunk out of her. That is what I am laughing at—Osa Johnson Ruark, girl adventuress."

"I was serious about the snakes," Harry said. "Touch more beer in the bottle. Have it? Knew a girl once was bit on the bottom. Hell's own trouble trying to decide where to put the tourniquet."

"Not so much farther to go now?"

"Ought to make the permanent camp on the Grummetti sometime after dark," Harry said. "Must stop off and see the Game Department bloke. Nice lad name of Thomas. Sign the register and that sort of thing. He'll buy us a drink. Then I want to stop in the village—the Wa-Ikoma *manyatta*—and pick up old Kibiriti. He's wired for lion, and I've a hunch we'll need what he knows. Maned ones, shootable ones, getting tougher and tougher to come by. Here's the *mem*. Let's be about."

"Who's Kibiriti?" Jinny asked as she got into the jeep and straddled the gearbox.

"Bit of a sorcerer," Harry said. "I expect his mother was a lion. He thinks exactly like a lion. He can find lions when other lions can't find lions. I don't know how he does it. One time I was in great trial and trouble with a couple of sports, must-have-lion-or-the-safari's-off type of blokes. I looked high and low. I put out kills and I said prayers. I consulted witch doctors and learned how to talk lionese. No lions. Nobody speaking in camp, just sitting there being surly over the gin-and-lime. Boys all unhappy. What's called lionitis out here. Whole *campi* upset. So I send out a hurry call to Kibiriti. He arrives, complete with three wives. God-awful ugly except the young ones.

" 'Simba,' I say. 'Mbile. Simbambile. Got to have two, in a hurry. *Pese pese* hurry. *Suria* hurry.' *Suria's* a bad word. Old Kibiriti looks around and sees his wives are happy with their new friends—shocking morals, these people have—and scratches his head. 'The Douma,' he says. 'We go there for the lions.'

" 'You been there lately, you heard anything about lions in the Douma, you know for sure?' I say to Kibiriti. 'No, *Bwana Haraka,*' he says to me, 'but I feel like there are two large black-maned lions in the Douma. We go to the Douma.'

"So," Harry said, "we break the camp and we go to the Douma. First night we shoot one fine *simba*. The next day we shoot another fine *simba*. Don't ask me how he does it, but you'll have a chance to watch him work. We'll pick him up in the village as we go through. He's having a little trouble with three wives and will be glad to take the trip. That last wife of his is awfully young and pretty and she's claiming most of his time. Others raising hell."

Bwana Thomas, the Game Department type, wasn't in his compound, being out after some poachers. The *askari* took our names and looked at the licenses and allowed us to fill the vehicles and the water bags with some of *Bwana* Thomas' nice fresh rain water, and we pushed off. We headed on a nebulous trail for Ikoma, a village of some half thousand, in God's back yard of Tanganyika. This was a lion-hunting village. Its young men all had their personally killed manes of big *doumi* lions, each killed with arrow or spear, of course, and illegal, of course, as illegal as the marabou stork plumage they wear when they dance, as illegal as the colobus monkey fur they wear when they dance.

The drums had been ahead of us. Kibiriti—which means "matches"—was expecting us. He made a big thing of seeing his patron saint, *Bwana Haraka,* once again, and was most hospitable about the premises of his newest wife's compound. They are impeccably considerate about wifely rights in Tanganyika. Each wife has her own hut, her own goats to tend, her own water to draw, her own mealie corn to tend, her own wood to fetch, and her own babies to have. She brews her own brand of beer for her man, who, in order to show no favoritism, stays only a week with each wife unless he is cheating, and Kibiriti was cheating at the time.

It was coming on for dark when we took Kibiriti away from his mud-wattle hut and his new baby and his euphorbia cactus *boma* and his pretty, shy new wife. He perched atop the lorry, his red fez cocked rakishly, as full of importance as Winston Churchill coming over for a new loan. I wished later we had kept him, for in the eighteen miles that separated us from our first permanent campsite, Mr. Harry Selby, the infallible white hunter, to whom I had entrusted my life and that of my wife, got lost. Hopelessly lost. Bitterness was added to the brew when that ungainly slut, Annie Lorry, the faller-in-pig-holes and sticker-in-mudholes, that slab-sided, over-loaded, weak-axled travesty of a truck, had to come and find us.

"This," said Mrs. Virginia Ruark, "is one hell of a way to start a safari. I am lost in Tanganyika with a child who does not know his own way, and a fool—meaning you—who was better off loaded at lunch at Toots'. Pass the last of the scotch. If the lions eat me tonight they will not eat me sober."

"I'm most awfully, dreadfully sorry," Harry said. "But the bush has changed since I've been here, and what with the high grass and all, I seem to have missed the little avenue I must use to get from here to there. Let's swing back again and see if I can't pick it up again. Meantime, I think I'll have a bite at that bottle myself. Been a long day to get lost at the end of it."

It was an eerie evening. The sky was dusted with stars against the incredible furry velvet blue of the African night. The bush bulked black against the horizon, making strange animal forms, like a fancifully trimmed yew hedge on an English estate. The vast plain of grass—shorter now—was silver in the night and glimmered like a field of wheat. A slim, graceful crescent of moon made the grass sparkle as we sped over it fruitlessly, seeking the harbor entrance to the camp we knew was over a long, low-bulking hill. Little bat-eared foxes scampered ahead of us and grimaced at Jessica's headlamps. Night jars whooshed and got up ghostily ahead of us, fluttering off like startled spirits. My knees ached. My back ached. My knees cramped. My eyes were full of dust and my beard itched. My irreverent wife began to sing a song to the tune of "How High the Moon."

"How tall the trees," she sang. "How green the grass. How skinned my knees. How tired my——— Pass the spirits, Buster," she said. "And where is Jack Armstrong, the all-East African boy, aiming to take us now?"

"Home to *Campi Abahati*," Harry said. "I see Annie Lorry's headlamps. She's waiting for us around that corner and just past that hill, damn her eyes. She found it first, and I shall never forgive myself."

"What does *Abahati* mean?" Jinny said. "Bugs in bed or rhinos in the john or what?"

"It means Happy Camp, Lucky Camp," Harry said, and pressed the gas. The jeep leaped and bounded at fifty miles an hour over the plain, occasionally loosening teeth as Harry struck a stone or a hole or a stick.

"Happy Camp, yet," Virginia said. "Lost in the jungle with two idiots and they call it Happy Camp. Ah well, a girl learns to put up with anything if she's married to a writer. Lead on, Mac-Selby, and tell the hyenas they got new food for thought, meaning me."

We couldn't make much out of *Campi Abahati* at midnight, except that seven hyenas, three lions, and an assortment of baboons and leopards seemed to be eagerly awaiting us. It looked pretty dreary.

"This doesn't seem like the happiest *campi* I ever *campi-ed* in," the *memsaab* said as we crawled under the mosquito nets and a lion voiced a certain amount of displeasure fifty yards away.

When we left it ten days later she cried. And not from relief.

I woke up in an Old Testament, or possibly Koranic, paradise. To estimate a paradise today you have to call it a place that God was happy to make, had not erred in the making, with the original creatures in it and not even man behaving very badly. The Happy Camp, the Lucky Camp, was on a grassy knoll overlooking the Grummetti River. We pitched the tents beneath big thorn acacias. Up the river a leopard sawed. Over the hill a lion spoke. The baboons came to call to see that we were doing everything right. Halfway between the camp and Harry's favorite leopard trees was a big anthill twelve feet high. Somewhere along the marsh there would be a couple of juvenile twin rhinos, especial friends of Harry's, and one old buffalo bull with a crumpled right horn.

"One of these days I shall have to kill that ancient character," Harry said at breakfast. "I have wasted more time stalking him than I have time to waste. I get up to him at last every time and he looks at me and leers. He knows that I won't permit the client to shoot him, with that ugly, stupid, worn-down horn. He wastes my time, but he is a friend of mine, and I've never had the heart to settle his troubles for him."

I am always amazed when I think of how much living can be compressed into a tent settlement. We had four major tents, not counting the toilet one. We had a big double-fly job for the *memsaab* and the *bwana*. Selby slept in a single double-fly. There was a big open-faced dining tent in which all the boxes of food were stacked. There was a tiny cook tent, and some of the boys had shelter-halves. It takes fifty minutes to set it all up, and the next day it bears the earmarks of a thriving city. Somehow it suddenly becomes logical to go to the john in a canvas cell and to wash your dirty body in a canvas coffin, in water full of living things, and to sleep soundly with the hyenas tripping over the tent ropes.

The sounds become wonderfully important. There is a dove that sounds like a goosed schoolgirl. He says: "Oooh. Oooh! OOOHH!" The bush babies cry. The colobus monkeys snort

like lions, except that it does not carry the implied threat. At
first it is hard to tell the baboons from the leopards when they
curse each other in a series of guttural grunts. A hyena can roar
like a lion. A lion mostly mutters with an asthmatic catch in his
throat. The bugs are tumultuous. A well-situated jungle camp is
not quiet. But the noise makes itself into a pattern which is
soothing except when the hyenas start to giggle. A hyena's giggle
is date night in the female ward of a madhouse.

"You will find yourself growing fond of old *Fisi*," Harry said.
"He's a noisy nuisance and a cheeky brute, but if you took him
out of Africa it wouldn't be Africa any more. He's a tidy one
too. Cleans up everything for you."

We slept late that morning, bone-sore from the three-day
drive, and along about elevenish Harry said we'd best go and
sight the guns in. We left Mama in the camp to repair the rav-
ages to her beauty and drove along the plain. The grass was
short. The grass was trampled. And all the animals in the world
were busy trampling it.

Our camp was cuddled in the crook of a low mountain's arm,
but behind was plain, a brilliant yellow plain dotted with blue-
and-white primrosy sorts of flowers. Wherever you looked there
was life. Five thousand wildebeest there. Five thousand zebras
yonder. Two hundred impala here. A thousand Tommies
there. Five hundred Grant gazelles there. A herd of buffalo on
the river. Harry's twin baby rhinos. A shaggy-necked, elky-
looking waterbuck with his harem in the green reeds. If you
grew grass on Times Square and cleaned up the air and made it
suddenly quiet and filled it with animals instead of people you
might approach some likely approximation of what I saw that
morning, with the sky blue and the hills green and the plain
yellow and blue and white.

The animals looked at us casually and with little curiosity.
We stopped the jeep beneath a thornbush and Harry motioned to Kidogo. Kidogo, wearing his floppy shorts on his
skinny bowed legs and his big cheerful grin on a face like an
Abyssinian king, picked up the *panga* and walked a hundred

yards away to another tree and chopped a big blaze off it with the *panga*. Harry took a couple of cushions out of the Land Rover and laid them on its bonnet. He spraddled his short thick legs, leaned the .375 against the cushions, and fired. Kidogo tapped a point of the blaze with his *panga*.

"High and left," Harry said. "We'll just rearrange these graticules." He did something to the scope and then rapped on it with a big .416 cartridge to see that the new setting was solid. He fired again, and this time the big Winchester was dead on.

"Good gun, that," he said. "Just remains to see if you can hold it as steadily as it'll shoot straight for you if you give it the chance."

We—he—sighted all the guns, the .375, the .30-'06, the .220, and the big ugly .470 double. I shot them all afterward. They all seemed to kick. The big .470 had a push, but it pushed you back two feet. I was beginning to feel nervous, having never shot anything more serious than a shooting-gallery duck with a rifle. These guns seemed to make a god-awful amount of noise.

"Tell you what," Harry said. "We'd best break you in easy and get you used to the light and the guns. On the way back to camp we'll let you shoot a zebra for the boys to eat and a Tommy for us to eat and a Grant and a warthog for a leopard bait. I've a very fine tree just down from the camp. Always seem to haul a leopard out of it. Harriet Maytag shot an eight-foot tom out of it three months ago, and the *manamouki*—the tabby—had a new boy friend in it the next night. A lot of blokes fancy just hogs for leopard kill, but I've had any amount of luck with Grants. To play the percentage evenly I generally use both a Grant and a pig. Been awfully lucky so far."

We climbed into Jessica and aimed for the camp and lunch. A herd of Grants looked at us and ambled slowly away, walking gingerly on seemingly sore feet.

"See the old boy, the last one, just over there?" Harry said. "He's an old ram and about ready for the hyenas. He'd be tougher than whitleather and his liver is full of worms and his meat is measly, but the leopards won't care. Get out and wallop him. *Toa* .30-'o6," he snapped over his shoulder to Kidogo. The Nandi gunbearer slid the bolt of the little Remington and handed it to me. I slid out of the car and crawled to an anthill. The jeep went away. One does not shoot from cars in Africa, nor until the vehicle is a good five hundred yards away. The Game Department aesthetically deplores car shooters and also puts them in jail.

I have shot at submarines and I have shot at airplanes and I didn't shake, but now I shook. The sight of the rifle was revolving like a Catherine wheel. It seemed to me my breath had ceased forever, and I was panting like a sprint horse extended out of class in a distance race. My eyes blurred. I aimed at the gazelle's shoulder, waited until the rifle stopped leaping, snatched at the trigger, and heard the bullet whunk. I aimed at the shoulder and I hit him in the hind left ankle. Great beginning, boy, I said. Steady rest on 135 pounds of standing animal and you hit him in the foot. I shot five more times, carefully. The last time I shot he jumped into the bullet which broke his neck. He went down on his horns, and the jeep drove up to get me.

"Nice shooting," Harry said.

"*Piga. Kufa. M'zuri sana*," the boys said.

"Nuts," I said. "It looks like I am a shotgun man."

"You broke his neck," Harry said.

"I was aiming at his behind," I said.

"It's like that for everybody at first," Harry said. "The light, you know. Everybody misses at first."

"Look, the light hasn't got anything to do with my shakes," I said. "The light doesn't make the gun wiggle like a cooch dancer. I got no guts. I shake and I can't control my breath. I aim at the shoulder and hit it in the foot. I am sighted in on his can and I break his neck. This we can't blame on the light. This we can't blame on the gun."

"Take it easy, take it easy," Harry said. "It happens to everybody. Even Hemingway. It even happened to Theodore Roosevelt."

(63)

"*Bwana Haraka,*" Adam, the Wakamba gunbearer, said. "*Pandi hio. Ngiri.*"

"Nice wart hog," Harry said. "We need him to go with the Grant. *Toa* .220, Kidogo. You can shoot this one from the car," he said to me. "It's vermin and legal and you can get a steady rest on the windscreen. Wallop him up the rear. Bullet ranges forward, and if it doesn't break his back it'll work into his chest cavity."

The pig was trotting, his antenna-tail straight up. I held the little hopped-up .22 on his buxom backside and it felt steady. I squeezed and peeled a ham off his right hip. He let out a squeal and went into the bush, leaving blood behind him. We tracked him and we never found him and I looked sadly at the .220 Swift and sadly at the boys and sadly at Selby.

"You can blame the gun on this one," Harry said. "The bullet broke up on the outside of the pig. Didn't penetrate. I have read a lot about these speedy little guns, but it seems to me they wreck the little stuff and just savage the bigger stuff. Let's try it once again on the hyena over there."

The hyena was watching us as we drove up, his big dog's face mean and sullen, his lion's ears pricked, scabby hide ugly in the sun. As we approached he gallumped slowly away, the hindquarters that God crippled sloping down from his bear's body, a dog's head with a lion's ears on a bear's body with the hind legs of a crippled beggar. *Fisi,* spotted and stinking and no friend to anyone. I shot him. I shot him nine times with the .220 Swift. I hit him every time, and every time the bullet splattered on his outside. One time I hit him in the face and took away his lower jaw and still he didn't die. He just bled and began to snap fruitlessly with half a face at his own dragging guts. I spoke my first command in Swahili.

"*Toa bundouki m'kubwa,*" I said. "The big one. Gimme the .470." The gunbearer snapped the barrels onto the elephant gun and slipped a couple of cigar-sized shells into it. I held it on the gory hyena and took his head off.

"They say it's a good woodchuck gun, the .220," Harry said.

Use Enough Gun

"I'm inclined to believe they may be right. But for pigs and hyenas and such it ain't much gun, is it?"

"I just fired it for the last time," I said. "I wouldn't even use it on a woodchuck. Or a skunk. Or anything else I had any respect for. Give it to the deserving poor."

"I am beginning to like you a little bit," Harry said. "I am completely caught up with clients who want to go out and slay a bull rhino with one of these silly freak guns with an ounce of lead and a lot of speed. I am strictly a heavy-bullet man myself. I cannot abide wounding things that could be simply killed if you used enough gun. But you'd be surprised how vain some of these sportsmen are. It gets us professionals killed. Some sporty type wants to do it all himself, wounds, doesn't want us to collaborate, it goes off into the bush, and then I wind up having to go after it."

"Pal, you are not hunting with a vain man," I said. "Anything I shoot that needs extra shooting you are invited. Be my guest. Collaborate, when and as necessary, and do not pause to check with your client. Shoot it first and I will argue with you later."

We shaped back to camp again and put up another hog, a biggish boar accompanied by the sow and six piglets.

"You'll kill this one well," Harry said. "Mind what I say. Use the .30-'06."

The boar was running diagonally across and ahead of us. The Remington felt comfortable in my hands. I swung it ahead of the boar's shoulder and squeezed her off. The pig did a forward flip and stayed still. One of the gunbearers exhaled sharply.

"*Kufa,*" he said. "*M'zuri sana. Piga m'zuri.*"

"Old *Bwana* Firecracker," Harry said, grinning. "The toast of the Muthaiga Club. You have now passed your apprenticeship. That is a very dead pig and a very nice shot and we will hang the pig in the tree next to the Grant and we will shoot us a very nice leopard, and now for Christ sake quit worrying about your shooting."

Just before we got back to camp we remembered that I was supposed to shoot a Tommy for our table. There was a likely-looking one standing and switching his tail. I got out of the jeep with the Remington and shot him. I shot at him fourteen times. My wife killed him three days later. He had horns good enough for space in Rowland Ward's records.

I did not speak much during lunch.

I don't think I ate any, as a matter of fact. All I could think of was the fact that the guy who couldn't hit a Tommy was supposed to shoot a lion.

We left the *mem* in camp again to do whatever it is that women have to do, and we went down by the reeds. We had Kidogo and Adam and Kibiriti along as ballast. We drove slowly along the wet edge of the high green reeds and we flushed a herd of waterbuck, but the bull wasn't much and you can't eat them anyhow, so we pushed on and then Kibiriti rapped Harry on the shoulder. A ripple showed through the reeds.

"*Kita*," Kibiriti said.

It was a hunting cheetah, and you could see his small round head plowing through the reeds, and he looked over his shoulder once and then took off like a shot.

"*Hapana*," Kibiriti said.

"He's right," Harry said. "This one we will not see again. When they go they *go*, and you have had him. Let's go shoot a zebra for the blacks to eat."

Kibiriti said something rapidly in Swahili. It was about a paragraphful of Swahili.

"The old boy's come down with one of his hunches," Harry said. "He's feeling liony. He says that, the way the moon is and what with the rains and all and the state of grass and economics amongst lions in general, he feels like a lion ought to be about three miles from here, comtemplating his navel under a tree hard by a rocky hill. To my certain knowledge Kibiriti has not been here for a year. But if he feels liony we'd best go and take a *dekko* at his hill. Don't let the fez fool you. This is a true savage, and he is finer with a bow or spear than anybody I ever met, and he *feels* lions. Are you up to shooting one today, your first day?"

"Christ preserve us," I said. "Let's hope this lion fancier is wrong. Today I would hate to go up against a bull butterfly."

Use Enough Gun

"You'll change your tune when you see your first shootable *simba*," Harry said. "You'll be awfully brave. You'll probably be so scared that you will mistake fear for bravery and do everything right."

"That's nice to know, Mowgli," I said.

"What's this Mowgli business?" Harry asked.

"He's a fictional figure," I said. "Kipling dreamed him up. He lived among the beasts of the field and seemed to like it. His mother was a wolf."

"Did he have fleas?" Harry asked politely, and swung the jeep toward Kibiriti's hunch, his lion-tenanted rocky hillside.

And it was that simple. We traveled the three miles. There was a rocky hill alongside the marsh. There was a clump of thorn, and under it there was a lion, catching a nap in the afternoon sun which slanted under the umbrella tops of the trees and struck some golden sparks from his blackish-yellow hide.

"*Simba*," Kibiriti said. "*M'kubwa. Doumi,*" as a man might remark that if you go east far enough on Fifty-fourth Street you will find the East River.

"I'm damned if I understand it," Harry said reverently. "This silly bastard is infallible. I *know* he hasn't been here in a year. I also know that three days ago there couldn't have been a lion in the neighborhood because the game is just starting to come in. But here we are. Your first shooting day in Africa and now you've got to shoot a lion. His mane is a little short on top and he's a little past prime. But he's the biggest blighter I've ever seen, and today a lion is a lion. I think you'd best collect this bloke, and maybe we can better him later."

I looked at Kibiriti's broad black face and saw the sun shining through the holes in his pierced lobes. I looked at his red fez and disliked him extremely.

"Why doesn't this idiot mind his business and stay home with his wives, they should cuckold him constantly?" I said bitterly. "Why has the son of a bitch got to go around finding lions on my first day when I can't hit a Tommy in fourteen tries and mammock up a wart hog and shoot Grants in the feet? I don't know anything about shooting lions. I couldn't hit myself in my own foot if I was a conscientious objector. I don't even know if I *want* to shoot a lion. Tell that grinning bastard to quit living my life for me and find his lions on his own time."

"Everybody wants to shoot a lion," Harry said. "That's why safaris cost so much. Even Aly Khan wants to shoot a lion. It's the high cost of lions that's ruining our economy. You can't mean you'd pass up a bargain lion your first day? Harriet Maytag shot one her first——"

"God *damn* Harriet Maytag, whoever she be," I said. "All I hear is Harriet Maytag. Harriet's leopard. Harriet's lion. So all right. Call me Harriet. Let's go shoot the damn thing and then I will be sick."

Harry grinned. Selby is an extraordinarily handsome young man with the kind of curly black hair and dark eyes that bring out the mother in women. He also has wrists as thick as ordinary men's ankles, and a hard mouth that turns down at the corners. In town he looks like what the fagot writers call a "pretty boy." Take him into the bush, among the blacks and beasts, and he is called *m'zee* by natives. *M'zee* means old man. It means respected, ancient sir. It means wisdom and courage and experience. At that particular moment I decided that I had met few people with so much to admire and so little to worry about. He swerved the jeep away from the lion and we stopped her on the side of a hill, five thousand yards away. I lit a cigarette and passed it to Selby. I lit one for myself. Looking at the hands, I noticed that they were not shaking.

Harry unbuttoned the left door from the jeep. He tossed it onto the grass. He said something to Kidogo, the bowlegged gunbearer. It sounded like *wapi hapa iko simba lio pandi hi m'kubwa bandouki bwana piga bloody nugu.* I didn't really listen. I was sending my soul away again. I hoped it was at Toots Shor's having a drink with friends.

"We will collect this *simba* like this," Harry said sternly, like an over-young professor lecturing the class. "Kidogo drives Jessica here. I sit in the middle. You sit on the outside. We will drive as close as we can without annoying this creature overmuch and taking care to observe the government's rule about five hundred yards away, et cetera. When I nudge you, fall out of the jeep. Fall flat and lie still and then we will crawl as close to this *simba* as we can, and when I tell you to shoot him you shoot him. The idea is to get close as you can—less danger of wounding him that way. You wound this chap, old boy, and he gets into those reeds, and we will all have a very nasty time. I'd *not* wound him if I were you. When you've shot him once, shoot him again, and then shoot him once more for insurance. Very sound rule. Old Phil Percival taught it me. All set?"

I couldn't say anything but yes. Kidogo had taken the telescopic sights off the .375. I slid back the bolt and caught the comforting glint of the bullets in the magazine. There was one in the chamber. Good-by, Mother, I said to myself. Et up by a lion in the bloom of youth.

"Well, let's go shoot him," I said. "What are we waiting for?"

"That's the spirit," Harry said. *"Pese pese. Suria. Kwenda."*

The jeep began to roll, Kidogo obeying motions of Harry's hands. We approached the lion deviously. We seemed always to be going away from him but actually were growing closer. Kidogo took his foot off the gas. Harry hit me in the ribs with his elbow. I fell out of the jeep. I remembered to fall with the gun protected and pointing away. Harry tumbled out behind me. He had a dirty, rusty-looking .416 Rigby bolt-action rifle in his hand. He had told me once that it could not hit anything but lions.

I was on my belly in the stiff, coarse yellow grass, and the lion was looking enormous now, staring in that oddly stuffed-shirt profile way they do, like bankers contemplating the future. A lion's hide is not tawny. It is yellowish-black. This one flexed the muscles of his forelegs, hooking his claws, and flicked his back hide to express annoyance at the camel flies that buzzed around him. I was humping along on my elbows, with the gun pushing out ahead of me.

We were close to the lion now. I could count flies on him. Harry reached back and touched me, pressing me down behind a hummock. The lion turned his head and looked straight at us. He *was* a little scruffy on top, but he had a fine dark mane below. His feet were as big as Satchel Paige's feet. His head was as big as a bale of hay. He yawned and I saw he had his right canine tooth broken off. He was huge.

"Wallop him," Selby whispered.

I got up on one knee and went for just behind his ear. He flopped over like a big dog, kicked once, roared once, and stretched out. I never did hear my gun go off and felt no concussion.

"This is the biggest lion I ever saw in my life," Harry said. "Also the deadest. But I should slip another one into him just behind the shoulder blade if I were you. I keep telling you, these dead animals are the ones that get up and kill you. Bust him again."

I busted him again. You could tell he was dead from the sound of the bullet hitting him and his bodily reaction to the bullet hitting him.

"*Kufa,*" Harry said. "My Christ, he's huge. An old boy to boot. Shouldn't be surprised if he isn't the type that citizen in Ikoma was calling a cattle killer. He'd be about ready for cattle now and mauling the odd native now and then. He's about ten years old. I might say you shot him rather well, chum."

"I always shoot lions in the ear," I said. "Like I always shoot Grant gazelles in the foot. I was probably aiming at this one's can too."

"No bloody fear," Harry said. "I was watching you. Old *Bwana Simba.* Old *Bwana Lisasi Moja.* One-Bullet Bob. The toast of the Muthaiga Club. Here come the worshiping throng. They want your autograph. Kill a lion, make friends, influence natives. Nice going, chum."

The boys knew the script well. They all gave me the special handshake, grasping the thumb, roaring asthmatically, and telling me that I was the one-shot *bwana,* the mighty *simba* slayer, the protector of the poor. I agreed readily and then went over behind a bush and vomited just a little bit. This was because of something I had eaten disagreeing with me. Then I went to look at my lion. He looked awfully rumpled. A dead lion has no dignity. All the majesty leaks out of him with the blood. He looks like a moth-bit rug, and after a while his mane drops off.

"This is a hell of a lion," I said.

I looked at my lion. The top of his brainpan was off. We walked off his measurements and he was ten foot six. That is a lot of lion. His paws were as big as pumpkins. It suddenly occurred to me that I had crawled up on this thing as close as I had to get and when I had to shoot him I shot him and didn't wound him and of a sudden the boys were admiring me and Harry was kidding me and I felt real good. I hadn't spooked. I hadn't butched it. I hadn't looked bad in front of the boys.

I am a hell of a fellow, I said to myself. I am a slayer of Simba, Lord of the Jungle. And anyhow, I didn't run or fire into the air. Whisky is indicated.

We wrestled the corpse into the back of the jeep, on a matting of rushes so he wouldn't bleed up the Rover. I talked a great deal on the drive back to camp and accepted congratulations freely. One of the camel flies bit me painfully, and I didn't care. I was suddenly free of a great many inhibitions. Every man has to brace a lion at least once in his life, and whether the lion is a woman or a boss or the prospect of death by disease makes no difference. I had met mine and killed him fairly and saved him from the hyenas which would have had him in a year or so if one of his sons didn't assassinate him first.

When we hit the camp the boys knew. They surged over the jeep and me and mauled us all and told us *m'zuri sana, bwana*, and waited for the money tip to the whole camp. They did a sedate lion dance and ran me for alderman of metropolitan Ikoma.

I went down to the tent to collect the hero's bride. She was taking a nap. She bubbled gently as she snored.

"Get up, you lazy slut," I said. "While you are sleeping your life away I have been out slaying lions and protecting the honest poor. Come and see what Father done done with his gun. And bring your camera."

Virginia came with the camera. We posed the defunct *simba*

suitably, his chin arrogantly on a rock. The blacks told me again that I was one hell of a *bwana*. Then the lion's eyes opened. Then his ears twitched. Then he uttered a grunt. Then I found myself alone with a lion and Mr. Selby. The admirers had achieved trees. I am not ashamed to say I shot my *simba* once more in the back of the neck. Like Harry says, it's the dead ones that get up and kill you.

The night we got lost coming into the camp I looked at this brawny child who was going to run my life for me with a slightly new interest. I had lived in the same car, the same camp, with him for three days. We had had some drinks in the Queens' bar in Nairobi and lunch together at the Traveller's Club and I liked the way he tackled the check, like a man used to reaching for it. He had no impediment in his reach, I thought, and snickered at the pun. I would have liked it better if it had been *my* pun.

I had seen him shoot the little Tommy, and I had heard lots of tales about Selby. They told me how he could tie two rocks to strings and start them swinging, like counterpendulums, and then dash off to fifty yards away and wheel and shoot the two twines as they passed in their pendulum swing. They told me how he took a Rigby .450 No. 2 and shot the two swooping kites, the swiftly sliding scavengers, with a right and a left. A man who shoots flying birds with an elephant gun shoots pretty good. They told me about the last buffalo too. The one that Bob Maytag shot and they thought it was dead. It got up and Harry hit it over one eye and Maytag hit it under the other eye and it still kept coming. So Harry shot it through the *pupil*. I presume he wasn't aiming elsewhere.

He seemed the kind of kid girls might like to marry or mothers might want to raise. He was polite to excess, extremely courteous to Virginia, and he always offered a cigarette when he smoked one himself. He blushed rather easily, and when he swore, it was self-conscious. Virginia after three days was just a little bit in love with him already. With the tumbled curly hair and the deep eyes and the self-confidence and the reputation behind him for being all man, and clean man, you would wonder how the women left him single that long. And shy, too. And modest.

He was a long way from the fictional idea of the professional. The popular conception of a white hunter, built largely in the American mind on film portrayals by Gregory Peck and Stewart Granger, is almost as erroneous as the movie and popular magazine accounts of African safaris. According to what you may have seen or read, the basic idea of a professional hunter is roughly this:

He stands about six foot five, sports a full beard, and is drunk (off his client's liquor) most of the time. He always makes a play for the client's beautiful wife and/or sister, and always scores. He shoots lions with pistols and wrestles with snakes and buffalo for fun. When he is not out on the safari he hangs around bars in Nairobi, ogling the girls and thumbing the big cartridges he wears in the loops of his jacket. He does all the shooting for the client, while the client sits comfortably in the shooting car. He is always taciturn in a me-Tarzan-you-Jane manner. He has a secret sorrow which drove him to a life among the wild beasts. His business is regarded as butchery, and it takes a superhuman man to be a competent butcher.

This is about as accurate as the average movie presentation of high life in New York, or the general supposition that all Englishmen have no chins and sport monocles. In some respects the white or professional big-game hunter, African variety, is the toughest man in the world, and in others he is as gentle as a dead dove and as unsophisticated as Huck Finn. He is competent at his job, which is why he is alive, but you will see more rugged types on the dance floor at El Morocco. And he is the last of a breed of men who have such a genuine love for the wilds and such a basic hatred of civilization that they are willing literally to kill themselves with backbreaking work and daily danger, on a nine-months-per-year basis, for less pay than a good waiter in

New York draws. They forswear matrimony, generally, because no wife lasts long when the old man is off twisting the tails of leopards for most of the calendar year. They save only a little money, for the upkeep on their hunting cars largely outweighs their income, and they blow the rest in Nairobi between safaris or in the rainy seasons when hunting is impossible. They are referred to as a vanishing breed because there are somewhat less than thirty practicing top pros in British East Africa today, and in a very short time there will be little big stuff left to practice on. It is thought by most of the smart ones that the next three or four years will see the last of safari in the old sense, when a man went out to kill a lion, a leopard, an elephant, and the more elusive big antelopes with some feeling of certainty.

Harry Selby is possibly the best of the current bunch—certainly there's no better about, and his popularity is such that he is booked up five years ahead. He was not yet twenty-seven at the time I write but has been an able pro since he was twenty. He was born and raised in East Africa, on a cattle farm in Nanyuki, Kenya Colony, and had killed his first elephant before he was fifteen. He looks like a public-school boy and speaks an impeccable British English in such a gentle voice that even an occasional "damn" sounds very wicked.

Tony Henley, whom I had met, was raised on the slopes of Mount Kenya and was an old pro at twenty-three. He is a blond youngster who looks like a substitute end on a high school football team. Tony Dyer, at twenty-six, looks like the valedictorian in a junior-college graduation exercise. Donald Ker, a partner in the firm of Ker and Downey, is a small, thin, mild-seeming man in his forties. His partner, Syd Downey, looks like an ordinary businessman, is pushing fifty, and still is rated one of the best in the business. Andrew Holmberg, the expert on mountain game, is a strapping, rosy-cheeked six-footer who might very well be a junior advertising executive. And the now-retired dean of the bunch, Philip Percival, who raised Harry, is a plump old gentleman with stubby legs, who looks about as fierce as Colonel Blimp.

Yet all these men have made a business of mingling daily with lions, leopards, and the most dangerous trio—buffalo, elephants, and rhinos—and have managed to stay alive, although nearly all have horn wounds and claw scars, and all have considered death as a daily diet. They have a tremendous respect for dangerous animals. When they are hurt, ninety-nine times out of a hundred they are injured trying to protect a client who has just shown arrant cowardice or complete stupidity. Yet no client is ever publicly branded a coward. No client is ever tagged as a kill-crazy meat hog. No lady ever misses her lion—not for the record anyhow. The code says that the hunters don't talk, once the safari is over. That is ridiculous, of course. They talk plenty, mostly among themselves, but occasionally to customers they have come to know and respect.

The function of a professional hunter on safari is almost god-like. He is responsible for the safety of the whole shebang—you, himself, and the black boys who make up your *shauri*. He is the guide over trackless wastes. He is the expert on finding game and seeing that his dude is in the best possible position to shoot it.

If you ask him, he will shoot it for you, but he will quietly despise you as a man, and the contempt he feels will be mirrored in the black faces.

If you wound an animal, it is the hunter's responsibility to go into the bush and finish it off, both out of humanitarianism and caution, since a wounded lion or buffalo is bound to kill the first unlucky local who crosses his path. At all times he is the servant of the Game Department, whose laws are strict and in whose employ are many spies.

The hunter stands at your side to backstop you on dangerous game. His idea of a pleasant safari is one on which he is not forced to fire a gun once. But if the going gets nasty, his big double is your insurance.

"I don't care a damn about these people who can split a pea at three hundred yards," old Phil Percival once remarked. "What I want to know about a man is how good he is on a charging buffalo at six feet."

The heavy work for a hunter is not so much the location of

game and the supervision of the final kill as the camp routine. He supervises a tiny portable city—administers loading and unloading in exactly the right order, ordains the pitching of camp, selecting camp, looks after the water supply, supervises the skinners and trackers and gunbearers and porters and cooks and body servants. He must be an expert mechanic—he must be able to rebuild a motorcar from the spare parts he carries and improvise those parts he has not.

The hunter is responsible for correct victualing of an expedition that may be out from town three or four months, so that he needs a dietitian's knowledge of supplementary canned goods and a balanced menu. He is directly responsible for providing an average of ten pounds a day, per man, of fresh meat. In most cases the ordinary day's killing will keep sufficient meat in camp.

As the head of a safari, the hunter finally combines the duties of a sea captain, a bodyguard, a chauffeur, a tracker, a skinner, a head-waiter, a tourist guide, a photographer, a mechanic, a stevedore, an interpreter, a game expert, a gin rummy partner, drinking companion, social equal, technical superior, boss, employee, and handy man. The difficulty of his position is magnified in that he lives in the pockets of his one or two clients for long weeks, and unless he is a master of tact, nobody is speaking to anyone else when the safari pays off in Nairobi. The old-timers had a phrase to describe a safari gone sour.

"I'm still drinking their whisky," the hunter would say, meaning that all social intercourse had ceased and the safari was operating on a basis of frigid politeness, with the hunter keeping himself to himself except during shooting hours.

More dangerous than an angry cow elephant with a young calf, Harry had said, is the woman on safari. She is generally rich and spoiled, old and full of complaints, or young and apt to fall a little bit in love with the hunter. In a tent community, this puts rather a strain on the young man who is accepting the husband's pay to hunt animals instead of wives. Living *à trois* can be a difficult operation in the midst of Tanganyika when the *memsaab* has a tendency to cast goo-goo eyes at the professional and invent ways to catch him alone. "Even the best of the sporting ladies," Harry said, "even the most rugged of the female hunters, has a tendency to woof at the monotony of the food, the lack of toilet facilities, and the prevalence of bugs, snakes, and scorpions. Africa is dusty, and Africa is wet and hot and cold, and a tent is not the Norfolk, nor is a canvas tub a Grecian bath. Warm martinis can irk on a delicately reared lady. A girl gets tired of hearing incessant conversation of guns and game and grass. I know of no hunter who is delighted at the prospect of setting out with a lady who may turn out to be either shrew or nymphomaniac."

Some of the ladies can be fun, though, he said. Selby was out once on a more or less photographic safari with the Duchess of Grafton.

"We were taking some snaps of impala, or something tame," Selby said, "when we spooked an old gentleman rhino who was very cross at being woken from his nap. As we'd no license for rhino, I didn't like to shoot it, so I said to the Duchess: 'Your Grace, you'd best make for yonder tree.' The old girl took off at the speed of knots and went up the tree like a squirrel, camera and all. Then I entered into a delaying action."

Back in Nairobi, however, the Duchess told the press a different story.

"I was safely ensconced on my limb," the Duchess said, "when I heard a small, polite voice below me. It was Mr. Selby, who was running round and round the tree, with the rhino's horn just behind him. The small voice said: 'If you please, Your Grace, would you mind moving up another branch? I may need the one you're sitting on.' "

Selby denied this. He says it would never have occurred to him to address her as "Your Grace" under such trying circumstances.

Harry was talking on as he shoved the jeep along. "The sense of humor of these men is rather amazing. We have an old-timer, Murray Smith, who once dived into the bush with his client after a wounded rhino. The old rhino boiled out from behind a thorn tree, and as old Murray squared away to face it, he went tail over tip into a pig hole and sprawled flat. The *faro* came at him, and all Smith could do was seize its horn with both hands and hang on for dear life, with the *faro* bouncing him up and down. The client, who, I expect, wasn't a coward, ran up and stuck his gun in the rhino's ear, and saved old Murray from a very sticky finish. Later somebody asked him what he thought of when the rhino had him down.

" 'All I could think of,' Murray said, 'was that now I had hold of it, the horn seemed *longer* than I thought it was when I told the client to shoot.' "

Harry was saying that there are clients who are too brave, who insist on shooting everything themselves, and who also insist that the hunter not shoot under any circumstances. These are the people who generally get the hunters maimed, since they are prone to shoot too fast and from too great a distance, wounding the game and making it necessary for the professional to go and collect it from the thornbush.

There are the too timid, who shoot wildly, run away, drop their guns, and generally foul up the detail. They refuse to take advantage of the old safety axiom: "Get as close as you can, and then get ten feet closer." They bang away from afar and gut-shoot the lion or merely annoy the buffalo, and the poor old pro has to make amends in the name of the Game Department.

There is the complete phony, who gets out of the city limits and says: "Look, you shoot it all, but don't tell anybody." This is a fairly simple type to handle, since a competent pro can round up the fraud's complete bag, on reasonably mediocre animals, and send the fellow back to brag in his club in no time at all. But a hunter spits when he mentions a client of this sort.

From the hunter's standpoint the ideal customer is a man who is scared enough to be cautious, but brave enough to control his fear. He follows instructions, knows and is frank about his own limitations on stamina, and quits when he has had enough of mountains and swamps and dust and bumps for one day. He shoots his own game but is not averse to a little help when a buffalo or something else large and fierce needs some extra killing. I learned about this one later.

"You know," Harry said, "there's hell's own amount of clients

Use Enough Gun

who carry on frightfully if the hunter collaborates. They won't even accept the animal, won't even let the boys skin out the head. Lot of bloody nonsense, of course, but there you are. They're the chaps who get us killed."

The true professional hunter has something of the bullfighter's philosophy, in that he has no guarantee he will see the bright lights and pretty girls of Nairobi ever again. In the final analysis he has to stand and fight. Each man I came to know has had a dozen slim squeaks, mostly from elephants and buffalo. When the crisis occurs, there is no place to run, no tree to climb as a rule, because the wounded animal usually starts his charge in thick bush, from a few feet, and he nearly always sees you before you see him. Some remarkable escapes from certain death have occurred.

Frank Bowman, an Australian and a very fine hunter who is now retired, once sat on the ground with a twisted ankle and no bullets for his gun while a wounded buffalo got up and staggered, sick but still furious, toward him. Bowman screamed for a gunbearer to fetch more bullets, waited until the bearer had run to the car to get them, slapped two fresh bullets in his double, and shot the buff at a range of about one foot. It fell in his lap. The time between no bullets and two bullets must have been the longest recorded wait in the history of hunting, at least from Bowman's angle.

"This gunbearer, Adam," Harry said, "was elevated to the aristocracy in the following manner: Old Phil Percival, with an empty gun, was being chased round and round the hunting car by a wounded buffalo, and all the natives in the back—save Adam—panicked and went over the side. Adam was a porter then. He sorted through the dozen different varieties of cartridges in the back of the car until he found a couple of slugs that fitted old Phil's gun. He handed them to the old boy as he went round the car for the umpteenth time. Percival loaded his weapon in full flight. He settled the animal. As of then Adam was promoted."

Percival, Harry told me, in his later days as a hunter, had still another narrow squeak. Three rhinos charged him and Tommy

Shevlin, an American sportsman and a fine shot, penning them in a narrow avenue cut through the thorn. Shevlin's killing shot dropped the nearest rhino across old Philip's legs.

Anyone who hunts elephants, rhinos, or buffalo is a candidate for catastrophe. It is occasionally necessary, in a buffalo stampede in high grass, to whack the nearest animal and *climb up on him*, so that the other great beasts can swerve aside and pass around you. Both elephants and rhinos will charge, unwounded and unpredictably.

The point is that what is one client's rare thrill is routine for the pros. I imagine Murray Smith has been hurt three or four times. Selby has already had six or seven scrapes with buffalo, several with elephants, and a couple of do's with lions and leopards. Syd Downey has been tossed twice by buffalo and has contracted sleeping sickness from tsetse-fly bites. Nearly all East African hunters have a chronic malaria that reduces them to bone-breaking agony and pitiful shakes several times a year. Their lungs are abrased from constant inhalation of lava dust, and their eyes are permanently bloodshot from dust and glare.

Their average day starts at 4:30 A.M., and they rarely bed down before 11 P.M. During the course of a day they will drive a hunting car an average of 125 miles over trackless, tough terrain. They will walk an average of ten over mountains and through swamps, and they will crawl from one to five miles on their bellies. If you are hunting elephants you will walk from twenty to thirty miles a day over dry river beds that suck your shoes into the sliding softness and make every step a mighty effort. The sun smites like hammers all day long, and the nights, in most parts of huntable Africa, are bitter cold. After a full day's work they are still supposed to supervise the constant necessary repair of the hunting vehicles, see that the camp is in good order, solve the problems of from one to two dozen natives, tend the sick, and still be jovial drinking, talking, and card-playing companions to the paying guests. Added to the general chores is the task of explaining the same things, over and over, to a succession of clients who want to know (and rightly) what is that tree, what kind of bird is that, why do we camp here instead of there, and what were the boys saying in Swahili? The hunter also must listen to all the alibis, again and again, as to why the shooter missed the topi at twenty-five yards from a steady rest, and must soothe the injured pride of the man who is paying a hundred dollars a day to do something he would really rather not do, such as crawling through thorns after a sick and angry leopard.

The question, then, must be: *What do they get out of it?* They don't shoot unless they have to, and mostly they take no delight in killing, but rather regard it regretfully as the logical end point of an exciting adventure. They are the greatest of game conservationists—the strictest abiders by the rules. They'll average five or six hundred bucks a month, plus free food and whisky, but they'll spend three or four hundred fixing up the cars they wreck in their mad dashes over rocky hills and pig-hole-riddled fields. They put up with boors and bores and bitches and cowards and braggarts and creeps and occasional homosexuals who have the eye more on the hunter than on the game. They work harder than any of the blacks in their retinue. They have no home life—they don't even share the canvas latrine tent which is set up for the client. They consider death as calmly as life, even when it applies to themselves. They drink too much, like sailors off a long cruise, when they are in town, and they mostly throw away their money. There is no real future in professional hunting—when you get older you get too cautious for your own safety, and your slowed reflexes make you a liability to yourself and to your party.

I believe I already knew what they get out of it. There is a simple love of outdoors and of creatures, as against a hatred for the contrived living of cities, for the claustrophobic connivances of civilization, that drives a man to the vastnesses of Africa to fulfill some need of basic simplicity in himself. My friend Selby, hopelessly lost in the jungles of so small a town as Nairobi, is Moses leading his flock when all he can see is horizons and a lion or two. The complete love and trust of his blacks are testament to this.

He is happy in the dawn and in the tiny-gleaming fires of the camp, and secure in his knowledge of domination of his element. He worships a buffalo or a lion or an elephant because he knows it can kill him painfully if he is not very careful. He builds his own bridges, makes his own roads. He still has the thrill of providing his own food and the food of his friends. He recognizes the inevitability of death as an adjunct to life.

There are no more jealous people in the world than hunters. They have an intense pride in their work. A good white hunter will work himself into a breakdown to scare up a record bag for a man he despises. Hunters criticize each other constantly, and each man has his secret ground, a territory where he endeavors, as long as possible, to keep from shooting the easy animal—what he wants is "heads."

"You are not shooting an elephant," Selby told me. "You are shooting the symbol of his tusks. You are not shooting to kill. You are shooting to make immortal the thing you shoot. To kill just anything is a sin. To kill something that will be dead soon, but is so fine as to give you pleasure for years, is wonderful. Everything dies. You only hasten the process. When you shoot a lion you are actually shooting its mane, something that will make you proud. You are shooting for yourself, not shooting just to kill."

These few surviving men are largely Jasons in search of the Golden Fleece, and they do not care who brings it down, so long as they are present at the chase. Selby and his companions will actually work harder for a man they loathe than for a man they like and admire, because the ultimate end is noble in the mind.

When you are out in the bush for any considerable length of time you do not remember days by date or week or weather. You reach backward to the day of the buffalo or the day of the lion or the day the lorry busted her axle. The day of the waterbuck was quite a day. It got to be more of a day as it went along.

We headed out of camp with the dew still bright on the grasses, looking for nothing. It is a gorgeous way to hunt, looking for nothing. You spin along in the jeep and just look. The breakfast is still warm inside you and the second cigarette is tasting almost as good as the first. The sun is just beginning to take a touch of chill off your face, and the woods and plain are alive, vibrant with tentatively stirring animals. The birds, just wakened, are starting to scratch and fly and complain. You drive along by the wood or the river or out along the veldt and you almost hope you will see nothing worth working for that day because it is more fun to watch it than to chase it or shoot it.

"I think we'll check down by the river and see about that waterbuck," Harry said, driving around a herd of impala that seemed trying to set a record for altitude in their leaps. "The ones we have seen have been fairish, but I seem to remember an old gentleman from the last trip who's got more horns than he needs. They must be making his head ache. He used to live over here," Harry said, driving through some reeds and coming out of the reeds to draw up to a small grassy hill with trees and shrubs that looked considerably more like woodcock country than waterbuck country. As we drove up to the summit of the little hill a herd of perhaps a dozen waterbuck broke from the rushes and loped leisurely up the hill and across a small pastury-looking field and stopped just short of a wood.

"That's the gentleman I had in mind," Harry said. "I believe he's the best I've ever seen, but I've never yet had a good look at those horns. Suppose we walk a bit and investigate this fellow."

We climbed out of Jessica. Kidogo handed me the Remington, and Harry started a stalk in that half crouch which looks so easy at first and then forcibly reminds you of age and girth as it continues. I was puffing when Harry held his hand, palm down and pushing backward, in the stop sign. We were in a small copse of trees and thick lianas as big as your wrist, with the dew still heavy on the grass underfoot and on the leaves that brushed your face. Harry reached around, grabbed my gun arm, and pointed with my arm. The herd of buck was in the pasture, feeding straight at us. You could feel the fresh brisk wind blowing directly into your face, curling back your eyelashes and causing a

constant rustle in the trees—which is always fortunate if you are
the kind of man who steps on dry sticks and goes through bush
like a bull buffalo in a hurry.

They were beautiful. A little suspicious at the extra rustle I
made, maybe, but with no scent of our presence and no real
worry about the snapping and crackling in the clump of trees.
The bull was looking straight at me.

Waterbuck are awful to eat, since they are tough and carry an
insect repellent in their hides, a greasy ointment that comes off
on your hands and smells like hell. Their fat is made so that it
congeals swiftly in the cooking and winds up in hard balls, stuck
in your teeth. But there is no more ruggedly handsome animal
in Africa.

The bull will weigh nearly as much as an elk. He is not so
rangy, nor does he stand so high, but he has a thick, tufted elk's
neck, a noble face, a compact, heavily furred body. He will
weigh around seven hundred pounds. He is beautifully marked
in black and white and grayish-fawn, and his horns are slim parentheses that are heavily gnarled at the base and finish off in
four inches of clean ivory point. Perhaps a kudu is more beautiful, but he does not own the compact, rugged, swell-necked mas-
culinity of a mature waterbuck.

My boy was walking steadily toward me. My breath had come
back a little. The Remington was braced in the crotch of a small
scrubby tree. The gun was shaking again, and the limber limb
was moving gently to match my shakes. The buck kept coming. I
put the post of the telescopic sight on his chest, sucked in my
breath, and started what I hoped would be a squeeze.

The squeeze was two-thirds complete when Harry's hand
came back and closed over my trigger hand.

"Watch," he said. "Wait."

The magnificent bull separated into two animals. What I had
been aiming at suddenly became a cow, who sidled off to the
left. My bull had been standing so directly behind one of his
wives that his horns had appeared to be growing from her head.
In a hundredth of a second I would have shot the cow. When

they separated, it was exactly like watching two images merge and move apart in the sighting machinery of a Leica. The cow sidled off. The bull looked me straight in the eye at thirty yards and snorted irritably. His horns appeared to be the size and length of two evenly warped baseball bats.

Harry's hand came away from my gun hand. The post went back to the old gentleman's chest, and the unseen force which fires guns operated. The waterbuck went straight up in the air and turned at the top of his leap. He must have been a good six feet off the ground. The herd of cows and yearlings went off with a snort and a crash. There was nothing to be seen.

"I hit him," I said to Selby. "I hit him where I was holding. I was holding just to the right of his breastbone. If this boy ain't dead I am going back to Nairobi. This is the first time since I've been here that I felt confident about anything."

"You hit him all right," Harry said. "I heard the bullet smack. But where you hit him remains to be seen. Christ, wasn't he something to see standing there with that head thrown back? Let's go see what happened to him."

Kidogo and Adam had come up. They looked at Selby.

"*Piga*," Selby said. "*Kufa*—maybe. But he was a big one. A real *m'kubwa sana*."

"*Ehhh*," the boys said without much enthusiasm. Kidogo stopping, tracking, walked over to where the animal had been when I shot him. You could see the deep scars his feet had made in the turf when he jumped. Fifteen yards away Kidogo stooped and picked up a stalk of yellow grass. It was brilliant scarlet for three inches at its tip.

"*Damu*," Kidogo said. "*Piga m'uzuri*."

"That's heart blood," Harry said. "Not lung blood or belly blood. The lung blood's clottier and pinker. The belly blood's got more yellow to it. You got this bugger in the engine room, I think."

Everybody tracking now, including me, we followed the bright slashes of blood for fifty yards or so, turned a sharp L around the patch of bush, and almost stumbled over my fellow.

He was completely dead. I had taken him through the heart squarely as he stood with his head up and his chest thrown out. Harry took one look at him and let out a yell like a Masai *moran* on the warpath. He threw himself at the animal, seized it around the neck with both arms, and kissed it in the face. Both gunbearers fell on their knees. Kidogo picked up the great noble head by the ears, and he kissed the buck. Adam ran his fingers up and down the chestnut-colored horns, rubbing his fingers over the ivory tips. He said a short prayer in Wakamba. Selby hit me a punch in the chest that nearly floored me, and both boys grabbed me by the arms and danced me around the water-buck.

"I don't suppose you know what you've got here, old boy," Harry said. "Unless I am mad or drunk, you have just walloped the best waterbuck that anybody ever brought out of Tangan-yika. If this one isn't thirty-four inches I will carry him back to camp on my back. This one you can hang on your wall, chum, and Mr. Rowland Ward's records will be very pleased to include him at the top of the heap. Very nice shooting, *bwana*. For one dreadful split second I thought you were going to loose off at that bloody cow. I would have sworn she was the bull. Those horns of his were sticking right out over her ears, and it wasn't until she moved just a fraction of an inch that I realized she was standing square in front of the *doumi*. If she hadn't moved you'd have shot her, the bull would've spooked and would have been halfway across the Serengeti by now. You're a lucky lad."

This was quite a creature, this buck. You couldn't close your hands around his horns at the base. They were serrated and very clean, and they curved inward at each other in a nearly perfect ellipse. His big bull's neck was thick and shaggy with a chest mane. He had a big deer's face, although he was an antelope, and his hairy hide was gray-fawn like a good tweed suit. He was very heavy. It was all the four of us could handle to heft him into the back of the jeep. He smelled like hell, with his insecticide coming out of his special glands and making sweat splotches on his hide.

"We'll take this baby back whole," Harry said. "I want better pictures of him than we can get here. We'll go back to camp and let the *memsaab* do her stuff with the color box." Harry patted the buck on his poll. "You beauty," he said. "You lovely, lovely hunk of horn."

He wheeled Jessica around and we headed back to camp. We were driving slowly across the blue-and-white-flowered plain, full of self-congratulation and the yearning for a celebration drink, an afternoon off to gloat, an afternoon free of hunting, for no man likes to cheapen his achievement by doing something competitively else that same day. A miss on a good head can spoil the hit on the other. This waterbuck was all I wanted from that day or that week, for that matter. I was a little drunk already with the wine of the fine fresh morning and the first real good shot that I had actually made on purpose. I was warmed by the sun and by excitement and by the approval of the boys. They grinned when I turned my head and offered cigarettes. Like Charlie MacArthur when he offered Helen Hayes a bag of peanuts, I was sorry at the time that my cigarettes were not emeralds.

The plain was like a great wheat field, and Jessica went smoothly along in it, her windscreen down. Cloudlike flocks of weaver birds swarmed in masses, dipping and twisting like a miniature tornado. Kidogo braced his bowed Nandi legs around the waterbuck's horns and leaned over to seize me on the shoulder.

"*Simba,*" he said. "*Kishoto kidogo, Bwana Haraka.*" Harry swung Jessica left a little, and there the *simba* was. My neck hair was lifting again. There is no other word in Swahili that carries the electrifying impact of *simba*. Away off, making a gentle ripple in the sea of yellow grass, two rounded ears were flattened to a yellow skull as a lady *simba* stalked a herd of zebra. Her ears looked like a Portuguese man-o'-war sailing along on a quiet ocean. You couldn't see her slither as she moved, belly flat-pressed to the ground, and just her nose and ears showing.

"Let's go and have a look-see," Harry said, wheeling the

Rover. "The old girl's stalking a kill. You very seldom see a solo lioness. The old boy has got to be around somewhere, probably upwind from her, letting his scent float down to distract the zebra while she sneaks in for the kill. Very sensible arrangement. Make the wife do the work, what?"

We drove in narrowing circles through the grass and came up on the lioness. The zebras spooked and took off. The lioness looked annoyed. She curled a disdainful lip and made a half pass at a charge and then bounded away into some scrubby thorn acacia. We circled the bush. On the other side of the prickly island we turned up three more lionesses. And four unsteady, spotted, clumsy cubs. The first lioness growled and started toward the car.

"Mama *simba*," Harry said. "Old boy's bound to be about somewhere. Wouldn't find four *manamouki* and young *mtotos* together without the big fellow, unless he's just been killed, and nobody can've hunted here since before the last rains. Must be the fellow we've heard roaring 'cross the river at night. Nice one, I'll promise you, by the sound of him."

We widened the turning circles, and suddenly Kidogo tapped shoulders again. *"Doumi,"* he said. *"M'kubwa sana. M'uzuri sana."*

He was, too. He was *m'kubwa*. He was real *m'uzuri*. He was male, all right, and he was very big, and he was awful good. His ginger mane sparkled in the climbing sun, and his gray-tawny hide glistened. He looked very burly and handsome against a backdrop of green bush, the yellowing grass just matching his hide. He looked at us and yawned as we drove slowly toward him, with all the bored disdain that a prime lion can muster. He spun on his heel and sauntered into the bush.

"Beauty," Selby said. "Much better than the one you've got. Let's go and have a spot of lunch, pick up the *memsaab*, and after we've eaten we'll come back and collect him."

I said nothing. I had been out long enough to know that Harry thought like an animal, and while I didn't know how he expected to find the lion in the same spot, or how he figured to get him out of the bush, or just how we'd shoot him, or how we'd cope with the others, I shut up. Anyhow, that waterbuck was enough achievement for one day.

We drove the bumpy eight miles back to camp, took black and color pictures of the buck, knocked off a pink gin or so, and ate.

"Come on, Mama," Selby said to Virginia. "We are now going out to collect a lovely lion"—in the same tone as a man who says he is going to walk down to the corner for the papers.

"Yes, master," Virginia said. She had quit asking questions, too, some time back. "Just so long as it's a *lovely* lion."

We drove away. Two miles from where we'd seen the lions Selby stopped the car. A big bull topi was standing sleepily under a tree.

"Get out and shoot him," Harry said. "We need him in our business." I got out and shot the topi. We opened up his belly. One of the gunbearers hitched a rope around his crooked-ended horns, and we headed for the lions, the topi bumping along behind the car.

"Hors d'oeuvres," Selby said. "The lions must be hungry, otherwise the lady wouldn't have been out after those *punda*. Can't have killed lately. We will ask our friends to tea. Fetch'm out of the bush for the party."

We drove up and saw all the lionesses and the cubs where we'd left them. Mama lion snarled.

"Unpleasant sort," Selby said. "Got an ugly face for a lion. Disagreeable. Oho," he said, "look there."

Here was Papa, all right, and he was about twice as big, twice as massively maned, and twice as fine as the other we'd seen that morning. He raised his heavy head, looked at us a very short second, and leaped into the bush. His mane was bright cherry-red.

"Shy type," Selby said. "Wants coaxing. We'll coax him." We drove back and forth in front of the bush.

"Smell it, chum," Selby said. "Smell it good. Smells nice, what? Pray do come and dine with us."

(89)

He drove then to a broad, clear, grassy oasis in the bush and dropped the topi. It was at least a couple of hundred yards from the nearest thorn. Then we drove a couple of thousand yards away and killed the motor under a mimosa. Harry got out the binoculars.

"All we need now is a few fine vultures or a noble hyena or so," Harry said. "If just one vulture drops, or old *Fisi* comes bouncing out to feed off that kill, you'll see more lions boiling out of that bush than you'll know what to do with. They just can't stand to see anything else chewing up that nice, fresh topi. They're greedy, just like people."

The vultures came and circled slowly and warily in the clear blue sky. The sun was boiling down now, and everyone was sweating—me especially. The executioner's job was mine. I'd killed my first lion ten minutes after I'd spotted him and hadn't really had time to think about him before I was tumbling out of the jeep with a gun in my hand and crawling toward him. But now it was past three o'clock and I'd been thinking about this fellow for four hours.

"Damn birds," Selby said. "They know the lions are there. You can't depend on vultures. If they work for you they're fine. If they don't they can bugger up the whole bloody issue."

Finally, after half an hour one bird dropped his flaps and vol-planed down to approach the kill warily. We beamed him in on a prayer. He sank his beak into the topi's belly.

"The rest'll come now," Selby said, "and then the parade'll start. Consider that we have a dead lion. Watch, now."

A half dozen, then a dozen vultures skidded down. Now the sky was blackened with birds.

"Thank you, *ndege*," Selby said. "*Asante sana*. Here comes the parade."

Four lionesses came out of the bush, finally followed by the big male. The younger male did not appear. They went quickly to the kill and commenced to feed.

"Young one's lying doggo, licking his wounds," Harry said. "He and the big boy had a fight after we left, or else he'd be out

Use Enough Gun

there feeding with the rest of the pride. If he's not dead he's awfully discouraged. Shouldn't wonder if we find this one marked up a touch when we collect him.

"Hmmmm," Harry said. "Old boy's got his head stuck all the way into the topi's paunch. Guess we'd best go and terminate his troubles for him. Mind, I'd really *not* wound this un if I were you. Any lion's troublesome enough in thick bush when he's hurt, and if this bloke gets into that thorn we'll have *two* wounded lions, a mother with cubs, and three more lionesses to deal with. That's a lot of lions. Let's go."

We took the door off the jeep, and Harry gave the wheel to the car boy, Chabani. Kidogo was carrying the big .450 No. 2. Harry checked his .416, and I slid a second look into the bolt of my .375. The bullets were there, all right.

We passed fairly close aboard the five lions, who never raised their heads. Chabani swung the car round behind some bush, and Harry and Kidogo and I fell out of the open door. The car took off, and we commenced to crawl. We crawled to within forty yards and crouched behind a small tussock. The lions never raised their heads. These were hungry, disdainful lions.

"End of the line," Selby whispered. "Wallop him."

I got up on one knee and set the sights on the back of Gorgeous George's neck and squeezed off. He turned over with a roar and began to flop. Three lionesses lit out for the bush. The nasty lioness inaugurated a charge toward us and then halted. Gorgeous George got up on his front feet and began to shake the earth with noise.

"Clobber him again," Selby said.

I had to stand now, and as I stood, the lioness charged. I was not uninterested in a charge of a lady lion, but the papa was galloping around, roaring and carrying on, and I was having a hard time getting the gun on him. He held still for a second, finally, and I socked him again, this time directly behind the ear. He flopped over with a grunt, and I was free to use both eyes on the lioness.

She had come to us, was still coming at twenty feet, and came again another five. I switched my gun toward her and noticed Selby still casually on one knee, his scarred old .416 held rather carelessly to his cheek. At about twelve feet she put on brakes, stopped, but her tail was still waving and she had a mighty big mouth. Selby got up. He advanced toward her, and I advanced with him, feeling rather lonely. The cat backed up a yard. We walked again. She retreated another yard.

Harry said quietly in Swahili to Kidogo, who was standing by with the spare rifle, "Get into the car. Then cover the *bwana* with your gun." He said to me in English, "Cover me. Then get into the car. Keep covering me from the car."

Kidogo got into the car, which Chabani—who had thoughtfully stalled it into a dead end of bush—had revived and driven up to us. I got into the car. The lioness stopped. Harry stopped. He made a step backward. The cat seemed inclined to follow him, but stopped, her face flat on the ground, her chest on the ground, her tail waving gently, her rump in the air. Harry walked backward slowly. He came alongside the jeep. He slid in. Chabani slid over to the center of the seat. Harry eased out the clutch. He hit the side of the jeep a tremendous whack with his hand and roared. I jumped. So did the cat.

"Begone, you surly slut!" Harry said, tramping the gas and whacking the door again. "Go back to your babies! Go back to your other boy friend! Away with you!" The lioness sneered and backed up. She walked reluctantly to the edge of the bush, across the broad savanna of grass, and stood at the edge, still looking unpleasant. We drove up to where the dead lion lay, his head pillowed on the haunch of the considerably disheveled topi. I looked then for the first time at Virginia.

"I hope you got pictures of all the commotion," I said. "It is so seldom that you have five lions to play with at once, one of them charging, in easy range of a camera."

Virginia stared at the camera in her hand as if she were seeing one for the first time. "Pictures," she said bitterly. "This idiot" —she pointed at Chabani—"drove this car into a dead end and stalled it. I looked over the side, and there was another lioness, with *more* cubs, right by the front fender. I have to watch my insane husband standing off another lion while three more bound around and one is flopping all over the landscape roaring and there is one more practically in my lap and then you two fools drive another one off like she was an alley cat and I am not accustomed to this many lions on an empty stomach and you ask me if I got *pictures*. No, I did *not* get pictures. I forgot I had a camera. I want a drink, and I will try to forget that my fate is in the hands of fools."

I looked at Harry. He shrugged and spread his hands.

"Too many lions at once apt to be unsettling," he said. "That was a very nasty lion. Thought for a second I'd have to shoot her."

"Why in the name of Christ didn't you?" I said. "By the time I'd finished with the big fellow she was practically sitting in your lap. I could see her come out of the corner of my eye and I kept waiting for the sound of a gun going off. Why didn't you belt her when she made that last jump?"

Harry looked at me in something approaching horror.

"My dear man," he said, "she had *cubs*. One doesn't go about shooting females with children—not unless it's absolutely necessary."

"When is necessary?" I said, bitter myself now, and still shaking.

"Oh," Harry answered. "I thought I'd give her another foot or so before I shoved one down her gullet."

"The *memsaab* is absolutely right," I said, sticking a cigarette into a dry mouth. "She is surrounded by idiots and fools."

We went up to see the dead lion. As we approached Gorgeous George in the car, Harry spoke over his shoulder to the gun-bearers. "*Toa* .220 Swift," he said, and to me, "When we get out, give him one more behind the ear."

I got out and popped the old boy again with the little gun. It wasn't necessary, but it didn't do any harm, either. We walked to this fine red-headed gentleman, and sure enough, there was a fresh, ragged tear across his forehead.

"Thought so," Selby said. "Fight with the young bleeder after we left. I'd hate to see the other fellow. . . ."

He prodded the lion with his toe while the boys shook my hand.

"Very fine *simba*," he said. "Dead, now. Comes of being greedy. Never let your belly rule your reason."

We jabbered, released from tension, all the way back to *Campi Abahati*.

"*M'uzuri sana, bwana*," old Katunga said. "*M'kubwa sana. M'uzuri, m'uzuri. Piga m'uzuri. Bwana Simbambile.*"

It sounded very fine to be called *Bwana* Two Lions that night, which is maybe why I am today dissatisfied with cocktail conversation and stale talk of politics and football scandals and congressional investigations. Also, my taste in sports has been somewhat spoiled.

This was a very fine *simba,* this last lion that I shall ever shoot. He had this real red mane, as red as Ann Sheridan's, and bright green eyes. He was absolutely prime, not an ounce of fat on him, no sores, few flies, with a fine shining healthy coat. He was the handsomest lion I had ever seen, in or out of a zoo, and I was not sorry about the collection of him. Already I was beginning to fall into the African way of thinking: that if you properly respect what you are after, and shoot it cleanly and on the animal's terrain, if you imprison in your mind all the wonder of the day from sky to smell to breeze to flowers—then you have not merely killed an animal. You have lent immortality to a beast you have killed because you loved him and wanted him forever so that you could always recapture the day. You could always remember how blue the sky was and how you sat on the high hill with the binoculars under the great umbrella of the mimosa, waiting for the first buzzard to slide down out of the sky, waiting for the first lioness to sneak out of the bush, waiting for the old man to take his heavy head and brilliant mane and burly chest out of the bush and into the clear golden field where the dead topi lay. This is better than letting him grow a few years older, to be killed or crippled by a son and eaten, still alive, by hyenas.

Use Enough Gun

Death is not a dreadful thing in Africa—not if you respect the thing you kill, not if you kill to feed your people or your memory.

ONE DAY in Tanganyika I was crawling after buffalo, the big, rope-muscled wild ox with horns like steel girders and a disposition to curdle milk. I had walked through a swamp that was full of water and snakes and rhinos. I had crawled and stumbled over two young mountains to reach a herd of buffalo that I didn't really want to associate with. I had already shot a buffalo and figured that was one thing I wouldn't have to do any more of. But Selby has a mad affection for the *mbogo,* a sort of perverse love and a completely unmanageable fascination for the big beasts. We had come back to the high plains under the Rift escarpment by Kiteti, back from a fruitless kudu expedition, back for one more try at rhino. And there was no rhino. But on the steep side of one of the hills reaching up to the escarpment there was a sprinkling of tiny black worms.

Adam, the Wakamba gunbearer, pointed. *"Mbogo,"* he said, and I could already feel my stomach start to knot. It was the same feeling I used to get when the lookout on the bow would reach for the phones and ring the bridge. "Periscope," he would say. "Periscope bearing so-and-so many degrees off the starboard bow," as if he were pleased at having done me a favor.

Harry looked at the buffalo through the glasses.

"There's a damned good bull in that herd," he said. "Better than the one you've got by six inches at least. I think we'd best go and collect him."

I didn't say anything. I just prayed inside me and hoped we

would not have to crawl too far in order to scare me to death. I don't know what there is about buffalo that frightens me so. Lions and leopards and rhinos excite me but don't frighten me. But that buff is so big and mean and ugly and hard to stop, and vindictive and cruel and surly and ornery. He looks like he hates you personally. He looks like you owe him money. He looks like he is hunting you. I had looked at a couple of thousand of him by now, at close ranges, and I had killed one of him, and I was scareder than ever. He makes me sick in the stomach, and he makes my hands sweat, and he dries out my throat and my lips.

These buff were a herd of about two hundred, feeding up the edge of the hills below the escarpment and following a vague trail that meandered up the side and led eventually straight over the top. They were about two miles away, and it was walking all the way, walking when you could and crawling when you couldn't, and slipping on the loose stones and fighting through the wait-a-bit thorn, puffing and blowing and sweating and cursing in the hot sun in the middle of the day. And finally wiggling along on your belly, pushing the big gun ahead of you, sweat cascading and burning into your eyes, with your belly constricted into a tight hard kernel and your hands full of thorns and your heart two-blocked into your throat. And then the final, special Selby technique of leaping to your feet and dashing with a whoop into the middle of the herd, running at the bull, and depending on that thirty-second bewilderment to hold the buffalo still, like cattle, before you shot and hoped you hit him good so you wouldn't have to follow him into that awful thick bush he was certain to head for. And wait for you in it.

We crossed the mountains and were in the crawling, wiggling stage now. We had a good wind and the buff were just a few hundred yards ahead, looking blue-black and clean, as mountain buffalo are, instead of scabby and scaly and mud-splotched like the lowland fellows, or rusty red and scrubby like the herd that hung around Majimoto at Manyara. There were two good bulls —the old herd chieftain with a fine sweep of deeply rutted, heavy horns, and a younger gentleman, almost as good, who would be pushing the old boy out of the mob one of these days. Harry and I presumed to save him the trouble of a fight.

You judge a buffalo by the configuration and curl of horn as well as by the distance between his horn tips, and also by the depth of the horn boss as it rides his forehead, and by the degree of close-fitting joining of the two segments of boss as it comes together like a part in the middle of an Italian hoofer's head. Our bloke was very much all right on all counts. The boss covered his skull like a helmet, and the dividing line was as tight as a piece of string. The horns were shaped very well, not crooking in too much, and worn down evenly at the tips. He would be forty-eight inches or better, and forty-eight inches between those tips is a lot of buffalo. My first fellow was only forty-three and a bit, and he was impressive enough for me.

We were in the herd now, creeping on our bellies and pulling ourselves forward by digging elbows into sharp rocks. The buffalo were grazing unconcernedly all around us. The herd bull was lying down, resting, and there were a couple of cows obscuring him. It is a difficult sensation to describe, to be surrounded by two hundred animals weighing from eighteen hundred to twenty-five hundred pounds each, animals as testy and capricious of temper as stud fighting bulls, capable of killing you just as dead accidentally in a stampede as on purpose in a charge.

A buffalo close up is not handsome. His body is bulky, shortlegged, and too long for symmetry. He smells of mud and dung and old milk. His patchy hide is scabby and full of flat ticks. Bits of his own excrement cling to him. Dirty moss grows on his horns, which are massive enough to bust everything up inside you if he even hits you a slight swipe with the flat, and sharp enough to put a hole in you big enough to hide a baseball bat in, and dirty enough to infect an army. He has the big bull's cloven hoofs, for he is a true unaltered ox and the progenitor of the Spanish fighting bull, and he delights to dance on your carcass until there is nothing much around but spatters of blood and tatters of flesh. Even his tongue is a weapon. It is as rough and harsh as a wood rasp. If you climb a tree or an anthill on the *mbogo* he will crane his ugly neck and lick the meat off you for as far up as he can reach. His tongue erodes your flesh as easily as a child licks the point off an ice cream cone.

As I crawled along just behind Selby, with Adam and Kidogo following me, I was thinking these things. I knew a lot about buffalo by now. I knew how fast they are, despite their apparently lumbering gallop, how swiftly they can turn, how they stop cold on a dime, and how they go through bush at a spurt—bush that an elephant wouldn't recommend. I knew how much lead they would soak and keep coming, especially after being wounded. You may kill him easily with one bullet, but if you don't, the next fourteen .470s serve mostly as a minor irritant. And you cannot run away from a wounded buffalo. You have to stand and take him as he is, shooting at his nostrils as he comes at you with his head high and his horns swept back, his neck stretched and his cold eyes unblinking at you. You shoot for the nose and hope it gets into the brain, because if you shoot too high the bullets bounce off his massive horn like rubber balls off walls in a New York stick-ball game.

A leopard will possibly claw up more people and is faster and tougher to hit when he lies back on your trail and begins to stalk you, but you can change his charge with a shotgun blast and he dies very easily, as all cats with thin hides and delicate bones and soft flesh die. You can change an elephant's mind, too, by shooting him in the face, and you can change a rhino's mind by shooting him anywhere that he's biggest. But the reason my friend *Mbogo* is generally rated as the toughest piece of all the African furniture is that he is a single-minded type. You got to kill him to discourage him. He scents very good and sees very far and hears marvelously. He keeps the egrets around to eat his ticks off him but not because he needs them for anything but ticks and society. The rhino and his tickbird sentries are another matter. The *faro* uses birds for eyes, and the ticks come in as a bonus for the bird-dog job they do for the rhino. The buff really fancies the snowy egrets because their white plumage looks nice and decorative on his black back. They are the only pretty thing about him.

Use Enough Gun

God, as I was crawling and creeping and cursing and sweating, how I remembered all the buffalo I had met and the first one I had shot. Maybe the reason I was so sensitive about buff was that I took two stampedes and a dozen stalks before I finally shot one, and I had been in three more stampedes since. *This bloody Selby,* I said. *Him and his fascination for this awful animal. Him and his get-up-and-run-yelling technique of making the last fifty yards at a gallop, standing and shooting in the middle of the herd while the animals snort and explode past you, not wanting to run over you but not caring if they do run over you.* They wall their eyes with mad panic and stream past you, each one bigger than a pair of Brahman bulls, each one with two inches of skin thickness to cover the steel cables that make his muscles an armor plating, each one with enough obscene vitality to run for five miles shot through the heart.

As I crept along on my belly I remembered *Mbogo Moja,* the first one. We had stalked across a swamp and I was bitterly out of breath, the stomach muscles jumping and a piercing pain in the chest and a great tremble in the fingers that wasn't a fear-shake but a nervous reaction to fatigue. We walked as far as we could walk, with the long withes of grass tripping you at every step, and then here suddenly was an old bull and his *askari*—an expelled herd bull, driven off from the cows by his son, with a neophyte to run his errands for him and learn all his wisdom so that someday he could go back and kick the bejesus out of the reigning bull who had driven Papa off from his wives and his family security.

So we crawled this one, too, like you creep geese in Louisiana, stopping and freezing occasionally when the *askari* raised his head to stare at you with a colder stare than any actress ever wasted on an enemy.

This *askari* was mighty nervous. He felt that everything wasn't happy. He kept feeding away, edging off to the nastiest patch of thornbush in Tanganyika, with the starting of the Serengeti reserve on the other side of the swamp. If the one we shot got hurt and went across he would not only be sick and angry and venomous in his sickness, but he would also be illegal.

We crept to a bush and froze behind it, and there were the animals, fifty yards away and moving steadily out of range. Harry had his palm down behind him, and suddenly he lifted it in a curling beckon. I crawled, still blowing, up to his shoulder. He turned his head slightly and whispered.

"We're not going to get any closer," he said. "That *askari* is nervous and leading the old boy away. You better bust him now, although he's too far off for my pleasure. Try to take him just where his neck comes down into his chest."

Selby, when he is working with dangerous animals, always wears two stalks of extra bullets sticking like cigarettes from his right hand. Harry had said: *Do what I do.* I had two stalks of extra bullets sticking out between the second and third fingers of *my* right hand. At this time it had not occurred to me that Selby was left-handed.

I got up on one knee and sighted low into the old bull's chest, and the heavy Westley-Richards settled handily in balance and I squeezed off the trigger, and then the bull was gone and I was on the ground, my nose full of cordite fumes and my head full of chimes. Away off somewhere a gun exploded, and then there came a mournful bellow as morose as a hunting horn, a cow's horn, lonesome sounding in the Carolina woods when a Negro cropper is lost and blowing hard on the horn to keep himself from being frightened blond until he finds the dirt road again.

Selby was standing now, spraddle-legged, with his hands on his hips and looking down at me.

"For Christ sake," he said, jerking his head toward the wood. "*One* of you ought to get up."

From this I assumed the buffalo was down too. It appeared that *right-handed* shooters are not supposed to store their spare ammunition in their shooting hand. In the effort to emulate Selby it never occurred to me that the guy was a natural southpaw, and that bullets contained in a shooting hand would ride back against the second trigger and touch off the other barrel simultaneously, loosing 150 grains of cordite against your face.

"You all right?" Harry asked. "What happened?"

"Both barrels," I said. "At once. Dropped me. Did I hit him?"

Use Enough Gun

"You knocked him tail over tin cup," Harry said. "He turned completely over. Then he got up and departed."

"I thought I heard somebody else shoot," I said. "Away over yonder."

"Me," Selby said. "This bugger was flat out for the bush. I'd not taken the time to check his blood pressure, you know. I didn't know how good you hit him. I thought I'd best break his back before he got stuck into that patch of bush. Very nasty in there. Actually I shouldn't have bothered. Hear that bellow? He's dying now. You'll find you got his heart. They don't bellow from a spine shot. Hope you don't mind, old boy, but once in a while a little collaboration saves all hands a lot of trouble. I know how to pull a sick one out of the bush. But it's just that I don't fancy it as a recreation."

We walked up to the buffalo. He was dying, bellowing, making mournful sounds, and trying to drag himself toward us.

"Slip one bullet into the gun," Harry said. "I still don't trust that sear. Take him just behind the horns in the back of the head."

I slid a single bullet into the right-hand barrel of the .470 and squinted carefully at the back of this boy's neck, where the muscle roll humped out like the back of the neck on a retired prize fighter. I was gun-shy. I pulled instead of squeezing, but the bullet went in and poor old *Mbogo* stretched his neck forward to its full length. Blood crept out of his nostrils and he was dead. Dead and ugly. Uglier dead than alive, and four times as ferocious.

My God, but he was immense. He was muddy from rolling, and the ticks were working on his scaly hide and it was a hot day and the flies were coming down. Maybe he was only forty-three inside the horns, but to me he looked like a hell of a lot of bull lying there in the yellow grass, his ugly face pointed straight out and the long striated lines of his horns and his ax-edged hoofs and the solid butting weight of his heavy casque of boss making him look like a contrived machine of destruction.

"Frightful brutes, aren't they?" Selby said. "We'll just take his marrow from a couple of legs. Tommy Shevlin says it tastes like *pâté de foie gras*. Rest of him too tough to eat. Except the tongue's wonderful. Boys'll take his belly fat, and we can make a tobacco pouch out of his scrotum. 'Less you want his hoofs for ash trays, we've had him. Except the horns are lovely. Not big but beautiful. I'm interested to see what you did to him with the first shot. I think you'll find you wrecked him, but I couldn't know that before you touched off the second fusillade, could I?"

Adam and Kidogo unsheathed a *panga* and a sharp skinning knife and started the postmortem. They took out a rib section, which they would eat themselves, and they removed the heart and the kidneys and the liver. They snipped the fat from around his intestines, and we finally burrowed into his chest cavity in the interests of science.

This *mbogo* had accepted a .470 bullet, five hundred grains of hardnose bullet powered by seventy-five grains of cordite. He had taken it through the jugular and into the heart, where it smashed all the major arteries and crushed the whole top of the heart. It had ranged backward through him and destroyed the lungs. When we opened him up about ten gallons of black lung blood gushed out. Yet he had gotten up off the ground with this terrible wound and taken off as blithely for the bush as if we had pinked him in the fanny with a .22.

"Nobody ever believes it," Harry said. "Sometimes I don't. But these creatures are damned near indestructible. Look there at the mess you made with that bloody cannon. And remember that he was two hundred yards away and rolling off like a steam engine when I popped his spine for him and put him down. He'd have gone half a mile and still had enough gas left to scare us green when he came from a piece of bush not big enough to hide a hare."

"I don't ever want to shoot another one," I said. "This is all the *mbogo* I need this day, or any other. Like the *memsaab* says: '*Hapana taka piga mbogo lio.*' Nor any other day. Any man with one buffalo doesn't need another. It's like what David Green says. A man with a Rumanian for a friend doesn't need an enemy. David's a Rumanian."

"You'll shoot another," Harry said. "You will always hunt

buff. It's a disease. You've killed a lion and you don't care whether you ever take another. But you will hunt buffalo until you are dead, because there is something about them that makes intelligent people into complete idiots. Like me. They are the only beast in Africa that can make my stomach turn like it rolls over when you've had too much grog and don't know whether the bed will stay there for you. You'll hunt more *mbogo,* all right. Kidogo! *Taka headskin kwa bwana.*"

That was a long time ago as we measure time in Africa. That was practically in another century. There was another lion and a leopard and a cheetah and all sorts of the common stuff and some rhino we didn't get and some kudu that we butched and a lot of travel in between it. There was a stampede in between it. Like yesterday.

We were driving back to the camp in the latish afternoon, with the oryx and the cheetah done now and out of the way. Where the road dips low and the hills begin to slide down away from the escarpment there is a big swamp, a long, wide flat, full of high reeds, with the hills moving up on the other side into a tiptilted half bowl of land. This was just a few miles away from Kiteti, where the camp was pitched and where the hippo grunted in the front yard. This was two turns in the road and one baobab tree away from camp and a *bathi* and one of Dr. Ruark's nutritious deliciouses, the bone-building gin.

The sun had slipped a little in the sky and the evening nip was coming into the air when Harry slowed the Rover to an easy stop. Across the marsh, only a quarter-mile away, the big fat black worms were crawling down the hill.

"*Mbogo,*" Harry said. "My sainted aunt, *what* a head on the big fellow."

They were probably the same herd that I was working on this moment, and thinking about now, but out of focus a few miles and feeding very quietly down the side of the hill and into the swamp. I was bitter enough.

"I know," I said. "*Kwenda.* Let us go and collect it. Let us struggle through the marsh and go and collect it. By all means. *Pese pese.*"

"Right," Harry said. "I was just going to mention that possibly we should go and collect it. Haven't much time, though. Past five now. What we do we will have to do in a hurry. *Kwenda. Pese pese.*"

We fought through the high grasses, in some spots eight and ten feet tall, and treacherously mucky underfoot. We slipped and sloshed and stumbled and fell and bogged. The mosquitoes were in very good form. By the time we'd got across the swamp the buff had all fed down off the slope and were in the grass. We scouted carefully around them. You could see where they fed by where the egrets fluttered, zooming up into the sky and returning to settle on the animals' backs. One time we got too close on the way across. An old bull, his horns worn down by use to fists, was feeding out from the main mob and I almost tripped over him. Again the wind was right and he never cared that we were there. Big knob-billed geese flew over us and honked. Teals dipped and whizzed around us. We hit the far shore finally, wet and bug-bitten, and stumbled along its rocky outcrop to a big thorn tree. Harry went up it like a monkey. He could see from there. He could see very well from there. He was up the tree a long time.

He came down.

"How are your legs feeling?" he said. "Are you up to a bit of a sprint?"

"As up as I'm ever apt to be," I said. "Where are we running and from whom?"

"Look," he said soberly. "I don't kid you much. There are two hundred buffalo out there in that high grass. They are feeding down toward the neck of the marsh. We have to get back the same way we came. It's wet in there and sticky. There are going to be about five hundred yards where we have to run. We have to run in order to get past two hundred buffalo. If the wind twists and they catch a scent of us they may stampede. Charge they won't. You know this. But in that high grass if they all start running we won't be visible to them until they're already swarming over us. That's why I want to know if you're willing to chance a run for it."

"What happens if they do take off?" I asked Harry. "What do you do when two hundred buff come bearing down on you?"

"I would *try* to shoot one," Harry said. "I would try to shoot one so we could climb up on him so's the others could see us and run around us. It would call for a bit of lucky shooting to drop one so we could use him in a hurry. You've seen how hard they are to stop."

It was nearly six when we headed back through the marsh where the car was and camp was and booze was. Off to the right as we slipped through the reeds you could hear the buffalo chewing and snorting and grunting. You could see the egrets and hear them squawk. We were doing fine and were nearly out of the thigh-high water and into the muck when we walked right up on the back of an outgrazing bull buffalo. He let out a large bellow and took off, galloping awkwardly, out to stir up the animals and alert the town. You could hear the sudden loud, harsh rustle in the reeds when he alerted the town.

"Run," Selby said in the smallest and most distinct voice I ever heard a man use. "Run. That way."

We ran. We ran through the stinking ooze, tripping over the long grasses, hearts hitting hard in chests and breath gasping in rattles, and over to the right other things were running. Two hundred buffalo were running. They weren't scenting us because we were still downwind, but old Uncle Wilbur with the knobby horns had passed the word and two hundred buffalo were galloping like a spread formation on a football field. They ran and we ran. You couldn't see them run because the grass was twice as tall as they were, but you could hear them breaking it down as they pounded steadily through it.

We reached some reasonably high ground and some shorter grass. As we hit it fifty buffalo, the right wing of the spread, passed just aft of us at full gallop, something under fifty feet behind us. I was completely winded. Harry was short of breath. We still had the black boys with us.

"Jesus loving God," Harry said.

I didn't say anything. Kidogo said something in Nandi. Adam said something in Wakamba.

"I'd not like to have to do that again," Harry said. "Bit of a near thing there at the end."

We walked toward the other shore. I was walking slowly. Harry was out in front by twenty feet. All of a sudden his cupped hand reached out and drew me up to him. This one I wasn't really anxious to believe.

The damned buffalo had run the length of the marsh and had turned in formation and charged again, this time straight into our scent. They were standing like a Roman battalion, feet firmly rooted, heads proudly high, and noses sniffing, no more than twenty yards in front of Selby. I came up behind him on the run.

"Him on the left, by the cow," Selby said. "That one. The good one. Not the first one. The second bull."

I was gasping like a boated fish when I threw the .470 up just as the entire battalion wheeled to run the other way. I went for the big fellow's rear end, having read somewhere that if you shot at the root of the tail you either broke his back or discommoded his kidneys. The gun said bang and the buff went away and there was no whunk after the sound of the shot. It was almost dark now.

"Thank the Lord," Selby said reverently.

"Thank the Lord what?" I said peevishly.

"Thank the Lord you didn't hit him," Selby said. "Or else we'd have to go and find him in the dark."

"This has been quite a day," I said.

"*Ndio, bwana,*" Kidogo said, although he had not been asked.

Virginia was waiting for us when we came into the camp in the soft black night, the fires going cheerfully and what seemed to be a gin bottle on the table.

"I don't know why you let me do these things," I said. "Why the hell don't you keep me home like any decent wife would if she loved her husband?"

Virginia looked at us, thorn-torn, wet to the waist, tsetse-bit, mosquito-chewed, suicidally tired, sunburned, and out of humor.

"Buffalo again," she said. "Idiots."

I was thinking about this as we crawled into the middle of the herd, the herd of buffalo I didn't want anything else to do with ever, ever again.

We had to pause for a long time behind a big thornbush, waiting for the herd bull to get up and for the cows to move away off from in front of him. I got some little breath back and summed the situation. A big fat tsetse was biting me on the bite another big fat tsetse had created as an art form earlier. The sweat was running down in solid sheets, the salt of it burning my eyes. Grass seeds were secreted in my socks and chewing on my ankles like bugs. I had more thorns in my crown than any man needs. This was costing me a minimum of a hundred dollars a day after transportation.

At this particular moment an old cow with an evil expression, a cow I had not seen, looked right over the bush I was hiding behind. She looked at me cynically and hostilely.

"Woof!" the old cow said. "Garrumph!"

I got up on my feet. I had the gun with me. When the bull lurched up, crooked-kneed, I walloped him. The bull went down. He got up again. "This has gone far enough," I said. I squeezed on the bull again, and the gun was jammed. Then I heard Harry shoot, and the bull went over. He got up. He took off. All the buffalo took off. It was sort of like crossing Park Avenue against a light. Animals went past us like taxicabs.

"We killed him all right," Selby said. "We turned him over twice. Why don't we have a cigarette and give him a little chance to get slightly sick before we go after him?"

The cigarette tasted brassy in my mouth. Harry was looking cheerful again. The boys were not. Nor was I. I had a hunch a compliment was coming. It came.

"Well," Harry said, "let's go and pull him out by the tail."

"Okay," I said.

We checked the loads on the rifles and we dived into the bush.

Adam and Kidogo were spooring ahead of us, crouched, sniffing like dogs on a scent. There were lots of places in the bush for buffalo to be, grown-over *dongas* and patches of tangled impossibilities where any buffalo in his senses would stop and wait for killable people to come by. The bloody dung and the bright gouts of heart blood always led into a cul-de-sac and always led out again. This was a peculiar buffalo. He never stopped once to bleed and sulk and build his hatred into a fever. He moved. He was a traveling man.

We tracked this bull for three hours and over three miles of mountain and bush. Sometimes you would go for several hundred yards without a single holly berry of blood to tell you what you were chasing. We sometimes found a sudden spatter of the pinker lung blood. Then we would find nothing at all and would be forced to recast our steps, working backward on the trail until we picked up the old blood trail, and heading in a new direction. Harry and I walked this boy up to tangled retreats that he had to be in and wasn't in, but we had to sort him out of it as though he was in it.

For three hours my safety was off the gun and it was carried at halfport. For three hours I was mentally and psychologically girded to stand flat-footed and spraddle-legged and shoot this ton of fury until there wasn't anything else left to shoot him with. For three hours I was nerve-edged to a sort of superperception, where every sound, every scent, every blade of grass, every rustle of breeze, every upturned stone and disturbed piece of earth meant something with a sick and angry buffalo on the end of it.

We found him dead.

He was lying dead like a damned old cow in a pasture, under the shade of an acacia. The flies were already at him. He had taken my bullet and Harry's through the lower heart and he had gone the three miles in the three hours and he had not even contemplated standing to make a fight. Here he was, dead, carrion, a hunk of meat, a slow trickle dried on his nostrils, looking beautiful in the horn department and just as dead as the Democrats, for more years than the Democrats will be dead. The buzzards were coming down.

"*Hapana,*" Adam said, looking disgusted.

"*Ehhh,*" Kidogo said.

"Bloody fraud," Selby said. "Never knew one before who wouldn't at least entertain the idea of standing and fighting. This one didn't. Never even paused long enough for the blood to collect in a pool."

This was a big buff and a handsome buff, but the littler one, the uglier one, is the one I got hanging on the wall.

The last days of Kiteti, after the buffalo, were an odd mixture of things. There was the business of the scopes all going out at once. I missed a bull oryx, as big as a house, three straight times, holding on his shoulder and never touching him.

"I can't be that bad by now," I said. "I was on that baby as solid as ever I was on anything. You saw me knock that hawk out of a tree with the same gun yesterday. He was two hundred if he was an inch. I think the scope's gone crook."

"We'll see," Harry said, and drove on, circling crabwise up the side of the tilted shallow hill that runs up to the Rift escarpment and then plunges sheerly down for thousands of feet to a flat valley. The blue of the sky was blinding, this day, the sun was a solid brass ball, and all over the country you could see the grass fires starting, darkening the sky early and lighting up the dusk with a rosy, far-seen glow. The time was all gone. We would be off and away tomorrow or the next day or the next, depending on luck.

We came onto a herd of Grants, slow-grazing, unafraid, new to the country, and just off a reserve somewhere. There was a fine herd ram.

"I say," Selby said. "Would you mind awfully if I shot this fellow? I've not much of a collection, but I'd like him in it."

"Fire away, Junior," I said. "I got all the Grants I'll ever need. Take the Remington and wallop him, as Harry Selby says to the clients."

The boys *toaed* the .30-'06 and Harry got out. He crept up on the Grant, getting to within thirty-five or forty yards and resting the rifle barrel on an anthill. He fired. There wasn't any bullet-hitting sound. The Grants took off, and Harry let them run. At about three hundred yards they stopped. Selby fired again, and the ram went over on his horns.

"*Kufa,*" the boys said in the car. We drove off to collect Selby, who had walked over to the Grant and was looking at the precise hole in the geometric center of the gazelle's shoulder.

"Bloody gun's a good foot high, maybe more," Harry said. "I held on this fellow at thirty yards and missed him clean. I held on the same spot at three hundred and clobbered him. Let's sight her in."

We sighted her in. She was fourteen inches high and a little left. No wonder I'd been blowing them past the oryx bull. I had been aiming high to get the spine if possible, because the oryx is awfully hard to kill, and had been slipping them over his back. We moved a couple of graticules, and now she was accurate again.

She wasn't accurate long. We knocked up another oryx, a fine one, in the low meadows where the Rift dwindles, and I held steady on this one from another anthill. He was standing broad to me, and the shot was alarmingly simple. The welcome whunk came after the boom. The oryx leaped and took off, running hard with his horns laid back.

"You shot his jaw off, for God's sake," Harry said. "What's the matter with you, anyhow?"

"The gun again," I said, and bitterly, because I hadn't wounded much and hate it. "Let's sight her."

"Can't be out again so soon."

"Sight the gun."

This time she was a foot and a half to the right and another foot high. This, the gun that had gone two months so accurately that the boys just said "*Nyama*"—meat—when the gun fired.

Use Enough Gun

"Bloody gun is possessed of demons," Harry said. "Let's go put that poor *choroa* out of his misery."

We coursed the wounded animal and came up on him and I had two belts at him. I missed him cold. This time it was my fault. I was nervous and upset at wounding him and I didn't trust the gun any more and I was jerking. He ran and went over a high, stone-cobbled hill where Jessica couldn't follow, and crossed some mountains, and at dark we had to give him up. I felt like hell, sick and sorry and ashamed.

"Leopards'll have him in an hour," Harry said. "That's one consolation. Every cat in the community will be on that blood spoor. Quit feeling so bad. Everybody butches one now and then. You can't say we didn't try. And you can't blame yourself for the gun."

"These damned scopes," I said. "You can't trust them. But everything you shoot around here you shoot at some impossible distance, and most of us haven't got your eyes. I haven't anyhow."

"Forget it," Harry said. "Let's go get some *chacula* and hit the sack."

"You're beginning to talk like a bloody Yank," I said.

"Evil associations," Harry said, grinning. *"Kwenda."*

We got a fine oryx the next morning. I had checked the sights again, and when we jumped this big fellow running hard up the side of the hill, I led him two lengths and a shoulder high, aiming at where I thought he might be when the bullet got there, and sure enough he was there. There was that bone-hitting crack and he slowed to an amble. I belted him again and down he went. He was sort of snarling in a bovine fashion, and I had to bust him in the neck before we could come up on him. They are one of the two or three actually fierce antelopes if they're hurt, and will skewer you with those sharp, straight, thin stickers they wear on their heads. This was a fine oryx, one horn worn down a little from digging, as they always are, but the best horn past thirty-one inches, clean and black and sharp enough to go all the way through anything it hit. He was buff-gray, lying there, a stripe down his back, a black-and-white mosaic pattern on his legs, his big stupid donkey face oddly striped with black and white. They look bigger than they actually are, but they run five or six hundred pounds and are as tough as a destroyer's skin.

The gun was in again, but she went out again that afternoon. This was the last full day, and I wanted Virginia to see some of the lovely country she had missed. We were just cruising, enjoying the fresh breeze and the blue sky and the wonderful yellow plains against their backdrop of blue hill, when Kidogo pointed and said:

"*Kitambile.*"

There were two big cheetahs, both toms, in the middle of the yellow plain. The bigger was sitting on an anthill, profiling six or eight feet off the ground. Against the fierce blue of the early-afternoon sky, sitting on a yellow anthill in a sea of yellow grasses, his hide white against the black spots, he was something.

"I'd say this is a definite bonus," Harry said. "A *shauri mungu* sent to repay you for the no rhino, the bad joke with the kudu, the way your gun's been acting up. Magnificent, isn't he? You can remember him like this. It's a sight very few people get to see. Get out and ——"

"Wallop him," I said.

There wasn't anything to it. I got out, Harry tooled the Rover away, and I found another anthill. This was an eight-foot cheetah, about half dog, half cat, with a round cat's face, a long cat's tail, a spotted cat's hide, long dog's ears, and a dog's non-retractile claws. I put the scope's post on his shoulder at sixty yards, squeezed off, and missed him as clean as anybody ever missed anything. He went straight up in the air about six feet, turned a somersault, and hit the deck, running. I don't know if you ever saw a cheetah run, but when I slung another one at him on the gallop, I was just kidding myself. A cheetah flat out can catch anything that runs, and there are people who say that in a hurry he will be doing about seventy-five miles an hour. This lad was long gone.

The other lad wasn't. He got up, stretched, walked a short

distance away, and lay down in the grass. I could see his round head and hard, clear cat's eyes and the outline of his body as he lay. This time I held the damned gun low, pointing at the ground in front of him. I shot, and he jerked and stayed there. I aimed at the ground and I broke his back, so high up that another inch would have missed him clean. Now this bloody machine was shooting *two* feet high. I unscrewed the telescopic sight and threw it away. Then I walked up on the big cat, who was snarling and crawling toward me, and put him quietly to sleep. He was beautiful and would look just fine with the lions and the lovely, lovely leopard, but what I had now was not just a hide and mask but a complete capsuling of a country and a day, with the heat of the sun and the cool of the breeze and the friendship of the boys and all I loved of Africa in it. This was as good a way to end it as any, not shooting any more, with the oryx neat and the cheetah neat and the damned traitorous scope thrown away to rust in the long yellow grasses.

The next morning the boys were knocking the camp apart.

"Let's go look at it for a couple of hours," I said. "I'm not content to leave it alone. I'm like a woman in a war who follows you to the airport or the railroad station and wants to keep on saying good-by—stretching the agony and fattening off the misery until the last bitter second."

"Okay," Harry said. "We'll take the .470 in case we just happen to see a rhino, and the .375. You really ought to shoot another zebra or so for those hides your friends wanted, and the boys can use a little fresh meat for the trip home. Pity about that fat cow you wanted to buy them for a farewell feast. But Juma spent the whole day trying to buy one. You know these Masai. They'd rather sell their mother than a cow."

We rode over the hills, rode for the last time, looking for the last time at all the landmarks we knew so well now—the cobbled hills there, the green knobbly hills there, the long blue slopes there, the baobab here where the road crooks just before you turn in toward Kiteti, the rhino hill yonder, the lonely village of musky anthills, the broad yellow plain, the swamp where the buffalo were, the high hill where the other buffalo were, the sheer drop of the escarpment, the green strip of lush grass with the giraffes always standing solemn and ludicrous nearby, the little scrubby orchards of thorn, the fleets of ostriches running and pacing like trotting horses at Roosevelt Raceway in New York, the buzzards wheeling, the dew fresh on the drying grass, the flowers beginning to wither, the sand-grouse specks in the sky, the doves looping and moaning lugubriously, the brilliant flight of the jays, the guineas running, the francolin scratching like chickens in the low grass between the ruts the car made, the weaver birds swarming like bees and dipping and rolling like a tornado. This was what I wanted to remember of it more than what I'd shot, but the shooting was important, because the presence of the animals in my home would bring it back as fresh and sharp as the air of this last morning, this last, sad morning.

"*Punda,*" Harry said, pointing at a herd of zebra. "Best take one, anyhow, for the meat."

There was a big stallion loping along at the end of his herd. I scrambled out of the jeep with the .375 and stuck one up his broad fat fanny as he went away. It was a long shot, but I was shooting with open iron sights and I wasn't surprised to hear it hit and see him lurch and break into a furious gallop. I knew this shot. It had gone in him and all the way forward through him and it had taken his heart. He would run five hundred yards and would be dead when we got up to him.

He ran the prescribed distance and folded as if somebody had skulled him with a hammer. We drove up to him and he lifted his head. Adam jumped out to sanctify him for the eating with his knife, to *hallal* him for Mohammed. Adam cut his throat.

Throat cut, heart-shot, this zebra was dead and sanctified and ready to be skinned and eaten. But somebody forgot to tell him he was dead and approved of by Allah. He got up and threw Adam twenty feet. He reared on his hind legs and charged Selby and me. Harry was leaning against the open door of the jeep. I was leaning against the fender.

He was awful to see—bloody, fierce, making a stallion's angry fighting squeal with his mouth distended and those huge yellow teeth, which can snap off an arm, bared in an equine snarl and his mouth looking bigger and wider and fuller of teeth than any lion's. He was flailing the air with razor forefeet, each hoof capable of splitting your skull right down to your Adam's apple. And he had Selby trapped against the jeep, wedged against the door. He was biting at Selby's face and striking at him with hoofs, and Selby was yelling and shrinking backward into the jeep and trying to fend this monster off with one hand.

I ran round the front of the car and dived through the back seat, diving horizontally like we used to dive in bar fights when I was young and full of orneriness in Hamburg and Antwerp and the tough sailor towns of the depression. On the way back through the back seat I scooped up the .375 from the rack and pumped a bullet into the chamber as I dived. I stuck the barrel of the gun into the zebra's mouth and pulled the trigger, and the back of his head came off. This time he was *really kufa*. He fell forward on top of Selby, pushing Harry under the wheel of the jeep. There was Selby, wedged into his own car by a dead zebra, sitting there, looking ruffled and hurt-feelinged, with a lapful of dead *punda* whose gory head was laid lovingly on Selby's shoulder.

"Somebody get this goddamned creature off of me," Selby roared, his dignity shattered. And then we began to laugh.

The boys hurled themselves onto the ground and screamed with laughter. They ached with laughter. I fell down on the ground and began to hiccup with uncontrollable mirth. Finally Harry, still with a lapful of zebra, began to laugh, and the zebra's head moved up and down so it seemed he was laughing too.

The first hysteria played out a little, and the boys began to skin out the dead animal after dragging it out of the jeep and off the *Bwana Haraka's* lap. But one would say something to another, and then Harry would say something and the skinning would stop. The knives would be dropped and the entire pantomime of the semi-catastrophe would be re-acted, and everyone would fall on the ground and scream. It took an hour to skin out the zebra. It usually takes fifteen minutes.

"Fancy," Harry said finally, the tears still streaming down his face and his sides hurting, "fancy the flap in the Queen's bar in Nairobi when the word spreads that old Selby, after all these years, had been done in by a bloody zebra. My family'd never live it down."

"It's sort of like being gored to death by a Tommy," I said.

"Or beaten to death by a dove," Harry said.

"Or nibbled to death by moths," I said.

"Or tickled to death with a feather duster," Harry said. "But suddenly you think: You're just as dead if a zebra bites you as you are if an elephant steps on you. Anything they've got here can kill you, from a snake to a thorn to lousy zebra. That's why this job is so interesting. It's the unexpected does you in."

We headed down for Arusha to register the trophies, and in Babati they told us that Harry's friend, Tony Dyer, had been frightfully beaten up by a buff. We stopped in Arusha, the little Greeky-Englishy Arusha, registered the trophies with a fat Indian *babu* in the Game Department, and took the good fast road back to Nairobi. Nobody talked much.

We stopped once near an anthill, which Virginia loved, and three giraffes, which she loved, walked up curiously to watch us. I looked at Virginia and she was crying quietly.

All the way to Nairobi I kept feeling something familiar. I remembered suddenly: This was the way I felt when the Japs quit and the war was over and I was headed home. All the excitement and the dangerous security of the war were finished. Now it would be work and civilian frustration and complication again. All the neatness was gone with the war, all the feeling of complete fatalism was gone. Now the future was in my hands again. The Navy and fate were no longer responsible. If I got on a plane and it crashed and killed me I couldn't blame the Navy or fate. My *shauri mungu*—my God's work—was all over. That is how I felt as the jeep pressed on in the dust toward Nairobi, with old Annie Lorry, tractable for once, lumbering and creaking on behind us.

We hit Nairobi and found my friends, Tommy and Durie

Use Enough Gun

Shevlin, just back from an unsuccessful safari in Rhodesia or someplace, and Tony Dyer was there, limping around on crutches. Little Maureen at Ker and Downey's was just as pretty to look at, and there was a flock of other pleasant folk about. Old Zim, the taxidermist, oohed and ahed over the trophies, which were really quite fine and something to be proud of. Virginia bought a couple of leopard skins for some bags and shoes and a stole, and everybody drank a good deal too much. Harry's pretty airline hostesses were all over the place, and there was a party every night and one drunken South African Airlines pilot that I nearly had to slug but didn't.

None of it was any good. I was glad to leave. There was a part of me, of us, back there on a hill in Tanganyika, in a swamp in Tanganyika, in a tent and on a river and by a mountain in Tanganyika. There was a part of me out there that would stay out there until I came back to ransom that part of me. It would never live in a city again, that part of me, nor be content, the other part, to be in a city. There are no tiny-gleaming campfires in a city.

We got on the plane one day and pointed back to Paris and New York and work and cocktail parties and penthouses and expensive, fashionable saloons. Our first stop was in Addis Ababa. The natives were just as ugly, and there were even more flies than I remembered. I was sure New York would be worse.

PART THREE

THE
HARD
TRUE
LIFE

I KNEW *I could write columns. I knew I could write any sort of magazine article for any sort of magazine. I had a couple of just completed short stories accepted and I had just found a wonderful hunk of ground and was beginning to put up what I thought was a wonderful sort of a house. But another thing was burning me. Like nearly everyone else who writes for a living, I wanted to write a serious novel and I was willing to gamble that I would be miserable the rest of my life if I didn't have a bash at it. It was a strange sort of self-torment but I thought I had seen the beginnings of a story in East Africa that was going to torture the world for the next fifty to one hundred years to come. I was willing to risk being unhappy for the rest of my life as a lousy novelist and a good journalist to have this one crack at a tough field."*

This story has a happy ending because the book in question turned out to be Something of Value. *This huge novel*

set in Kenya was started on a boat on the way to Australia,
and bits of it got written somehow between magazine assign-
ments in New Zealand and India, but the serious work was
done in the second half of 1954 at the new house in Spain.
The house was at Palamos and was still being built and so,
as Ruark said, "we started the book upstairs in the guest
wing, progressed to what is now my wife's office and finished
it up in what is now the other side of the house, with the
carpenters gaining steadily on me." All the same by Decem-
ber Ruark was in New York with the manuscript under his
arm.

No novel is purely the product of an imagination. As
Ruark wrote in his Foreword, he had fallen in love with
Africa because he found qualities in the people, and some-
thing wild and grand in the country itself, that he cherished
and couldn't find anywhere else. After that first trip in 1951
he only wanted to get back as fast as possible. And he did, at
the end of the following year, when he made a film docu-
mentary called "Africa Adventure." It was this second trip
that made his mind up about New York. "I got home to
New York on Saturday from Africa and would have quit
then if I found anyone to quit to, but New York weekends
being what they are I had to wait until Monday morning."
He'd thought about settling in Kenya, but what with Mau
Mau and the general uncertainty of things he decided "it
was no place to take a wife who hadn't signed on to be a kind
of covered wagon pioneer woman."

"He thought about a day he once spent all by himself
under a cool mimosa grove in Tanganyika, where no white
man had ever been before him, and where the elephants
were tame and friendly, and where the sun came through

the patches in the green umbrella tops and dappled the ground with flecks of gold. The mimosa were spaced with tall palms with feather heads. There was a light sweet breeze and complete silence in the grove. The ground was yellow-packed with clean straw. A dove called somewhere, far, far away. There was a dim crash, also far away, where some big animal, an elephant or a rhino, had taken fright and moved swiftly. A little river flowed slowly down at the edge of the clearing, and he could hear an occasional gurgling splash as a croc slid into the stream. The air was lovely with the little white blossoms that smelled like tuberoses. He had lain on the clean yellow straw, packed where the elephants walked, and gone softly to sleep. He had dreamed then that he had died and gone to heaven. When he awoke and looked about him, the delusion persisted, and he had thought, for just a few seconds, that he was still in heaven."

P ETER McKENZIE stood leaning against the bar in the dim cool malty-smelling taproom of the Norfolk Hotel in Nairobi and flicked his thumbnail twice against his glass. "I'll have a martini this time, please," he said to the steward. He turned toward his companion. "Pimm's is fine to cut the dust, but I need something a little sturdier after this last business. The same for you, Little John?"

"No, thanks, I'll have a martini too, please. Just what is it you call them?"

"Martini *a maui mbile*. American chap I had out last year thought it up. Seems they have some sort of drink called 'on the rocks' in the States, when it's just ice and double booze with no mixing. 'Martini twice on the mountain' was as close as we could come to it for Moussa's benefit. Right, Moussa?"

"Yas, *Bwana*. That other *bwana*, he drinking very much. We call him the *Bwana Ginni-Bottle* here in the hotel."

Peter McKenzie was standing with John Thompson, another professional hunter, who had been second hunter with Peter on the safari from which they had just returned. John Thompson was a short, wiry, muscular blond man with bright monkey's brown eyes and a broken nose. He was Peter's best friend, and each was happy to defer to the other as second hunter on a big safari, although neither would serve as Number Two to any other hunter.

Peter was something of a legend in Nairobi, young as he was. The natives called him *Bwana Nyeusi*, the Black One. He had been hunting professionally for seven years. He was in love with Africa and with the animals he saw, the animals which he sought for other men to kill. He fidgeted in Nairobi after a day or two of wenching and heavy drinking. He did not feel completely happy until he was back again in the Rover, his hatbrim back-curled in the stiff breeze, and the dust of the Ngong Range puffing pink behind him, with the great blue scar of the Rift beckoning him past Longonot and turning him up toward the high green hills he loved in the Masai. Or maybe when he crawled past the red clay hills and wet green Kikuyu shambas past Fort Hall and Nyeri and on through Nanyuki for the long, short ride to Isiolo, where, apt as not, you would be likely to see a herd of strolling elephants in the D.C.'s boma.

The Northern Frontier, past Isiolo, was Peter's very special country. He began to breathe more deeply when he passed Archer's Post, where the South African airmen had bombed themselves a sweet-water swimming pool, and he was wildly happy when he turned off to camp at the Kinya lugger. With the lovely, square-headed old mountain Ololokwe bulking huge on his left, he could curve the jeep around and aim for the dry rivers, the luggers, that swept new channels for themselves each year as the floods came flashing down, drowning the red-ant-hill-studded desert in muddy torrents so violent that they slung huge trees twenty and thirty feet above the river beds and caused the D.C. to put up barriers on the Garba Tulla–Shaffa Dikka road to keep all men out, and in, for the period of the rains.

This was where the hard true life of Africa centered, here on the dry, lava-dusty plains or ocher-wet pits, with the huge knobs of blue-and-red-and-white mountains strewed aimlessly around with no regard for symmetry. Here on the gray, lonesome, heat-shimmering plains with their myrrh and sansevieria bushes, the wild Boran and the painted Samburu and Rendille and the slim, beautiful light Somali roved with their herds of camels and sheep and goats and donkeys. Here lived the Turkana, fierce little black men who went about naked and who wore curved knives as wristlets and who would as soon chop your head as thank you if a question of pride was involved. Here it was *big* enough—big enough for the elephants and the rhinos and the little lesser kudus and the leopards and the lean, maneless desert lions. Here it was big enough for the nomads to drift their cattle over a million square miles of territory that nobody but Peter and God and the elephants really loved. This was the land of the sand grouse pinpricked against a clear well-washed blue sky, whistling as they came to scanty water in the morning. This was where the heat trembled at one hundred twenty degrees at 4 P.M., but where you didn't find any mosquitoes and not many tsetses. This was where the dry river beds were highways of sparkling white sand, islanded with rocks and little green-lichened pools, and where a constant traffic of life surged fretfully in a search for the water that bubbled under the cool sands. On the dry oases Peter could see, in a strip of ten miles, thirty elephants digging earnestly with their tusks for the water that seeped foully under the sandy surface. He could count a dozen rhinos on any morning and follow their trails across a hard-baked plain to the start of their daily twenty-mile walk for water. Why they never stayed on the luggers neither Peter nor anyone else, not even the Turkana, could explain. But you could spoor them simply by riding along in a jeep, following a big bull by the serpentine bicycle track his penis made as it trailed the ground when the breeding season was on.

This was the country in which the dry river beds were thickly cobbled with the dung of a million animals when it was dry outside on the plains—the sign of cattle and goats, elephants and rhinos and zebras and giraffes and Grant gazelles. The dazzling white sand was a parade ground for the vulturine guinea fowl who ran with their cockaded heads held high like trotting horses, and where the big, yellow-necked francolin scratched like barn fowl and yelled raucously at sunset. There were always more birds in the Northern Frontier than anywhere else, great hornbills and long, sag-tailed lories, many vultures and slipping carrion kites. The birds kept up an incessant scream, the guineas hoarse, the lories going "Faa-aak, faa-aak," the francolin mournful at nightfall, and always the pleasant good-humored chuckle of the sand grouse as they carved jet-plane arcs in the brilliant blue sky.

With the exception of the nomads, you didn't run across many people in the Northern Frontier. It was all too big and it was always either too wet or too dry. If you knew the way the luggers interlocked, doubling back on themselves, you had a wondrous source of heavy ivory, but a man who didn't know the luggers could get himself lost and die very painfully in the N.F.D. Not many safaris came up this way, because the weather was too unpleasant and the angry red clay pits and dreary gray plains were not picturesque enough for a man who had only six weeks to shoot it all, including pictures. The rhinos here weren't nearly so high in the horn as the rhinos around Manyara in Tanganyika, at the mouth of Mto-Wa-Mbu, the Mosquito River, not half so long-horned as the forest rhinos who grazed on the slopes of Mount Kenya and in the Aberdares around Nanyuki and Thompson's Falls. Beyond the birds and a few Grant gazelles and gerenuk there wasn't much to shoot except the elephants. This is chiefly why Peter loved it so, because there wasn't much to shoot besides the elephants. Most clients didn't want elephants unless they were true hunters who were willing to walk twenty or thirty miles a day through the sucking sands and through the dwarf palms that slashed like swords and the thornbush that clutched and bit at the body.

The immensity of the North Country did something lovely and lilting to Peter's heart. Its very barrenness was beautiful, and its sere heat was happy, healthy. Of all the natives he knew, Peter loved the painted, Masai-like Samburu who roamed with their herds, and after them the ugly, black, squat little Turkana. He actively hated the Somali, but he loved them just to look at the arrogance of them. The women were so lovely with their huge iridescent headdresses, their wonderful small, proudly tilted bosoms and tiny waists and big swaying behinds. And the men so lean, so delicately hawk-faced, and completely treacherous and deadly fast with a knife. They would steal anything, and they worshiped their herds of camels. But they were all part of the North, like its overwhelming nights, when the sky actually took the texture of furry velvet and the stars swung low and melon-golden, not so remote and silvery-twinkly as they were up in the Masai, when the evening cold set in.

Of course a man could love the Masai too, because around the Mara River and the Telek River, up from the Loita Plains, there was country to make your mouth water at its deep-loamed richness. This was all Masai reserve, thank God, and buzzing-full of cattle-killing tsetse flies, so that the people and cattle stayed properly away. But the man who might someday put it into wheat and cattle, after clearing the harsh thorn that housed and nourished the flies, would own a swift agricultural bonanza unchallenged by the discovery of later gold.

This wasn't angry, frightening country like the N.F.D., but soft and beautiful country, once you got away from the alkali dust and the wind-dreary sere lava plains. This was Hollywood Africa, with rolling downs, now of the softest gentle green, against the background of deep black lofty forest, or long plains rolling yellow-grassed and heavy-headed in the pleasant wind like the ripple of wheat. This country had the pure cold streams, and the hot-water springs around Majimoto, and the wonderful graduated mountains, with Tanganyika off that way and the Rift's scar burning blue behind.

And all, all the animals that God put into the world were on parade. Here in the Masai was where you could see a half million zebras in a day, a half million wildebeests, when the great migrations started across the Serengeti Plain of Tanganyika. Here the bright golden impalas tiptoed dainty-footed in herds of five hundred along the Telek River, its bed brilliant white and green rock-studded. Here a herd of two hundred elephants unafraid. Here the Tommies roved the plains in bands of thousands, and here the protected prides of lions grew as large as twenty or thirty to one family. This was where the very big heavily-bossed buffalo lived, and where the dark-gold leopards fed nightly by the riverbanks. This was where you could see a million beasts any day, Tommy, Grant, eland, impala, zebra, wildebeest, all moving outward against the menace of the big cats who waited for the violent bloody sunset to die before they nervously whipped their tails, stretched lazily after their siesta, and began to search for the evening's meal.

This was the place where the long-dipping glades were green as in England, and where the acacia flowered in the spring with blossoms as white and fragrant as any English May haw or the dogwood in America. But somehow the Masai was soft country, although its natives were the fiercest and its animals the most numerous. It was a country for women and children and small, awkward, wet baby animals with knobbly knees and unsteady feet. It was not so big and raw and tough and fiercely beautiful as the N.F.D. It was candybox country, created specially for tourists and the movie-making safaris. When Peter was really fed up with clients he and John Thompson would take a Land Rover and a cook and a gunbearer apiece, and they would trek up to the North Country to shoot out their license on big elephants. They would sleep under the intimate stars on doubled blankets without bothering about beds, eating what they killed of birds and small game, drinking nothing, and then they could face another season of commercial safari again.

Fred Hall walked into the bar and joined Peter and John Thompson. Fred was a hunter, too, and he was just back from something or other involving a recently divorced maharajah and a French female singer. Fred was a lean, rangy, ugly man who rarely spoke much, except to close friends, when he was drunk, and who was accounted dull therefore. But he was a pure hunter in his heart, and he completed a close corporation with Peter McKenzie and John Thompson.

"Bad, was it?" Fred said. "I'll have the same as you. What did they do especially awful this time?"

"I don't suppose it was actually any more awful than usual," Peter said. "There was this proven son of a bitch and his son. The son was quite a decent chap. But the old man wanted it all, as usual, and in thirty days. You know. Don't care whether it's any good or not so long as it's dead. So the Little *Bwana* here and I proceeded to toil, and we collected it all. Two elephants, one a hundred, one ninety, two rhinos, two kudus, two buffalo, two leopards—the whole bloody issue. I dragged his arse from the Masai to Tanganyika and back up to the N.F.D. It was amusing, actually, especially in the North. There are ways of saving steps, but I didn't bother to save him any. John and I left them in the hotel at Nanyuki. The father already drunk. I have heard a lot of filthy tongues in my short time, but this man was downright horrid. And do you know, after he shot some mangy old lion or other, he insisted on having the lion's *balls broiled* for his breakfast?"

"Were you still drinking their whisky?" Fred asked, using the classic phrase.

"I was. The *Bwana* John wasn't. Tell him, boy."

"It was first when this visiting gentleman shot the baby zebra," John Thompson said. "Long as he shot it, I thought p'haps I'd use the poor little creature for a bait for some vulture photography he wanted. The birds came down and the hero got sick when the *ndege* started to poke into the carcass up the rear end the way they do. He'll kill it, sure, but he threw up when he saw what happened to it after it's dead. But it was the lion that did it for me, really."

"Another gin for everybody, Moussa. Lion?"

"An old boy. Really old. We were rattling around in Ikoma and we came onto this old gentleman, see, sick he was and starved and mangy, with his back broken in some recent fight with one of his sons. I judge the old chap'd been helpless there the best part of a week. The maggots had already started on him, and the blowflies were working, and he was skin and bones and really miserable. There were about a dozen hyenas circled round the old chap, their tongues hanging out, just waiting for him to get a touch weaker before they closed in and et him alive. I walked up to the poor old bugger with the .22 and was going to give him the one in the ear to put him out of his troubles, when this four-starred nobleman told me not to shoot. Seems he wanted to *leave* the beast there alive to see how long it would take for the hyenas to eat him.''

"So old John shot the lion, naturally," Peter said. "Then he called his client a dirty murdering swine and drank his own grog for the rest of the trip. Oh, it was a charmer, I can tell you. This father chap, at the Greek hotel in Arusha, tried to pinch some young girl off his own son. The girl set up a mightiful scream and the old man took a clout at his boy in the argument, and it was an altogether bloody delightful business. I think I shall get very drunk tonight and behave abominably. John and I've earned it, this safari. And I have a new group of heroes coming in tomorrow. Man and his wife. Young Americans named Deane. His father used to manufacture something or other in Chicago or Detroit or one of those places."

"Maybe they'll turn out reasonably human. The good ones usually follow the bad."

The big plane eased down on the runway, bumped slightly, braked, turned, and swung in toward the airport buildings. The uniformed black boys trundled out the disembarking steps, and the small caravan of porters, baggage trucks, officials, and *askaris* swarmed out toward the plane like efficient ants. The doors opened, the officials entered, there was the usual delay, and then the passengers began to totter down the stairs, carrying their flight bags and attaché cases and topcoats, and wearing the blinking, owlish look of people who have been trapped in a dark stuffy closet and are now tasting fresh light air. Peter had had a lot of practice spotting clients by now.

Use Enough Gun

There they were. Peter smiled. The crew-cut was blond. The man was six feet two and slim. He carried a covert-cloth topcoat and wore a Rolleiflex on one side, a Leica on the other, the straps crisscrossed over his chest like bandoleers. He wore a brown Cavanagh hat with a black band and with the crown undented on the sides. Shirt, oxford buttondown. Tie, black knit. Golden bar across tie, "21" Club. School, Harvard, Yale, or Princeton. Looked a pleasant type as did the girl. Coat, short honeybrown wild mink. Suit, severe. Either a Balenciaga or a Hattie. Peter knew all the names of the better couturières and could recognize their peculiarities as easily as he could tell a shootable head from an unshootable head, looking through the sweated glasses in the blurring heat.

This was a pretty girl, dark, but with one blond streak. She had compromised on the season. He couldn't see the color of her eyes, but the shape of the mouth was nice and the face pleasant. They walked purposefully toward the detaining room, and Peter got up to meet them.

"I'm Peter McKenzie," he said. "I expect you're the Deanes. I'm your white hunter, come to collect you and your stuff."

The Deanes smiled back and looked relieved. The man shook Peter's hand. So did his wife, gripping it firmly.

"Tom Deane," he said. "My wife, Nancy. God, I'm glad to see you. I'm new at this. We had all sorts of ideas about being stranded here with about sixteen cases, all full of guns and cameras and other hot articles."

"Well, if you'll give me your baggage checks I'll just nip around and see to the customs. I can't help you with the passports, but there's no trouble there. Just get in line and hand them to that chap with the turban and the whiskers, and then he'll pass you through into customs. See you in a minute."

"What a very nice-looking boy," Nancy Deane said as Peter walked away, striding largely, slightly pigeon-toed from tracking, his long arms swinging forward of his knees in a peculiar rhythm.

The babu stamped their passports and they went through to

(133)

customs, where Peter had stacked a vast array of gun cases and valises on the shelf.

"There's no trouble about the guns if the serials you sent me check. I pay the entry duty, and when you've safely gone they pay me it back."

It was all very simple, and in no time, it seemed, Peter had got them through customs and into the car. As they approached the native bazaars, Nancy Deane got her first look at Africa, heard her first African sounds, smelled her first African smells. She seemed stunned. The smell was enough to stun a stranger.

The smells hang in the air like a low cloud. The smells are inseparable and form one tremendous acrid essence in which the sweetish odors of rotted meat and decayed fruits blend with the sharpness of urine and the dung of animals and humans, mixing with the smell of curry and smoldering cow dung and the sharp nose-itching odor of goats and human sweat and hot sun and strong cheap tobacco and filthy vermin-ridden clothes and untended huts and unclean sickness and rancid cooking fat and drifting hashish and swirling red dust and cheap sick-smelling perfume and rank alcohol and musk. It lies over the bazaar like a dirty cloak and permeates the smallest cracks in the miserable mud walls. It enters your clothes if you pass on foot, or strikes a club-blow in your nostrils as you drive slowly past in a car.

Traffic on Delamere Avenue and Government Road thins out past islands on which plum-black native police swing their batons with military precision and savage grace. Their invariably skinny legs look strangely storkish in wrapped blue puttees under wide uniform khaki shorts.

It is rather an ugly, largely treeless city, except for the scabby eucalypti which line its dusty streets, but out toward the edges there is a sudden upthrust of damp green of fir and fig and acacia, of jacaranda and flame, of cedar and palm. The private homes are almost obscenely riotous with flowers.

The city's architecture is fantastic, square white buildings of several stories, slashed by sunlight and shade, and mostly all ugly; here the delicate minaret of a mosque, here a sprawling Indian school of a violent yellow, there a house of pierced plaster in the Arab mood, and on the edges, long, ugly, crumblymolding green wooden barracks. The suburbs toward Muthaiga and Limuru are rolling and wet-green and lush-forested, as in any good suburb. The better-class white dwellings are snugged by trees and flowers, and the best boast their swimming pools and clipped tennis courts. The richer Indians have their fine homes, too, but not in the white districts. The Indian homes loom square and hideous on the dusty plains on the road to Thika. They sit starkly like yellow boxes, plastered in the front for show, but revealing ugly gray cement block, unstuccoed, behind, and with their plastered porticos carven in Indian scrollwork.

They came into town, and as they drove down Delamere Avenue they passed Lord Delamere's statue. The little man's likeness captured quite a lot of his fabled audacity.

"Who's that fellow?" Tom Deane asked. "Him on the pedestal?"

"Old Lord Delamere. The one that opened up these parts for the white settlers. Wagered his fortune and wrecked his health trying to make this what he called 'white man's country.' Fought England tooth and nail when the Home Office tried to take away the settlers' lands back in '22. Led a delegation to London, a bunch of hairy settlers and a couple of Masai warriors with spears. Told the Whitehall chaps that unless they called off their dogs Kenya was going to do what you people did and bloody well declare war on England. Home Office backed down. England could hardly afford to get mixed up in a war with one of its colonies at that time, and the settlers were dead serious. They were going to kidnap the Governor, just for starters."

"He must have been quite a gent," Tom Deane said.

"It all sounds fascinating," Nancy Deane said. "Is that the Norfolk Hotel there, the red long building down the road?"

"Yep. That's your home for the next couple of days. I've booked you into one of the better cottages. This cottage has two bedrooms and a quite decent living room. You've got so much gear that if we try to put it all in the living room you won't have any place to sit."

Three days later they were off to the Masai. They ate the bitter alkali dust on the way to Narok, and stopped for a Coke and to say hello to the game warden in Narok, and saw the proud, slim, goatcaped Masai with their spears, and arrived at camp on a crook of the stone-studded, tree-hedged, sand-flatted Telek River, seeing the winking lights of the cook fire a long way off, and finally coming into a tiny tent city where the mess tent was already up, a Coleman lantern burning and hissing bright from a downbent branch of tree, the fire fast and noisily alight, a small circle of campchairs drawn round it, and the melodic hum of African voices blending softly off toward the other cook fire. Yusuf came out to meet them as they alighted from the Rover, his black face shiny in the reflected fire, his white night-gown spotless, his green-and-gold bolero rich in the firelit night, and his smile impudent and happy. There were gin and lime and scotch and orange and beer and Coke and sardines and crackers and cheese and pickles on the side table, under the lifted skirts of the mess tent. From the cook fires drifted a scent of something spicy. One of the porters, dragging out firewood, was singing a song under his breath that was vaguely familiar but for the words. Somewhere was the solid smack of maul on tent peg. One or two of the blacks, shy and apologetic, came up to say something swiftly in Swahili to Peter, ducking their heads and smiling beautifully over the filed teeth from blue gums.

"Over there's your sleeping tent," Peter said, pointing. "This is headquarters, the mess tent. Yusuf is your boss from now on, from here, because he runs the camp. You'll see your personal boys when they serve you at supper. The sanitary tent's that way. It's not very grand, I'm afraid. I live in that little green tent over there. Scream if ever you want me. Would you like a bath, Nancy?"

Use Enough Gun

"I'd adore a bath. I've got lava in my pores and in my soul. Can you arrange one?"

"Sure. Gathiru!

"*Ndio, Bwana,*" came from somewhere in the dark.

"*Letti hi happa majimoto kwa memsaab pese pese!*"

"*Ndio, Bwana. Suria.*"

"That is the bath being drawn, I suppose?"

"Uh-huh. They heat the water in petrol tins. Then they pour it into a sort of canvas coffin which you'll find in your tent, in the back part. There'll be soap and towels and the boy'll dry your back. Don't be shy; he never looks at you, and it's nice to step out of the tub into a warm towel. I suggest your uniform for this time of day be those heavy flannel pajamas we bought, a robe, and mosquito boots. Then when you're ready to sleep all you have to do is hold out a foot for Gathiru or Kariuki to pull the boot off it, and fall into bed. The boy'll fix the mosquito netting, not that you'll need it now, but for the morning. You'll not be frightened when you see a cannibal staring at you through the nets, will you? It'll only be Gathiru or Kariuki fetching you the morning *chai.* That's tea. You the bartender or me, Tom?"

"Me. You're the expert on what eats me, and I shouldn't like to tire you. Lovely, nutritious, delicious, bone-building, character-molding gin?"

"*Ndio.* Without olive, please."

"What are the house rules around here?" Nancy asked sprawling into a canvas chair and stretching her khaki-panted, ankle-booted legs out toward the fire. "Anybody got a cigarette for a lady?"

"Here. One of yours. I pinched a packet. No house rules. You're the *Memsaab wa Safari,* the boss. What you want, you scream for. What you don't like, you tell me and I fix. What you wish to eat and what you don't, you tell me, and any little extras we go and buy off the *ducca.* You're supposed to have fun on this thing. Point of protocol, though. Apart from routine, anything special, you tell me and I'll tell Yusuf. He loses face with the boys if we go over his head. Thanks, Thomas. There is really nothing like gin to fend off the evening ague. Cheers, and a happy hunt to you both."

"Is there any sort of hierarchy, like in the Navy, I mean a chain of command with these boys of yours? I wouldn't want to butch the detail," Tom asked, handing a cocktail to his wife.

"Works roughly like this. Yusuf's the overall boss, but he has no jurisdiction with the gunbearers. They're what you'd call elite troop and beyond the scope of a servant. They sneer at Yusuf. They tell him he's a ruddy coward, which of course he is, and the big joke round the cook fire is the plot to get Yusuf off on a buffalo hunt. He's stark silly frightened of the old *mbogo*. But you can tell the caste system by who eats with whom."

"Who does Yusuf eat with?"

"Eats with the cook, Aly. Also dines occasionally with the two personals, but they sit a little outside the circle. They're in his direct charge. Then you'll see that the gunbearers always eat together, except when occasionally they'll add a guest if they're feeling like company. Once in a while, me. If you're very good, you might possibly get invited. It's an honor to eat with the gunbearers, because they get first crack at all the best victuals. Fat's highly prized here; the boys are dead keen for it. They think it'll cure everything from gonorrhea—excuse me, Nancy—to impotence. Truth is, they're starved for fats and protein. Anyhow, since the gunbearers are always first on the scene when we shoot something, they carve off the fat and the juciest bits of meat, and so to dine with the gunbearers assures you of the best."

"Who are the poor folks?"

"Well, the porters eat together as a rule, and then the kitchen *mtoto*—he's the Oliver Twist of the bunch—he eats with the car boy. Whenever we get a visiting fireman in the shape of a game scout or a special tracker, he generally eats with the gunbearers. We must go and shoot something big tomorrow, though. The boys have been lying around town and are fair starved for meat."

"What something big do we—you, possibly, or maybe I—

shoot tomorrow?" Tom asked. "There's a little more martini here. Have some?"

"Yes, please. Thank you. Oh, first I thought we'd go out and sight in the guns. Scopes bound to be out of whack, and nothing puts you off so badly as aiming exactly right and having the bullet fly exactly wrong. We'll shove up a target and see that all the guns are behaving. Then we'll go and shoot a Tommy for us. They're that little gazelle you saw coming in, the one with the straightish horns and the black bar on his side. Then we'll go and shoot a zebra for the boys. They're fat as cream, and we might as well start shooting the odd *punda* here and there, because you'll want the hides, of course, and the boys dearly love the fat. Zebras are a bore, but I'd rather you got started on something that hasn't any importance. You might as well resign yourself to missing a lot at first. The light's very tricky here."

"Christ, I'm resigned to missing without blaming it on the light, tricky or not," Tom said. "I don't know anything about this. All I know anything about is a shotgun."

"Well, we'll do a little shotgunning too. Tomorrow night we'll go, say about five-six, and shoot a pig or so to put in a tree for your leopard—that's no trouble at all—and we'll take the shotty-gun *kidogo* and collect a mess of guinea fowl and francolin for lunch day after tomorrow. Old Aly boils 'em and serves 'em cold with mustard pickles and mayonnaise and salad, and there is nothing better, I expect, in the world, if you're hungry and there's a beer handy. We're having some tonight, as a matter of fact. Chalo told me he ran into a flock coming down—francolin, I mean—and took the liberty of assassinating a few. I'm afraid Chalo's no sportsman. His idea of sport is to find a troop of guinea running down a footpath and to shoot flat on the ground, aiming at their heads. Oh, Nancy. There goes your hot water. *Tyari*. That means ready."

"*Bathi tyari*," the voice floated from the tent.

"I'll go and remove the soil," Nancy said. "You bathing, Tom?"

"Sure. There's more water, Peter?"

"Sure. Soon's your good woman's decent, they'll dump the

bathtub and fill it for you. Then I'll have her all to myself whilst you get sanitary again."

"Right. You going to bathe?"

"Yep. When you've finished. I'll just whip into my slightly smaller facilities and take a swift cure."

Dinner was a memorable thing, when the men had bathed and they'd had the last martini and kicked the fire into a blaze, a horrid-looking old black man bringing a dead tree and dragging it over the center of the fire. The night was really cold now and the stars were lit and dancing, and the symphony had tuned. Hyenas, attracted by light and the smell of cooking meat, had ringed the camp and were just beginning to sound their various A's. Away off somewhere there was a rumble and a racking cough.

"Your first lion," Peter said. "Old boy's got the rheumatiz, like Pa. The cold brings out the grumbles."

Away down the river there was a steady sawing sound, *hah-hah-hack-huh-hack-huh* sort of sound, and Peter smiled.

"Leopard. I'm glad to know they're hunting about here. Sounds fairish, and a male, I'd say. We'll just decorate a Christmas tree for that chap and shoot him off it when he comes to collect the present."

A shrill cursing followed in the wake of the leopard's coughing, almost similar in sound.

"That's what?" Tom said. "Another leopard?"

"No, only monkeys—baboons, actually, expressing their displeasure. They're mortal enemies, the leopards and the *nugus*."

"I don't mind saying I'm excited. I've waited a long time for this. And now to be here, to actually be here, with tomorrow, just tomorrow, right here, I'm goose-pimpled." Tom got up and stood in front of the fire. Somewhere off in the distance there was a strangely abrupt barking. "That's what? Dogs?"

"Zebra. Possibly frightened by a lion close by. Funny to think a horse can make a sound that much like a dog."

"I'm scared to death," Nancy said. "I never heard so damned many different noises in my life. What's *that*?"

"A bush baby. Little soft furry thing, cries like a child. You can see its eyes glowing as big as flashlamps if you'll step over here. They show red in the night. Sad little bugger, what?"

"How long does it take to know all this about it? I mean, what all the sounds are and what kind the trees are and all the rest?"

"Well, Tom, we've grown up with all of it, and so I suppose it's like your knowing about how to get about in New York. I'm sure I would be frightened foolish in London or Rome or New York and perform as an awful ass, not knowing how much to tip or what to order or how to find my way about in tubes. Here I feel at home, and since I've heard hyenas and bush babies and monkeys and lions since I was a baby, I feel comfortable about them."

"What's the chances of one of these things creeping into camp and taking a nip out of you?" Nancy said. "That tent of mine seems to have very little in the way of protection from any really determined anything bigger than a rabbit."

"No fear. You'll find everything out here more frightened of you than you're frightened of it. I would form the habit of shaking out my boots in the morning, though. Tarantulas and scorpions and such sort of like to crawl into shoes for warmth."

"Good God. What about snakes?"

"Very few up here. You find them more in the jungly country. Might run onto the odd cobra or mamba, but they generally go the other way."

"I don't know about you people, but I'm tired," Tom said. "This has been a very exciting day for me, and I don't want to disgrace myself when we start to shoot tomorrow. I think I'll turn in, if Nancy's ready. I'm beat."

"Fine. Just yell if you want anything, or clap your hands. The lamp's already lit in your tent, and there's a torch on the table if either of you has to use the loo. I'll just walk round the camp and see if all's tidy. Good night, all, and sleep well. If you find anything in your tent it'll be a rhino. Don't move, and the chances are it'll go away."

"Thank *you*, Dr. Livingstone," Nancy said, and went off to

bed. She jumped into her cot and tucked the mosquito netting firmly under the mattress, and although a hyena seemed to be about to make her an indecent proposition, judging from the nearness of the noise, and the whole African bush seemed to be conversationally inclined, she went to sleep immediately with a great sense of security. She did not wake until the gray light of early morning, when a cannibal with filed teeth shook her by the shoulder, leered horribly, and said: *"Memsaab. Iko hapa chai."*

What a curious thing, Nancy Deane thought as she reached out her hand to take the steaming cup of tea, to be shaken awake by a man who only yesterday was eating his uncle, and to have it all seem completely natural.

"Asante," she said, smiling, using one of the few Swahili words she knew. "Thank you." And got up to inspect the day, which naturally must be fine.

T H E Y waited out of the rain, in the hotel in Arusha, and read old papers while Peter went off to clear the trophies with the Game Department. Mostly they thought about the trip with sadness, now it was finished. It had been, Tom Deane thought, the only time in his life when he had been completely happy and knew he was completely happy. There was nothing that he and Nancy did not know about Peter now, including the one bad love affair when Peter had got himself sentimentally involved with some young thing and had come back from safari to find another gentleman, a city type, in his bed. Peter knew everything there was to know about Nancy and Tom, as well. They had lived in each other's pockets for three months, away off in a land God hadn't paid much attention to for a very long time. The lorry had bogged down and had snapped springs, and the food had run out, and the gin had run out, and the scopes had gone crook, and the Land Rover had consumed bearings, and once some thieves had come and stolen all the cameras. They had been hot and tired and wet and cold and hungry and filthy and bugbitten. Nancy had often been frightened and Tom had been petrified on occasion, and Peter had got himself lost, and the hyenas had sneaked into the tent one night and eaten a camera bag. Lions had strolled through the camp and stolen meat from where it hung fresh-killed in trees, and in a camp up around the Yaida swamp the hippos had bellowed almost in the back yard. But in the three months there had not been a single word of real exasperation, an earnest recrimination, a single serious quarrel. There had been a lot of chaffing and much sober talk and a great many completely silly private jokes, such as the way they always kidded Peter dead-pan about certain mannerisms and tricks of phrase. They had talked roughly, freely, but without leering or using smut as a diversion. There was nothing, practically, that Nancy would say in bed to Tom that she would not say as freely to Peter when they sat around the campfire.

When the men were off hunting hard, hunting buffalo or rhino or kudu, and an extra person was a bother, Nancy either stayed in camp with the black boys or took Kungo and the lorry and one other boy to serve as gunbearer and went bumping off on a bird-shooting safari of her own. Sometimes she would be gone for two or three days, sleeping under a blanket on a pad in the back of the lorry, with the two savages sleeping at her feet. It never occurred to her that it was strange for a young white woman to be camping alone with two complete savages in the middle of the Tanganyikan bush, with lions roaring close by and elephants screaming in the thickets, while her husband was off God knew where doing something idiotic about buffalo.

Sometimes she loafed in camp for days while the men took a basic pack and went off reconnoitering, and she was completely, utterly happy and unbored and knew at the time that she was happy and unbored. Then she wrote long letters home, or read cheap Penguin or Tauchnitz paperbacks, with Yusuf doing her hair for her. She watched the baboons, who came to know her and were very little shy of her, and she loved to watch the ants toiling as they made their mountainous red clay castles. She had one of those hurry-up cameras that develop a picture in a minute, and she took portraits of all the black boys to send back home to their mothers and wives. It was the first pictures most of them had seen of themselves, because while all people on safari made them pose frequently, very few ever sent back snaps. It was a forgetful way people had. The word spread that *Memsaab Picha* owned a new magic which could make a man's face print on paper in less than a minute, so shortly Nancy and her Polaroid camera became famous with the surrounding tribes, whose people would straggle in every day to plead for a little special voodoo with the camera.

The blacks adored her. Once, when the Coca-Cola supply was running out and there was no prospect of getting more, Yusuf, the headboy, started to steal a bottle a day. When the end of the supply was announced, the men resigned themselves to a diet of warm gin and an occasional beer. Only after they left camp did Yusuf appear bearing a Coke, cold from last night's condensation in the bottom of the water bag. He grinned and handed it to the Mama, as he called her. "Plenty more," Yusuf said. "I steal very much from the *bwanas,* save it for Mama." Nancy was so touched that she forgot to tell the men they had a thief in camp, and so drank a secret Coke every day, until Peter found out about it over the cook-fire gossip and booted Yusuf unlovingly in the behind. Peter had become very fond of Coke. They unearthed the stolen hoard, and for punishment Peter and Tom drank it all up and didn't give Mama any.

They had captured for her a baby monkey, a shriveled little old man of a beast about the size of Nancy's fist, whom they called Tembo, meaning elephant, because he was so tiny. Tembo loathed Tom and Peter, who were forever teasing him and threatening to cut off his tail. He loved Nancy and clung to her neck like a limpet. The only time Tembo would associate with Peter and Tom was when they moved from one camp to another in the jeep. When Tembo had an urge to urinate he would leave Nancy, leap to one of the men, and void his bladder on their shirts before they could scrape him off. Peter said that he had done a lot of loathsome things for clients before but that he didn't feel that being a W.C. for a bloody *nugu* was necessarily entered in the articles. Nancy wept when a wildcat abducted Tembo one day. He had been a very dear little monkey.

The whole thing had been just wonderful, both Nancy and Tom kept saying as they waited for Peter to get back from the Game Department with the trophy clearances. All of it. Every minute of it. Nancy was completely in love with Peter, and Tom had developed a massive hero worship that threatened to murder him, because he would do anything at all, no matter what the hazard, to avoid appearing poorly in front of Peter or the gunbearers. In the narrow corner of their lives Peter assumed demi-god proportions. He was as tender with his blacks as a mother, but always with a mother's discipline. He dosed them when they were ill and listened to their troubles, squatting on his haunches at the campfire, and he chastened them when he thought they needed it. They seemed to love him with the blind respectful trust of dogs; they never questioned, never complained, even after many consecutive days of riding high-perched on the lorry-load, in choking dust and searing heat or driving rain and knifing wind. They ran the camp as meticulously as a fine restaurant is run; they pitched it in an hour and struck it in forty-five minutes. When they were out after kudu or buffalo or especially rhino at Manyara, sometimes the hunters would not return until ten, and then Nancy would hear a hushed murmur from the gunbearers as they sat up until three or four in the morning, cleaning guns and repairing the lorry, with Peter himself never going to bed until all was done. The boys would come and sing for her sometimes, and she loved especially one old Wakamba song, a derivative of some ancient Christian hymn, which they just called *"Golu, golu."* They would accept a half beer each, although it is forbidden to give alcohol to an African, and then they would modestly retire, anxious not to overstay their welcome or embarrass the Mama by taking too much beer and getting drunk. They even asked Nancy to visit their campfire for supper, an unprecedented honor, and gave her the choice bits of things to eat which would have horrified her if she had seen them in the original state.

She saw Peter daily in the jeep, in the bush, in the camp, and in the little towns, and she decided she had never known a young man so gentle, so basically clean, so competent at his business, and so completely without pose or pretense. She had seen him find game where there was no game. She had watched his knowledge of animals and grass and weather. She had seen him that bad day with the lion; she had seen him build bridges and fix hopelessly damaged machinery. She had seen him prepare a three-course meal on a wind-racked desert, where there was no wood or water, making the cook fire with petrol and sump oil in a hole in the ground, and draining the jeep's radiator for enough water for tea. She had seen him always quietly kind and really rather shy, and very, very polite always, as a habit and not a mannerism. "Peter?" Always, in answer: "Nancy?" even if she just wanted to ask him to pass the salt.

Tom's estimate of Peter was not based so much on the sweeter side but on the utter competence with which he tracked; the almost maniacal concentration on outwitting something which already knew all the answers; the religious dedication to locating the best before any effort was made to hunt it, and then the rejection of it if it had any flaw of shape or length or breadth or thickness. In three months they had shot nothing that was not eaten or, if inedible, was not a candidate for the Valhalla of game, the records of the Messrs. Rowland Ward of London. There had been some very tight squeaks, or so it seemed in retrospect, but the squeaks had been oiled with a foreseen preparedness for just this sort of squeak—twice with the buffalo, once with the lions, several times with the rhino. They had not yet fired at a rhino. They had run away from forty, because this one was too short in the horn, that one a cow with a wonderful horn but her calf was too young to orphan, another who was pretty good but not quite good enough. Tom had seen Peter drive in the dust, eyes reddened from it, face black with it, from dawn until midnight, spend the rest of the night repairing the lorry, and arise the next day, with no sleep at all, to do it over. He climbed mountains like a hill baboon; he would walk ten miles, leaving Tom under a tree with a book, to verify a vague suspicion.

The gunbearers were something, too, something you couldn't believe. They had no protection but Peter, for they carried no guns except Peter's guns, and of course Tom's guns, and when you reached back to take the gun the black man was then un-armed, but they would still walk into a buffalo herd or a rhino or a whole flock of lions with complete assurance, depending, like small children, on Papa to make it all come right. You never had to look for Chalo or Metheke when you needed a gun, loaded and ready, or if you ran out of shells there was a black hand on your arm with a fistful of fresh stuff. These men rode for hours crouched uncomfortably in the cramped back of the jeep, which was full of guns and glasses and chop boxes and am-munition boxes. When the jeep stuck in a stream, they got out and waded waist-deep into water that harbored, surely, snakes, leeches, and, very likely, crocodiles. The gunbearers were always quiet and they melted into bush like wraiths, in full sight one minute and forever lost to view if you flicked your gaze away.

It was not the shooting, although when the shooting came at the logical end—like this morning when they found the kudu— it was wondrous fine, and then it was thrilling and gratifying to have the boys beat you on the back and call you a firecracker. It was overpowering, the day of the first lion, to have the boys wait-ing in camp for you and, when they saw the great head with the blood-streaked tawny mane lolling out of the back of the jeep, to beat you with green leafy branches and sing some triumphant

song and hurl you about until you were bruised with their affection and sick from laughter. They didn't do it for the money,
either; Peter wouldn't allow any tipping on safari.

The finest of it all was getting back at night, tired to tears,
lava-filthy and bone-sick from the constant jouncing of the hunting car, feet bruised from stony hills, scratched and hungry and
tsetse-chewed, to see the fire a long way off and know that with
the fire there was a drink and warm water and clean clothes and
hot food and a chance to slump in a canvas chair in the frosty
night and watch the sparks whirl upward and mingle with the
stars. Then you heard all the noises and talked about that day,
or yesterday, or the war, or funny people you knew, or things
that had happened to you before the war or when you were a
little boy. Nobody talked gossip, there wasn't any gossip to talk.
You just talked sort of lazy and aimlessly, until it was time to go
to bed, with the food and the brandy-and-coffee still warm inside
you, clean again and snug in your pajamas, so you could die for
nine hours in order to get up and do it all over again the next
day. The talk was the best of it. The talk and the drinking.

Funny about the drinking. You made a rule without making a
rule. If you came back to camp for lunch, if you were hunting
close by, you might have one pink gin or a bottle of beer before
you ate. Or if you were going to be gone all day you found a
bottle of beer apiece in the chop box, with the coarse-grained
home-cooked bread and the flat-sliced cold meat and the rock-
hard butter and the cold baked beans and clammy spaghetti and
the pickles which made your lunch. You ate the lunch under an
old baobab or a towering fig or a thorn tree, snoozed a bit, waiting for the heat to drop, and then hunted on until seven, when
it got too black to shoot. Then it took you an hour, sometimes
two hours, to get back to camp, bouncing along in the grass or
on a disappearing track, the wind bitter, every joint with a separate ache, and birds and foxes and rabbits skittering ahead, with
Peter swooping the jeep suicidally to avoid running them down.

It seemed then in the last half hour that you would surely die
if you did not have a drink, an un-iced gin, a scotch with warm

water with little wiggly things and dusty sediment in it. Nancy always saw the jeep's headlights a long way off, and when you climbed stiffly down out of the jeep, full of triumph or despair, she would have the drinks readymade and beckoning and the fire reaching higher than the sagging flap of the mess tent, where the chairs and table and food boxes and the paperback books and the sputtering, hissing Coleman lantern lived. Black shadows shifted behind the mess tent as one of the personals freighted the petrol tins full of hot water from the boys' fire to the brown canvas tub with the thorns under it and the fish in it. You took the drink with you into the sleeping tent and collapsed on the edge of the cot with a sigh and let one of the personals haul off your boots and undress you, and when you settled down into the warm, foul water, all the day's fatigue flowed away and peace entered you through the pores, together with the soap. The personal toweled you and helped you into pajamas and mosquito boots and held the heavy robe for you, and when you got back to the fire Yusuf was already dressing the table for *chacula,* with a checkered tablecloth held firm against the breeze by clips on the corners. And Nancy had the next drink, the really unbelievably, indescribably magnificent drink, waiting. When you had finished that with a cigarette that tasted like all the extra benefits the advertisements claimed, you were happy-flushed with fire and grog, and the soup was smoking on the table. The three personals were dandified in their white night-dresses and colored jackets, and old Aly, the cook, had scored another triumph, even if it was a ten-year-old boar wart hog that he had somehow contrived to alchemize into a six-dollar steak. Nobody made coffee as Aly brewed it over his oven of flat stones. The only trouble with it was that it put you to sleep instead of awakening you, or maybe it was the fault of the brandy that you poured into it. Because after the second cup of coffee with the solid slap of cognac you never remembered getting to bed at all. Suddenly Yusuf was shaking you gently by the shoulder and saying: "Get up, *Bwana,* it is morning," and thrusting a cup of scalding tea at you, the cup as big as a chamber pot. Your boots were lined by the bed, freshly and moistly dubbined, with the clean bush jacket and pants laid out, the underwear on top, and the thick gray wool socks folded neatly over the top of the boots, and the tooth glass and toothbrush and towel on the little table. You dressed, shivering, putting on the cashmere sweater under the jacket, and then went out to where the fire had shaken down into loosely drifting ash, with a bright cherry core of heat glowing through it, and there would be Peter, having a private attack of malaria in the cold gray dawn, with the wind blasting icily for the last half hour before the sun would rise to smile the cold away and scatter diamonds on the grasses. Peter would always be seated forlornly on a piece of unburned wood, toasting his hands and looking much smaller than in the daytime.

He would say formally, "Good morning, Tom," and you would reply, "Good morning, Peter," and he would clap his hands. The car boy would drive the jeep around and the two gunbearers would climb into the back, and the car boy would give up the wheel. Peter would slide into the front behind the wheel and ease the clutch, and you both would sit, saying nothing, looking, for the hour or two-hour drive to where the hunting was. The sun would creep cautiously up, red or golden, according to the weather, and soon the cashmere sweater would be too hot and you would strip it off and hand it to one of the boys in back. Occasionally one of the boys in back would hand a jar of *peramente*—hard candies—over your shoulder to moisten your mouth, and you would hunt on, driving in great circles, seeing all the game there was to see, speaking never except when you stopped for a drink of water from the big-pored canvas water bag lashed to the front bumper. If something you saw through the glasses was a likely head, you got out and stalked it—sometimes a short stalk to an anthill or a patch of bush, sometimes a stalk of which the first five miles was just preliminary, sweating and stumbling and cursing and fighting thorns. When you got up to shoot it, you shot, in the later stages, with complete certainty, knowing that you could hold it where you aimed it, and if you hit it where you held it, it would die then with no more trouble.

But when you shot good there was the handshake and the gunbearers crooning "Oooeee" over the length of horn or color of mane or size of animal, and a cigarette handed round for everybody before you drove on, looking eagerly at everything you had come so swiftly to love. Every baobab, every knobbly butte of clustered green with gold outcroppings of rock, every umbrella thorn, every mottled fig, every sweep of lovely curving hill, every harsh cruel drop of escarpment, every animal and every cloud of weaver birds, rolling and dipping and twisting like a tornado, every flock of guineas pacing, all the lions you didn't shoot, and all the herds you did not molest—all of this was so special that you gazed greedily, anxious to see all of it before anybody else saw it. There was no time for talk and no necessity for it. Talking was for when you got back to the fire and Nancy, if she had stayed behind, and the first drink and the bath and the noisy fire and the hot dinner. Then you talked. You babbled, with all the words you had saved up all day pouring out of you in a great welling rush.

The best day of all was the day after you finally collected— funny how you got to use that word; you never shot it or killed it, you "collected" it—the big thing you were after, because Peter was a purist and wouldn't hunt but the one thing at a time. If it was rhino, you shot nothing but rhino, the same with lion and the same with leopard and everything else except the common game.

The day after you collected it was decreed a silly day. You knew you would be moving on, and so the three of you went out and had a lot of fine foolishness. You took the shotguns and the .22 and shot birds and took pictures and played with rhinos, with the jeep, letting them come up to range before you swerved, using the jeep as a bullfighter uses a muleta to turn a bull's charge. You chased monkeys and sang and laughed and chattered and enjoyed the day, hunting nothing, just playing around a land where the horizons were two hundred miles apart and a peak stood as freshly clear at sixty miles as it showed at six hundred yards.

Those were the best days of all, and the days you saw all the things you wanted most to remember later—a lioness cuffing her cubs, giving them a severe lesson in lion deportment; the baby topi that wobbled and staggered, enjoying no more than minutes' freedom from its mother's womb; the warthogs trotting mock-serious and stuffy stately, with their antennae tails all stuck high in the air, the zebras wrestling and the hyena away up in the tree where a leopard had taken him to eat him; the mother ostriches playing make-believe wounded and dragging their wings to lead you off from the chicks—chicks, for God's sake, chicks as big as turkeys—and the crazy wildebeests fool-galloping up and down for no reasons, and the two big male ostriches paddling through the lake, and the flamingos settling and rising like an unbelievable pink cloud; the doves calling and all the other bird sounds; that day some hyenas tried to take a piece of meat from some wild dogs, and one of the *fisis* ran into a tree and knocked himself cold—that was what a man got out of the free days, the holidays, where nothing was serious and you could loose off the shotgun without worrying about scaring away some monster something that you wanted badly, very badly, for your wall. Those were the fine good days, shining days of blue and gold and green and white, days of warmth and the breeze fresh, days of sheer joy of being there and being alive on that day and in that place.

PART FOUR

LEOPARD FEVER

O V E R *the last dozen years, I have been on possibly 20 safaris. That's to say I've hunted twice in India, once in Alaska, four times in Mozambique, once in Australia, once in New Zealand and about ten times in Uganda, Kenya and Tanganyika. I have shot three elephant of over a hundred pounds per tusk, killed a couple of lion and attended the death of a dozen. I lost count on leopard—maybe 20—and have no idea about buffalo; maybe a hundred. The small game—zebra, impala, Thomson Gazelle, Grant gazelle, wildebeeste, gerenuk, oryx, duiker—in general, camp meat, must run into a thousand. I have shot three tigers, been severely mauled by a leopard, shot gaur and water buffalo, cheetah cat and cheetal deer, wild dogs and hyenas and guinea fowl and sand grouse and bustard and francolin (all white meat, even the legs, a lovely bird, the francolin) and I have had cerebral malaria, infectious mononucleosis and have been poisoned by tse-tse flies and maddened by mos-*

quitoes. *I have walked a thousand miles, jeeped a hundred thousand, and have rung up another hundred thousand in light planes on home-made airstrips in deep bush. Tents I have slept in, as well as rondavels and native huts, and I have also slept on the ground in the pouring rain. I have eaten elephant, snake, and fried grubworm."*

Brian Dermott, the white hunter who is the hero of *Uhuru*, is an altogether convincing portrait not just because Ruark was a superb creator, but also because of his friendship with men like Harry Selby and because of his personal knowledge of the country. By *1961*, which was when *Uhuru* was being written, Ruark could almost have taken clients himself, had he cared to go into the safari business. He went back to Africa every year from *1951* until he died in *1965*, and he always tried to get some hunting; but there was another, grimmer side to the picture: as, for example, the series of articles he wrote on the spot in the then Belgian Congo for Scripps-Howard in *1960* in which he predicted with some precision the chaos which was to follow independence.

A word about the title. Ruark insisted that it was the only possible title for a book about modern East Africa. He explained it as follows:

"*Uhuru is a Semitic word used commonly in both Arabic and Hebraic, and it sneaked into Swahili, which is the lingua franca of East and Central Africa, via the slave trade. Uhuru is synonymous with* l'indépendance *in the Congo, or freedom in West Africa. It is employed by black and white alike in much the same sense that* liberté, fraternité, égalité *became portion to semi-modern France.*"

THE BIG BULL stood, rocking to and fro, his ears flapping flies with the sound of handclaps, his trunk raised and S-curved as the weaving tip tested the wind; making a tremendous *plop!* as he moved his bowels. There he stood, lonely and huge and the color of the red ocher in the naked patch of dusty clay, a little hard-baked island in the scraggy gray bush of sansevieria and scrub thorn-acacia; there he was standing as completely unaware of Brian and the client and Kidogo as if he had been a tame Indian elephant in a zoo instead of a wild African loose in his own terrain with two hundred pounds-plus of trophy ivory poking out of his lip. Brian sighed inwardly, feeling as ever the brief stab of regret over reducing that mighty living monument to seven tons of rapidly bloating meat. It had not seemed so bad when he was doing the shooting himself. But this was a good client, trustworthy so far, and he was paying to shoot an elephant.

"Take a rest on the hill here," Brian whispered. "Hold it steady on that line between the ear slot and his eye—just a touch, just a hair above that line. It's a perfect setup for a brain shot. Okay. Take him. He's yours."

The big double-barreled rifle had boomed. The elephant dropped, collapsed as quickly as if somebody had let all the air out of him. There he was, foreknees bent, his hind legs jack-knifed backwards like a man's, kneeling on the ground. The trunk had writhed up violently once, and now was stretched out straight ahead of the bull as he knelt, almost as if in prayer.

"Jolly nice shooting!" Brian yelled, walloping the client on the back. "Right smack on! But let him have the other half just behind the shoulder. We don't want him to get up and take off, so we'll have to chase him!" Out of the corner of his eye, Brian had seen the other bulls clear off, as he stood up in full view of them. That was good. Sometimes the *askari* hung about the fallen leader, making complications, and sometimes the complications were nasty enough so you had to shoot your way out of them. And that meant trouble with the Game Department.

The client fired again, and they couldn't hear the bullet smack, because they had been very close, no more than twenty yards away from the big chap, and the gun's blast drowned the meaty whonk of the bullet. But Brian watched the flesh flinch, and he reached over and took the gun from his client, passing it without looking backward to Kidogo, the gunbearer.

"Jolly good shooting, *Bwana*," Brian repeated to the client, with almost honest heartiness, and patted his shoulder once more. "I don't recommend that brain shot to most firsttimers. Too dicey. I can tell you now we didn't need that second shot. But you . . ." and then Brian stopped. The client was weeping. His shoulders jerked in harsh sobs, and tears made dirty runnels on his dusty cheeks.

Brian lifted a chin at Kidogo, who followed him a few yards away to the shade of a small, scrofulous-looking palm.

"*Hi ndofu m'uzuri tu,*" the gunbearer said.

"*Hi m'uzuri* bloody client *tu,*" Brian Dermott said, answering Kidogo's remark that this was a very good elephant with the flat statement that this was a very good client as well. And so the client was. Only the very good ones wept with the realization that they had just reduced the true king of the world to an untidy mess of bloated meat, fly-buzzing blood, dung, seminal slop, and corruption. If he wept he was a very good client and deserved the bull, Brian thought.

"*Mupa tembo yango,*" Brian said and Kidogo dug into his only adornment, a leather pouch, and handed Brian a flat, dented silver flask which contained *tembo*—scotch whisky. The time for tears was over. Now it was time for a couple of drinks to celebrate, and then they could drive back to camp while Kidogo returned with Katunga and Muema and Chalo to hew the tusks out of that vast skull with the big deep melancholy-looking dents in the temples. It was a long, hot, sweaty, bloody job, calling for great skill and delicate care, since the ivory was paper-thin and very brittle as it joined the skull, because of the great pulpy nerve inside. It was almost like eggshell china for a couple of feet, and could easily be broken or damaged. This was too fine a pair to muck up. Brian hadn't seen such a good pair for a year or more.

The client was over his emotional fit now. He scrubbed a wrist over his eyes. The tears had cut little rivulets in the red dust that covered a shamed face. Brian shoved the flask at him without looking at him.

The man looked grateful. One of the things which had made Brian Dermott a tremendous success with clients, both male and female, was an ability to convey strength and toughness and skill coupled with an almost feminine intuitiveness and sympathy. Right now this is the only man in the world who had ever shot an elephant and then felt sorry that he'd shot it. No need to tell him most people wished they hadn't, especially after they have done it well.

"Funny," the client said, wiping his mouth with the back of his hand and giving the flask back to Brian. "You look different to me now. You look smaller, more my size. When we first came out you looked ten feet tall and I felt like a midget." This, too, was part of the safari catharsis. Growing up to the country. It always happened one way or the other. Quite a few grew smaller as the country expanded.

"Same old me," Brian grinned; a big, white, square-toothed
grin that gave his baked brown face a fleeting little-boy look,
and gestured mockingly at himself. "Same old *shenzi* shanty
Irish. No change in me. It's you who've changed. The Wakamba
say that the whole world changes when a man takes his first
woman, hears his first lion roar, and kills his first elephant." *Oh
mama mia,* Dermott, Brian sneered at himself. Brian Dermott,
the African philosopher, who can make up exotic native prov-
erbs to fit any and all occasions.

Katie Crane had been in Africa exactly one month, and she
thought she had never been so happy.

She sat in the front seat of the Rover, between the two men,
her khaki-trousered legs opened immodestly to allow Brian
Dermott's brown left hand a free play with the gear shift between her knees. The merging days had melted and run into
four weeks now, and she felt that she had been born and reared
in this uncomfortable, unladylike, undignified position. She was
even able to sleep sitting straight up between Brian Dermott
and her brother, Paul. Pretty soon now she and Brian and her
brother would raise the new campsite in the new country, and
she would be almost sorry to leave the car. She felt welded to it.
She felt as though she had never been out of it. The Land Rover
had become her home. She took an inventory, now, and smiled.
Nothing seemed to be missing, or else she'd have noticed it.

In the long compartment formed by the dashboard in front of
her was a box of Kleenex, a roll of toilet paper, three disheveled
paperback books, a tin of peppermint Scotch humbugs, a glass
jar of hard mixed candies she had learned to call *peramente,* a
bottle of *"Off,"* the anti-bug mixture, a carton of cigarettes, a
small pair of binoculars, a broken carton of matches, a plastic
bottle of sunburn lotion, a small leather-covered half-flask of
whisky, an airmail copy of last month's *Time,* a dirty roll of ad-
hesive, a bottle-opener-corkscrew, a tin box of aspirin, and a red
Swiss knife with a dozen varying blades of assorted exotic func-

One hundred and ten pounds each,
perfectly symmetrical, wonderfully thick,
and beautifully curved tusks.

He came—like a train. His trunk was straight out ahead of him, his tusks upraised, his ears back, and his feet high like a pacing horse.

The rhino is far and away the easiest of all African dangerous game to find and shoot.

Sighting the gun.

An eight-foot cheetah, about half dog, half cat, with a round cat's face,
a long cat's tail, long dog's ears, and a dog's non-retractile claws.

Bob Ruark with one very dead leopard.

Henry Selby and
a Grant gazelle.

He is a dreadful-looking beast, the rhino.

aterbuck are awful to eat, but there is no more ruggedly handsome animal in Africa.

u judge a buffalo by the configuration and curl of horn
well as by the distance between his horn tips.

The elephant lay stiff-legged in the bright morning sun.

The camp gunroom.

Bob and Virginia Ruark
in safari kit.

Lunch in the mess-tent.

Fellow hunter Ralph Johnston's Africa room in Texas home.

e memsaab adjusting
her new life.

I do not believe there are many
more impressive sights than a city man's
first glimpse at a live maned lion loose
on a plain in strange country.

Bob Ruark the one-shot bwana,
the mighty simba slayer.

tion. You didn't really need the bottle opener or the *maridadi* knife. You could easily snap the cap off a bottle under the curl of the Rover's dashboard.

Behind her she knew there would be a spare tire, a long tool box, and a picket fence of guns standing, upright, clamped into foam-rubber cushions. The extra artillery, mostly of the big-mouthed variety, slept well-greased in its jewel-cases against a declaration of war.

Also well-greased and permanently dark-fixtured in the back seat, always standing clinging to the crossbar onto which the up-right gun racks were bolted, was the team of Kidogo and Muema, the gunbearers, who seemed to have the vision of vultures and who constantly descried specks which meant nothing to her, but occasionally warranted a tiny tap on Brian's shoulder causing him to stop the Rover and reach for the little binoculars. Mostly he would say quietly: "I say, that's rather a jolly lion over there, just left of that little hill," and pass her the glasses; or, less frequently, "It's another Jumbo, nothing like so good as the one we've got, but decent enough for most people"; or, rarely, "That's a damned fine oryx; I don't think we're likely to see a better." And swiftly over his shoulder to the gunbearers. *"Toa three hundred kwa bwana,"* and then commence a devious approach at which she never ceased to marvel. Then, suddenly, he would say to her brother: "Right, Paul, just when we pass that anthill . . ." or thornbush, or acacia, and her brother would stretch his right hand backward to the gunbearers and she would hear the soft smack of the weapon as it was slapped like a big surgical instrument into a doctor's palm.

Paul would plunge out of the car as it passed the anthill, or thornbush, and usually Muema, the gap-toothed, grizzled, broken-nosed Wakamba gunbearer, would fall out with him. Then Brian would rapidly drive the car away to some small pimpling hill a thousand yards distant, and tell Kidogo to hand Katie the big binoculars from the back seat. They would stop, then, to get out and limber their legs and view the unfolding tableau through the glasses—to watch her brother and Muema, stalking from anthill to anthill, from low bush to tree, dwindling tiny black figures printed against vast yellow carpet, until finally she could see Muema touch her brother's arm. The gun would ride easily to his shoulder, he would brace his legs and lean against the side of the hill or bush, or else squat flat on his backside with upraised knees forming a steady, locked rest, as Brian had taught him. Then, usually, there would come the solid *tunk!* as the bullet struck before the sound of the gun's explosion reached them. Mostly the animal collapsed, or staggered in a shrinking circle before falling. Occasionally it raced dementedly away in a death gallop as the tiny bullet touched its heart without breaking bone.

Brian, standing beside her, always knew immediately from the sound. *"Kufa,"* he'd say, if it was a solid whomp—dead. Sometimes he'd say "Dead but it doesn't know it yet," when the animal lurched and then sped away. Once in a while he would say *"Piga,* but too far back," or shake his head and mutter *"Tumbo tu"*—"belly only." Then was when they would track, tracing sometimes the sprayed pink frothy lung blood or the yellow-bily stomach blood in little clots and ropy slashes. She was allowed to tag along when they tracked, and was invariably awestruck. Kidogo and Muema ranged ahead of Brian like circling dogs, each man pointing rhythmically with a stick or weed and nodding sagely at things she could not see—a scuffed bit of earth, a minute scrape on a stone, a back-bent blade of grass. She tried and she tried, but she could never track, although one day they had followed a wounded kongoni for nearly two hours and she never saw a sign of its passage after the first few bright berries of blood dried away under the hot sun. Brian was usually articulate about nearly everything that he did as a reflex, but he had tried to explain tracking to her and had failed, because tracking was neither a skill nor a science. As far as she could make out it was nine-tenths intuition, if not sheerest magic, and she noticed that neither Brian nor the natives ever really looked at the ground. They seemed to stare out in front of them, on a waist level—what Brian called "bringing the ground up to you," and followed in the general direction of where it seemed likely an animal might go if you were that particular animal.

After a time, generally short but sometimes unaccountably long, covering sweaty miles, they would come upon the animal, suddenly dead or occasionally down but with its head raised, its eyes hurtful with dumb, baffled anger. Then was when Brian would say quietly to her brother, "Best slip another behind the shoulder," or "Give him the other half in the back of the neck, please, Paul"—or, occasionally, the part she hated most, when one of the gunbearers would unsheathe his knife, and, warily approaching, seize a horn in one hand and sever the vertebra with a quick, short stab at the base of the brain. Only occasionally did he miss, and then the sight of twisting blade, probing for the spinal cord, made her actively ill.

But that was only the tiniest part, and Katie was no milksop. If you were there to kill, some unpleasantness was necessary and she could understand the necessity. She had long since realized that minks were not born sewed into coats and that sirloin steaks were not spun in test tubes, and that shoe leather invariably came ripped untimely off a cow. It had taken her a few days to conquer the first aversion to all the blood and slop that attended the death of a zebra which would some day be converted into a frightfully chic strip of upholstery for a modern sun room in Palm Beach.

She had watched, fascinated by the final awfulness of it; the automatic voiding of the bowels, the pumping seminal ejaculation, then the great spilling of hot stinking white shiny-bulging intestine as one of the boys "toa hi tumbo"—split the belly and plunged into the abdominal cavity with both hands to haul out the slippery stomach and scrape off the glistening globules of yellow fat which lined the great gut.

The hot sweet sickish smell of blood, the spilled green-spinachy contents of the paunch, the hordes of fat buzzing flies that came from nowhere, then the vultures circling and finally volplaning down from the sky to light with a bump of their undercarriage; birds looking like horrid sextons sitting in an evil,

crooked-necked circle, hopping and flapping with irritable impatience, or waiting lasciviously eager, like nasty unbuttoned old
men, waiting atop an anthill or on a dead bough of thorn tree
for the hunters to be done with their skinning and dismember-
ing. Then, as the bloody-handed gunbearers wiped their dripping fingers on a tuft of grass after loading the severed hams and
sections of ribs, and bundling the heart and liver and strips of
intestine into the blood-soggy package of the heavy fresh hide,
she could see the drooling vultures tense and hop closer even
before the people had all crawled back in the Land Rover. By
the time the car was in gear and crawling away, the birds were
already quarreling and flapping over the carcass, their bloodied
heads stuck obscenely into the dismembered mess. She knew
the buzzards were necessary to the scene—knew they were protected and even cherished as scavengers, but she consciously
hated the dreadful end of it; the sleek, sun-glistening animal,
alert and vibrant with life small minutes past, suddenly reduced
to a pile of brownish lumps and picked red-scabbed bones, the
yellow teeth ugly in the eyeless skull. She had never really considered the mechanics of death before, but had to admit that she
was more fascinated than shocked by the completeness of disso-
lution.

It developed that Brian was heavily in love with nearly all the
animals he knew, and it seemed to her that he deliberately post-
poned the killing of any of them—until, at last, he sighed and
suggested almost apologetically to her brother that the dimensions of whatever it was they were seeking did not figure to im-
prove with further search, and so Paul had best get out and wallop it.

She believed she understood a little better now that she knew
more. She had been more interested in photography than in
shooting—indeed, she had refused to kill anything with more
personality than birds, which seemed, like fish, to lie weightless
on one's conscience—and she and Brian had gone alone except
for the gunbearers on several camera expeditions when her
brother took an occasional day off in camp to ease his blistered

feet and skim through the batches of his business correspondence that overtook them fitfully when Brian sent the lorry into the *ducca* at Isiolo or Garba Tulla for petrol. She was fascinated by everything, but especially by the elephants, particularly the relatively "tame" ones on the National Park side of the road, where shooting was forbidden unless something was about to bite you.

It was with the elephants that she had first experienced shattering physical fear—the first time when an old dry herd-mistress had broken away from the straggling group and charged them, screaming, trunk-stabbing, ears pinned tightly back, and Brian had performed some new miracles of maneuver with the Land Rover. She should have caught tremendous moving pictures of that screeching charge—except that in her fear she had forgotten to take the protective covering from the lens and so had buzzed out several score unfertilized feet of nothing.

On another occasion, they had stalked close to an old one-tusker bull who had been rocking, snoozing, dreaming old-man's nostalgic dreams under a palm along the bank of the dry river bed. The wind had changed unaccountably, a stick had cracked under her foot, and the ancient bull had suddenly received their scent and blasted a trombone bellow. Perhaps he wasn't charging, but he was bowling full steam in their direction, and Brian had nearly jerked her arm out of the socket dragging her crosswind, her toes scraping only against the higher points of ground. They had come very close to elephant several times after, and always she felt the almost joyful flooding of fear that the great, rumpled, wrinkled relics of the Pleistocene Age created in her. They were never quite real, those plastic tons of gray wraith that melted in and out of elephant-colored bush with never a sound, or that occasionally played like happy huge pigs or naughty little boys when they came in the evening to drink and bathe.

"Where's this Loitokitok or however you call it?" Kate's brother Paul asked. "I'm sort of attached to this Northern Frontier of yours. I still think I'll go back to Maralal and buy those two little Samburu maidens and take them home with me. I like all your wild people up here—especially those fierce-looking Turkana. What've you got that's better in this Loitok-some-thing?"

"Heaps. You'll like it," Brian said. "We go down deep into the Masai area right round Kilimanjaro, but on the Kenya side. There's a big swamp there called the Kimani, which is rotten with elephant and buffalo. And leopard. And lion, even though you won't be shooting another. And of course the mountain—old Kili and her twin sister, Mawenzi—comes up bright every morning in your tent. You've had Mount Kenya for a spell. We ought to go and see how the other half lives. How's it sound?"

"I think it sounds delightful," Kate said. "I've read so much about the Masai I'd hate to leave without seeing them. You say they're related to our Samburu here?"

"Kind of cousins—Nilotic, Hamitic. Beautiful people, and utterly useless for anything at all in this world except what they do beautifully, which is nothing. Maybe that's why I like them. They're kind of a special luxury—like your Red Indian," Brian said.

So now they had left Mawingo, left the stern portrait of Mr. Ray Ryan staring in the reception hall, left the huge drums, left the big suites with the oily-smelling cedar fires, left the hot baths, the view of The Mountain through the enormous glass windows of the big lounge.

Katie said, "Much longer, *Bwana?* My posterior is one long solid ache."

"Not much," Brian said. "A few miles only. That lovely swatch of green under the knobby hills on your left is part of this Kimani swamp."

"I really don't care about shooting much of anything any more except maybe some birds and—of course—the leopard," Paul Drake said. "You've thrown so much leopard talk at me that I'm about to get a fixation. You've got me thinking they're bewitched, and only come to special magic."

Brian laughed. "Just wait until you see your first one," he said. "You won't joke. Leopards have a most profound and frightening effect on people. Known to sunder old friendships and break up solid marriages. Well, just round this bend and over the hill and across a stream and up another hill and down and right and there we'll be. It's a lovely spot—and stiff with friendly lions and inquisitive rhino."

As they came to the top of the last hill, he pointed down. The lorry and the power wagons were long black slugs against a carpet of tender green. Standing also green and cool to the eyes, the mess tent peaked light against a black bulk of trees. A long line of deeper green, lacily friezed against the sky by towering, flat-topped acacias, hedged the outer edges of what could only be a low, wet, vividly verdant swampland which spread flatly until it ran up a yellowed hill which turned darker and darker green as its rounded summit stopped brusquely, clearly superimposed on a higher hill of soft purplish blue. A cottonroll of clouds tumbled over the plateau of the long blue range, and behind it one corner of Kilimanjaro showed a strip of snow. Its top, however, was lost in a solid cloud bank of dazzling whiteness over the clear azure of sky.

"Home," Brian said, grinding to a halt. "Everybody out. Lady's room going up, I see. Mess tent pitched, tables out, chairs out, booze box unlocked, fire in 'arf a mo', other tents a-raising. Dermott organization triumphs again. You'll have your bath as soon as your tents're up, chaps. Have a drink and take it easy while I just go *chunga* up the boys."

He ran at a lope over to where they were unloading the lorry, leaped nimbly over the cab to the top of the load, and standing, fists on hips, began to give orders like a ship's first mate supervising cargo discharge. Paul Drake wandered down a game path to a little bluff below which he could hear the gurgling exciting scurry of a river.

"This is going to be a very happy camp, I think." Brian had come back now from his overseeing chores. "Boys like it. Plenty of water in the river for washing and cooking. Won't have the water chore to bother them. Plenty of dead wood, too. Always a help when those two commodities are easy to hand."

He poured himself a small scotch and added water.

"What do you think, *Memsaab? Bwana?*" he asked. "How about these fever trees?" he waved a hand at the towering canopies of the dappled umbrella thorns, barely visible now against the sky as sudden darkness plunged on the camp. "Just like the movies."

"Wonderful," Katie said.

"You suppose there're any leopards along this river?" her brother asked. "I thought I saw tracks down there."

"Oho. Leopard fever already, like I said, eh?" Brian grinned and sipped his drink. "Yep. Bags of 'em here. I just had a word with Muema, who's been down casing the joint. One big male and a largish female, fresh today. Not surprising. They'll always stick close to the water and the larder. Masses of impala—I guess you saw that one herd—and plenty of pig, Paul. No trouble."

They slipped into luxurious, coffee-warmed silence now, as they always did when they actually hunted. Brian drove effortlessly, as always, leaving the clay track as soon as they turned out from camp, following game or cattle trails, Katie couldn't tell which, as he gentled the Land Rover smoothly around rocks and fallen logs.

They drove tilted along the sloping side of the hill that reached down toward the river, and every hundred yards a group of spurfowl scratched and scurried, occasionally to lift and fly squawking, sailing on stiffened wings a hundred yards before they put down indignantly again. Doves looped lazily up in front of the car, settling again a few score feet ahead. Starlings and bee-eaters were flung jewels in the lower trees and clumps of bush, flashing burnished purple and brilliant blue and red. Black ground hornbills walked grumpily, their enormous red faces and beaks making them look like W. C. Fields leaving a barroom. A brace of Kavirondo crested cranes danced, their gilt filigree of head plumes nodding; secretary birds used a lot of runway before they took off, only to settle again with a bump and almost a spoken curse, and the majestic greater bustards, as

Use Enough Gun

big as overstuffed Christmas turkeys, paced like trotting horses. A honey guide rose and flitted enticingly ahead, blandishing; metallic-blue–feathered, yellow-helmeted guinea fowl ran by the hundreds in the bright new grass, which carried its night dew still gleaming in diamond droplets on its short stiff ends.

An inexplicable tameness afflicts wild animals in early morning and late evening, Brian had told them, and so it was with a herd of impala that was performing a delicate minuet on the fresh sparkling sweep of green dell which stretched from the cobbled hillside into pasture and led up to the reedy edges of the river, with its dark thick stand of big trees and tangled underbrush. The impala were the color of new-minted gold, with gleaming white bellies, and they kicked and leaped out of sheer frosty morning exuberance, butting at each other. This was a large herd of ewes and slim-necked young ones, feeding and caracoling apart from a smaller herd of rams, whose lyre-shaped horns bespoke youth and whose play was more bumptiously boyish.

"The old gentlemen are over there," Brian pointed to the thicker rushes, under the shadows cast by the radish-rooted wild figs and massive rough-boled gums that strode the river. "See."

Three sets of horns, backswept, almost square in the classic brandy-snifter shape of mature ram impalas, sailed along the wind-bending grass like ship masts seen across a levee. The impalas never seemed to walk—they glided, when they were not springing into the air or nearly turning somersaults. The horns of these gazelles slid through the green like a barge on the Nile, Katie thought, showing only occasional glints of gold where the sun burnished their skins.

"Leave these in peace," Brian said. "Although about here seems a likely place to hang one kill. We'll shoot the bait elsewhere and bring it back to the scene of the eventual crime."

It was funny how much alike all the animals looked when you first came, Katie thought, as the Land Rover lurched on, wallowing slightly and only occasionally shaking her with a rattling bump. Now, after just a month, even I can tell the difference just from the way they walk. The little Tommies run like hell—except the babies, who pronk up and down on stiff legs like springs. The big white Grants all have hurty feet and too much horn. They walk with their heads hanging as if the weight of the horns was more than they could bear. The zebra gallops and wheels with cutting-horse purpose and trots with dignity, exactly like a horse. The female ostriches fluster and lift their skirts when they run, like a group of old maids heading for the john. And the giraffe moves on two dimensions in slow motion.

Two gray-blue shapes flashed out of a bush and dived across their path. Brian stopped the car. One of the blurs had stopped, solidified, and turned to look over his shoulder. His horns were double-curled and the color of nutmeats in the sun. Streaks of white ran down from his *kohl*-rimmed eyes, and white Vs formed two sparkling chevrons on his swollen throat. The blue-gray body was streaked in vertical slashes of white, and when he turned to run, he flicked a big white-fluffy tail.

"Lesser kudu," Brian said. "Not many of them here. Not so good as yours, Paul."

"Why, he's painted exactly like a Masai," Katie said. "I hadn't thought of it before—the white strips coming from the eyes and the design making the Vs on his neck."

"I think they're the most beautiful of all," Brian said. "They're protected here. Not for long, I imagine."

He put the car in gear again. They were running parallel with the swamp, and in a moment Brian stopped the car and pointed.

"There's your rhino from yesterday, Paul," he said. "Mama and young son—but sonny's damned near as big as the old lady. He'll have a shootable horn on him some day; not bad now. And oh, I say, away over to the left—about a thousand yards. Jumbo."

Brian called for the extra glasses and Katie swept the yellow ripple of tall grass which grew up and away from the poison green of the rushes. The gray-mud-colored rhino were quite close, mother and son standing staring with irritated weak-eyed intensity at something they could hear and smell but could not see. The unalarmed flocks of tick birds were easily visible on their backs and heads. Through the glasses Katie could see one bird upended, picking dedicatedly at the female rhino's ear.

The elephants looked like flat brown grubs, or old anthills, or shifting formations of sand as they stood eye-deep in the tall grass. Through the glasses she could barely make out a glimmer of ivory, but there was a snorted *"hapana ndoumi"* from Kidogo in the back, and a disgusted-sounding *"mwanamuke mtoto tu"* from Muema.

"Cows and calves," Brian said. "Old bulls still back in the hills, likely."

They drove again, this time turning up stilted knock-kneed giraffes, long disembodied necks craning stiffly above the short thorn bushes on which they were feeding, and two black-plumed ostriches poised like huge puffballs on a hillside.

"Male ostriches about to breed," Brian said. "See how their legs are turning bright red. Necks, too. Make your own moral. Up north the legs turn blue."

There were impala everywhere, and pale illusions of the ghostlike Grants, with occasional pairs of the fantastically long-necked gerenuk, rearing as they browsed. An occasional wistful-looking hyena sat staring hopefully at healthy animals he would always be too crippled in the hips to catch until some day they became sick or wounded or weakened from childbirth.

They kept to the river, still seeking a warthog, and several times Brian halted the car by bare patches of ground to get out and scan the earth for tracks. Twice they saw leopard signs, three times lion, and always the great broad platterdents of elephant. Brian grunted at the elephant sign at precisely the same time and in the same way the Africans grunted. Katie had reached the point now where she could almost translate the grunts. This particular grunt was a disgusted grunt, meaning women and children only.

They had driven perhaps five miles when Brian jammed on the brakes swiftly, sending Katie forward against the dashboard. Muema was already twisting the thumbscrews that kept the guns wedged in their padded brackets.

"There's your pig, *Bwana,*" Brian said. "Quite a nice old boy. Get out and clout him. He's over there by that fallen log about one-fifty, no more. See?"

Her brother scrambled out of the Land Rover, accepting the loaded gun in one motion as he almost fell to the ground.

Kate wondered briefly at the transformation that came over men at the prospect of killing; her brother's eagerness to get out of the car achieved a sort of graceful ballet scramble, and he did not even look too silly as he threw himself violently to the ground, bringing up the gun to shooting position, his elbows braced on his upcocked knees. Katie found that her breath quickened, too, and she searched for the pig against the dark background of bush—searched and had just found him, standing three-quarters on, big, roach-maned reddish head turned toward the car, abnormally big ears perked and outflanging, white curves of ivory reaching upward to the bumps in his impossibly ugly politician's face.

The report of the gun and the smack of the bullet merged in her ears, and the pig had disappeared from view.

"Jolly nice shooting, *Bwana,*" Brian said as always, lighting a cigarette. "That's one more we won't have to chase. Right over. You got him smack on the point of the shoulder. Look, see him kick?"

They drove slowly over the mossy excrescences of rock to where the dead warthog lay, thin-haired, tick-ridden and hideous in a spreading pool of blood. He looked ludicrously ugly at close range, with the great knobs like leper-lumps on his hog face, the tusks long and yellowed, a little worn down from rooting, and smoothly grooved underneath from being constantly used as a whetstone for the razored lower ripping teeth.

Brian jerked his head at the boys. "*Tia ndani gharri,*" he said. "We'll stick him in the car for the moment, and hunt on. We'll go up on the high plain and pick up a kongoni for the boys' camp meat, and if we see a likely impala with lousy horns and a general look of being tired of life, we'll add him to the bag. Another pig if we see one. Sorry, Katie. But it *is* shopping day."

"I'm all right, *Bwana,*" Katie said. "Having seen this warthog at close range, I don't feel so badly about the tribe. I'm fascinated only by the piglets. We do *have* to shoot one of those lovely impala?"

" 'Fraid so. There's still a couple on the license, and they're in long supply here anyhow. The pig's in," he said as the gunbearers jammed the back latches on the Rover's drop-apron. "Let's go."

Brian turned the Land Rover in a wide circle and drove in a meandering fashion up toward the top of the hill, where, he said, they'd find a road and follow that until they got up to the high open plains where they'd see topi and kongoni and very probably a few Thomson gazelles—plus, with luck, some sandgrouse for their own private menu. They located the road and had gone no more than another mile when Brian stopped the car again.

"Might as well do that poor blighter as any," he said to her brother. "See him?"

Katie looked and saw flecks of gold dappling through the woven green of the thorn scrub.

"That last one," Brian whispered, "it's a small bachelor committee of old rams. The chap we want is old as Kidogo and has only one horn." He grinned. "Unlike Kidogo, who has many antlers due to being away from his women all the time." The old gunbearer grinned back at him as Brian touched his head.

Katie watched her brother get out of the car and disappear into the thorn following just to the right and behind Muema. They were both walking in a half-crouch and picking their way from bush to bush. In a moment she heard the too-familiar *tunk* and then the blast of the rifle.

"Unless he hit a tree he got his impala," Brian said. "I must say it's nice to hunt with these one-shot blokes. Saves me a power of walking." He turned the car off the road and drove twisting, with mighty wrenches of his arms, between tree and rock until he bumped the Land Rover to the top of a cobbly knoll, where Paul and Muema were standing over a red-splashed old-gold body which carried only one horn.

"Time we collect the other *nyama* we'll be a proper meat

wagon," Brian said as they drove on, crossing two streams of swift-rushing black waters, the Rover going in the water up to the floorboards and clawing on the next bank to gain a foothold. It was cool, cool and frightening, there in the heavy shade as they wallowed in the pebbled stream, with monkeys jabbering the length of the dark, tree-thatched watercourse, the birds screaming and the eye unable to penetrate more than a few feet into the black depths of the thick-laced undergrowth.

"All this is leopard country, gorgeous leopard country," Brian said. "A really smart *chui* need never leave this swamp, because the water never dries, and there's an unending source of pigs and impala always coming to drink. Like living in a free supermarket. But I'd hate to go after a wounded one in that stuff. Thick, very thick stuff, and I have thin, very thin blood."

The car struggled up and out of the water onto the loose-shaled road of the steeply rising hill, and Katie could have sworn that the vehicle paused to shake itself like an old retriever emerging triumphantly with a fetched duck.

Once they'd cleared the summit of the long hill, the track straightened into a reasonably navigable thoroughfare, rutted by the hooves of cattle and worn smooth by the pads of elephant coming miles to drink. Katie had made a quick-peel job of the sweater while the men were hoisting the dead impala into the car, and now the sun, slanting strongly down, was burning benignly through the light drill and warming the bare skin of her stomach underneath. The air was still sparkling and fresh, and the dust had not yet risen, and she felt a languorous, almost sexually excited sense of well-being.

"We'll just stop here and have a little look round," Brian said, taking the glasses and leaping out to stand on the hood of the car and sweep the plateau and the valley below with his long binoculars. Kate got out with him, and climbed up on the other fender.

She stood with the breeze brisk in her face, perched atop the metal skin of a Land Rover that was already sun-hot through her crêpe soles, seeing the country's sweep of endless miles of undulant wheaty plain, with its capriciously strewn granite knobs and turreted hills of careless boulder, its huge sentinel rocks and in the arroyos, the *dongas,* long stands of trees. The plain was not treeless, it was clumped like an old, rundown orchard with the scrub thorns and *masuaki* bushes and strange cacti—rounded bushes that made little mock apple trees of gray-green against the yellow grass.

The building-size boulders never ceased to fascinate her; some were blue and some red or black in certain lights, and they blurted from the earth with no reason, scattered spend-thriftily by the volcanic upheavals that had made the great rift which cracked East Africa apart, which had formed new mountains and extinguished volcanos and made sere plains of what had been enormous lakes. Then there were always the long green hills; deceptively swelling as gently as breasts until you tried to climb one and suddenly found it full of ankle-twisting loose cobbles and vindictive thornbushes, and what seemed at first so enticing a stroll suddenly steeped to rise straight up as any wall.

Across the plumed grass, at the bottom of the valley, before the valley tilted like a lifted bowl into a really vast grassed swamp which was nearly dry now—and which should be maggoty with elephant and buffalo, according to Brian—there were some moving spots which showed white and red among the black; these had to be Masai cattle.

"God damn it, Paul," she heard Brian saying. "I was afraid so. The Masai are in the swamp. And they're beginning to move up to our hills. There's a *manyatta* over there; I'll just see how long they've been on the rove. Rains certainly coming now, if they're trekking out of the swamps and heading up high. Probably march right through our camp."

He jumped down.

"That finishes any elephant or buffalo in bulk in this swamp," he said. "By my reckoning, the Masai must have been grazing down there a couple of weeks, with anything that's wild scared back up the mountain and into the park. Oh, well. We didn't really need anything else. It's just that we might have picked up a really spectacular buffalo, and buff hunting is always good fun. Full of surprises and sudden frights."

They drove to where Brian said he had seen the Masai *many-atta*. Its *boma* of thornbush had been burned, and scorched twigs still showed in the black scarring of fire and loose gray smear of ashes. The little flat-topped huts still smoldered slightly, but most of the walls stood. A smell of goats and cow manure still hung over the tiny deserted village.

"A proper *manyatta* burns like peat, for a long time," Brian said. "This was a kind of hit-or-miss one. More mud than cow dung. Shoddy job of construction." He kicked a hut wall and a piece of the smoked plaster broke off. "They've been gone about two days. I expect we'll run into a lot of the migrators as we hunt this country. Tracks I saw back there were all heading up in our direction."

He started the car again. The sun was pounding down now, and the dust was beginning to lift off the plain as the animals moved. As they bumped along over the rocky track, Katie could almost feel the earth hardening under the steady soaking of the sun. It would be really bumpy on the way home, she thought. The tires swelled and the earth got like rock, and driving was no fun any more until just before dark when the sun dropped and the dew started to cool things in preparation for the savage swift plunge of nightfall.

Brian had saved the dead pig for last. He had settled on a site for the hanging in the first glade they had seen and admired in the early morning—the unbelievably lovely Fragonard dell by the rush-bordered little river, no more than a few thousand yards from the camp. It was latish evening when they arrived, tired and very dusty, having hung two other baits—Paul had added another seedy old impala ram to the general bag—after a slapdash lunch out of the chopbox. The whole day, it seemed to Katie, had been devoted to finicky care in choosing just the right tree, with just the right branches in just the right relationship to prevailing wind, water, cover, and even the position of the setting sun. Brian had explained that all this was vitally necessary or there'd be no leopard coming to the blind.

The greening glade was occupied again by the same bouncing herd of impala they'd spotted that morning, and also by a mother warthog and a small fleet of antenna-tailed progeny. The guinea-fowl hordes had increased, and the big yellow-necked spurfowl, the francolin, scratched and clucked and stood on tiptoe to flap their wings. They seemed almost as tame as barnyard fowl.

"There's your perfect leopard tree over there," Brian said, pointing, as he stopped the jeep and motioned to the boys to see to the pig, which had bloated horribly from the heat, was abuzz with flies, was setting up an awful stink, and was considerably battle-worn from having been towed behind the car for the last mile. "I spotted it this morning. We'll shoot a leopard out of this tree, I think."

"It looks just like any other old tree to me," Katie said. "What makes it so special? I've seen thousands of fever trees today that look just like this one."

"Well, it's got a nice slanting trunk, for one thing," Brian said. "You have to remember that the leopard's lazy. He can streak up a greased pole, if he wants to, but he'd rather have a tree he can saunter up instead of climb. And then the first fork is a very nice one—he can sit there and scan the scene before he nips upstairs to tackle the pig. You don't shoot him in the first fork—you wait until he gets to the feeding fork."

"*I'd* shoot him in the first fork," Katie said. "Why don't you shoot him in the first fork?"

"Because it's not done. It's a difficult shot, with not much target area except his head, and you'd ruin the mask if you hit him at all. But apart from that you don't put your gun up until he's in the tree, and if you move while he's casing the countryside there'd be just one flirt of tail and that's the last you'll see of that particular *chui* on that particular day."

"And so?" Katie didn't know why she persisted in being flip, since both her brother and Brian seemed to take all this very seriously. "Why don't we shoot him on the ground then, before he jumped into the tree?"

"You won't see him on the ground," Brian was patient, a teacher who'd been through this drill several hundred times. "That's one of the reasons I chose this tree. It's got plenty of thick cover under it, behind it, and both sides of it. Leopards don't like to cross open spaces. The best leopard tree is generally in a hellish position for following him up if you don't kill him dead. This is in a dreadful piece of bush, so I'm depending on Paul to kill him dead."

"Thanks," her brother said, rather feebly.

Brian continued the lecture doggedly.

"I've selected a tree with the right kind of second fork. There's a branch we can tie the pig to by the hind feet, and a lovely branch below and just behind it so the cat can sit comfortably and gnaw his way into the pig's backside and belly—they always like to go in hind-end to, into the soft stuff."

Katie made a mouth.

"But the important thing is to put the branch he *must* sit on close to the pig but to leave the pig hanging clear so he can't actually hide himself from you by feeding from behind the pig on another branch. And you have to see daylight behind the pig or you won't be able to spot the leopard when he comes, which is generally very late in the afternoon. So your tree has to be located with clear space behind that feeding branch, and also in a position where you'll get the setting sun behind you, or to one side, which will give you shooting light but not glare in your eyes, and which *will* get in the leopard's eyes. And your blind has to be fixed so that there's dark stuff behind *you*, so the leopard can't see you move against the daylight, for the reverse reason that you want light behind him."

"You mentioned wind before. Why do you pay any attention to wind if the leopard can't smell? And if he can't smell, why did we bother dragging these dead animals around in circles?" Paul asked.

"The leopard can't smell much, if at all, but he can hear, and there are other animals who *can* smell," Brian said. "Hyenas will follow the trail I made with the pig. Leopard hears them and gets curious and comes to investigate. Now that's enough; I have work to do." He nodded curtly to the gunbearers. Kidogo went over to the big tree and almost walked up the slanting pole, his prehensile heels gripping the rough bark.

Muema picked up the rope which had been passed through the reeking pig's slit hind legs when they towed him bumping behind the Rover. Muema took the coil in his right hand and, walking over to the bole of the tree, tossed the coiled rope upward like a lasso. Kidogo caught it, and passed it over a branch, paying off the free end until it snaked back to the ground again, whereupon Muema seized it and made it fast to the front bumper of the Land Rover. Brian crawled into the front seat and reversed the engine until the line tautened, then dragged the pig over to the foot of the tree. Then he accelerated, still in reverse, and the pig shot upward to the lofty branch on which Kidogo stood like a black angel awaiting the arrival of Little Eva in an amateur dramatic show.

They began to build the blind, now, using a fallen log and one standing dead acacia as a base, and the structure grew rapidly. In perhaps half an hour's time, the dead branches and one small green tree had been tugged into position so that they formed a kind of bower, the daylight-showing spots being plugged with the long grasses. The bower was open behind, but the rear was protected on both sides by curving arms of brush, and the front was a solid wall of branches and leaves.

Brian took the machete and went into the blind. He carefully chopped the underbrush and roots from the enclosure, and then scraped the earth level with his palms. Then he used his hands to part the thorny front foliage, facing the leopard tree, to make apertures from which the dead pig would be visible. Then he shouted at Muema, who trotted up carrying a branch which he had chopped into a rude fork. Brian dug a hole in the ground in front of the largest aperture, and planted the sharpened end of the stick until its crotch was level with the peephole. Squatting, he sighted through the fork out toward the hanging bait, and then ran over to the base of the tree, where he stared critically at the blind. While he was looking a dove fluttered down from a neighboring tree and perched atop the blind, teetering up and down on one of the topmost branches of the bower.

"It'll do," Brian said, walking back over to the blind and fussing with a few stray branches in the front. "It's fooled the bird." The leafy structure now seemed to Katie's eyes to be exactly like any of the hundred old brush heaps she could see within a few hundred yards—one green tree surrounded by grass and blown-over dead thornbush.

"There's no halfway on this blind business," Brian said. "It's either perfect or useless. Paul, crawl in with your rifle and see if you can line your scope on the bait and the feeding branch comfortably. And move around—I want to see if I can detect any movement. You comfortable in shooting position? Not cramped or anything? It's important."

"Sure. That pig is so close through the scope you can see the maggots already starting to work on him."

"It's a little early for the mags," Brian said. "Tomorrow or the next day. We'll sight your rifle tomorrow so it'll be dead on for fifty yards. Let's shove off, now."

"It's a lot of trouble to go to for just one leopard," Katie said, as they climbed back into the car and headed home. "I hope it's worth it."

"It's worth it," Brian said. "I say, this has been a day. Tomorrow we'll just rattle around and shoot some birds, maybe—I spotted the water where the sandgrouse drink—and check the kills to see if any of the leopards are feeding. Well, children, there's the prettiest sight in the world for my sore eyes. Campfire going and everything neat and shipshape by now. It takes them about a day to really get sorted out after a move, but everything ought to be perfection now."

He pulled up in front of the mess tent. The cocktail doings had already been arranged on the table in front of the blaze, and the camp, as he said, was truly sorted out into a city. Freshly washed clothes hung on thornbushes, lanterns had already been taken to the sleeping tents, and the debbie tins of water were spitting steam.

"I'm for a bath before grog," Brian said. "And after we get cleaned up, Paul, I'll give you the rest of this leopard business in one gulp, if Katie can stand it."

"I can stand anything," Katie said. "I'm bathing too—and right now." She hurried down the path to her tent, where her personal boy was already filling her tub.

"You realize," Brian said as they sat before the blaze and sipped their drinks, watching a slim horn of moon cocking over the mountain and smelling something delicious being wafted from the cooktent. "Of course you realize that this is about moving time for the average leopard. He's a nocturnal animal, by habit, and the trick is to rebuild those habits and seduce him into being a daytime boy. This frequently takes a bit of doing."

"You make it all sound so simple, Brian," Paul Drake said.

"I was thinking the same thing," his sister said.

They slept late. Paul Drake was just rising with the sun high when he heard his sister whistling outside her tent next door. She was drying her hair with exaggerated vigor as she whistled.

Brian was sitting in the mess tent with what appeared to be his fourth or fifth cup of coffee, judging from the cigarette butts in the ashtray. He looked enormously pleased with himself.

"Hello, you two," he said and called Mwende to bring fresh coffee. He smiled his small-boy happy smile at Paul and said: "I've wonderful news for you. Early unsuspected action. Kidogo and Muema skipped down to the pig-tree, that last bait we hung yesterday, and guess what?"

"I know," Katie said. "The leopard ate Muema and Kidogo."

"Hardly. But the big fellow came last night, and gobbled all of the stomach and most of one hind quarter off the bait. They don't usually feed the first day."

"How do you know it's the big one?" Paul Drake asked.

"Couldn't be anything else. His tracks all over the foot of the tree, and the trunk fresh claw-scarred, Kidogo says. No female tracks at all. The old gent's keeping his women folk out of the commissary until he's had his fill. I think with luck, him being so bold and all, we might collect him today, Paul. If they feed that soon they usually get confident fast."

"I'm beginning to feel excited in spite of myself," Katie said. "I hope he's enormous, Bro, and I hope you wallop him right through a ragged rosette, so's you won't spoil his hide."

"I hope I hit him at all," Paul Drake said. "Let's have that coffee again, please, Brian. We sight the rifle?"

"After you've finished the coffee. I thought we'd take a little reccy and check the other baits. Ordinarily we could sight the rifle here in camp, but we're awful close to the kill. Best drive off a mile or so."

They had sighted the rifle to Brian's satisfaction, the scope adjusted to zero at fifty yards, and had gone to inspect the other two kills. Brian glassed the first from several hundred yards away, and shook his head.

"Nothing so far," he shrugged. "However, sometimes they don't come for five or six days, until you can smell the bait for five miles. Oddly, they seem to be overbold when they wait a long time, too. It's the in-between ones that practice the most caution."

They drove on four or five miles to the other tree, which was almost a replica of the blind arrangement of the feeding bait near camp. It too was pitched near the river's edge, but in much thicker country. The kill-tree was surrounded by bush, and was set more deeply back into the jungled trees and tangled dense underbrush of the river than the other two.

Brian stopped the Land Rover on top of a high rise.

Use Enough Gun

"We made an awful lot of noise clanging and ganging this jeep going down through those rocks and trying to navigate those Grand Canyon gulleys yesterday. If we try a car-approach to this blind we'd scare any leopard that might be hanging around clean back to Tanganyika. And if we stay in the blind until nightfall, Muema'll never get this car down over all those boulders in the dark. I guess we'll just have to walk about a half mile, very, very softly. But maybe we'll be lucky with our camp blind, where the big chap's feeding. He trained his glasses on the tree.

"No . . . no . . ." he murmured. "Hey! There's your Bateleur eagle!" he said, as a smallish eagle sailed out of the tree and circled on stiff wings, looking almost like a vulture in the blue sky. "And . . . oh, Christ! Muema! *Darubini ingine!*"

He took the long binoculars and handed them to Paul, then gave his own short glasses to Katie.

"He's in the tree!" he whispered. "Look, count up from the bait—one, two, three branches just to the left of the kill. See him? He's lying full length on that branch. You can see one paw and his tail hanging down! He's a beauty, Paul, really a beauty!"

"Jesus," Paul breathed, as he looked.

"Christ," his sister added reverently.

The big cat was sound asleep above the kill, his golden black paw-printed hide gleaming through the delicate dark fretting of the acacia's leaves. Blue sky showed behind him, and the tail swung curved at the end like a thick question mark. One big paw hung indolently, and the big cat was obviously sleeping off a large morning meal.

"I'll try to slip us away from here without waking him," Brian said, starting the car. But as the engine came alive Katie could see the leopard stand, yawn, stretch, turn toward the noise of the motor, then streak down the bole of the fever tree like a big lizard. He paused a semi-second at the fork, and then leaped to the ground in a graceful limpid blur of yellow and was gone from sight in the thick bush at the foot of the tree.

"Well, we don't have to be cautious any more," Brian said,

raising his voice to normal as he turned the car. "He'll lie up in the bush again before he comes to the tree to work on that meat some more. By God, Paul!" His voice held honest excitement. "Isn't that something to see? Katie?"

"I'm shaking all over, and I'm not even in the blind," her brother said. "But tell me, isn't this rather unusual? Actually catching him in the tree in broad daylight?"

"Yes," Katie said. "It seems to me we're fair swarming in leopards. I thought they were awfully rare and you never saw them by day unless you went through all that business you told us about yesterday."

Brian gave his attention to bumping the car along the hillside, weaving around the bigger boulders and lifting the car gently over some of the smoother, flatter stones, before he spoke.

"I've only seen half a dozen asleep in a tree by high day in my life," he said. "Mostly all you ever see is a flash when they jump down if you see them at all. Our girl Katie's brought us luck."

"That's awfully thick stuff in there," Paul said. "Awfully thick."

"Too thick, as a matter of fact," Brian replied. "And so's the non-feeding one we just looked at. But I'm hoping we won't have to sit for this gentleman or bother with that last blind at all. The other feeder's as big, judging from his paw-prints, maybe even bigger. We're just plain lucky. I expect we'd better go now and collect a few more guinea fowl at a decent distance away from these kills, Paul, and then let's head for the barn. I'm thirsty, and it feels like a long gin-and-tonic morning."

They were shaken gently awake from their post-lunch siesta by the room-boys. Brian was waiting with the afternoon tea when they washed their sleep-damp faces and came to the mess tent.

"Leopard time," he said cheerfully. "Hot, ain't it?" The flat pound of the afternoon sun on the mess tent's canvas was almost audible. The air was very close, and now cloud masses had piled, obscuring the mountain, baling up on the horizon. The rainbird's three-note call was clear in the still heat.

Use Enough Gun

"It's sticky, all right," Katie said. "My neck hair is sopping. I sweated a real good stain on the pillow—first time since the North."

"Feels like what we used to call a weather-breeder," her brother said. "Is it?"

"Wouldn't be surprised. That's solid rain tucked away in all those black puffballs, right enough. It'll wool up a little more each day, now, and then, wallop! Time to pack up and go. I assume we'll have the old *chui* down and dead and scraped and salted by then, with his wishbone sandpapered nice and shiny to make Katie a lucky brooch. Well, shall us up and away?"

They drove leaning sideways along the slope of the hill. The same green meadowland, as they worked downhill and then flat along the river's edge, was empty now of game. No dainty-footed golden impala fed; no birds scratched or ran. Silence hung tangibly, oppressively, and in the distance, past the purple hills, the sky had darkened from its clear wash almost to sulky violet.

"Yep, she's a-building, all right," Brian said again. "Look over there." He pointed to a low collar of black cloud around the throat of a small mountain. A bluish vertical haze seemed slanted beneath the cloud, almost like a slightly leaning tower of striated stone. "That's the rains, chums. And every day they'll march closer."

He stopped the car and walked around to the side. Muema handed him a double-barreled shotgun. Brian broke it, squinted through the barrels, and then looked closely at the two fat black cartridges Muema handed him.

"Buckshot," he explained, inserting the shells. "Wanted to be sure that they weren't fives or sixes. I'm betting you don't wound him, Paul, but if you do and I have to go pull him out by the tail, I don't want to discover in the hospital that we used birdshot instead of buckshot in this blunderbuss."

Brian climbed in the back, and Muema moved up front to take the wheel. As the car started to move, Brian said: "Jump out into the blind when I tap your shoulder, Paul, and Katie, you scramble in behind him. Sit on Paul's right. Don't forget

(201)

your cushions. That ground gets awful hard about an hour from now. And if you want one last smoke, have it now."

The Land Rover jounced along, Muema driving as carefully and quietly as possible in second gear, following the track that they had made when they first sighted the area and then, later, when they had hung the kill in the tree. They turned right and went slightly more steeply downhill and now Katie could see the brown beehive of the blind, already looking comfortably weathered after only a day, already almost indistinguishable from the other rubbish-hummocked fallen trees and dead-grass-rimmed rocks.

Muema was slowing now, shifting to low gear, and she could feel her brother stir beside her, then spring out of the doorless Rover—almost like the paratroops; she thought *Geronimo!* as she plunged blindly out of the car behind him. She landed harshly on her hands and knees and scurried crawling into the blind. Paul passed her a pillow, which she slid under her backside and then arranged her legs spraddled wide, tucked in and crossed Indian-fashion at the ankles. She stole a quick peek through the little porthole in the leafy barrier of the blind, and found that she could clearly see the dead pig hanging, his hide whitened by the afternoon sun that struck sidewise into the deep-shadowed tree.

She turned her head very slowly—Brian had warned her to make no abrupt motions in the blind—and saw that Paul had leaned his rifle against the front of the blind, next the forked stick which would hold the gun when—and if—he fired it. He was sitting looking intently through his peephole over the crotched rest, his knees drawn up and his arms clasped around his legs. Every muscle in his body seemed tense and his eyes strained to the opening in the thatched branches.

Brian was not tense. He was lounging well back behind them both, leaning on one elbow, one knee drawn back to rest his other arm. Presently he eased himself a little farther to the rear, turned comfortably on his side, and straightened both legs in front of him. He saw her looking at him and winked.

Use Enough Gun

Katie swung her chin back slowly and stared through her peephole. There was nothing in front of her but a patch of meadow-smooth green ground and a rim of trees lining a rushy river and a tall big-boled yellow-black-mottled thorn tree with a dead pig slung into its rigging. She could hear birds, though—away behind her came the goosed-girl *oohoo-oohoo—oohoo—* OOO! of a dove, and a silvery tinkling bell-bird she'd never heard before.

There was a slight, comforting chittering of monkeys in the bush ahead, where the leopard must come, and the lazy *fa-aak* of the long-tailed bird she could now identify as the lori. And away down the riverbed she heard a harsh castanet clatter of guinea fowl. There was nothing more of any real interest except the lazy hum of locusts. It was hot though, hot as blazes in that little leafy oven they sat in, hot except for the cool feel of the shaded ground coming up through the fiber sweat-pillow they used in the front seats of the Rover.

A drop of sweat ran down Katie's nose and fell with a frighteningly loud plop. She cut her eyes sidewise to see if either man had noticed this unplanned disturbance, but her brother was still pinned to his peephole, and Brian, leaning backward on his brown bare arm, resting his chin on the heel of his hand, had locked the impossibly long fringes of his lashes, and seemed to be asleep. Katie noticed for the first time that the scarred twelve-bore shotgun was resting with its trigger guard on an old gray turtlenecked sweater which she remembered seeing Brian wear one cold morning. My God, but silence was noisy when you listened to it objectively.

Already one of her feet was going numb. She looked at her watch—five of five. Brian said the leopard probably wouldn't come before six, usually sometime between six and seven. That meant an hour, two hours more, before the crash of her brother's rifle or the climbing shaky beam of Muema's headlamps would rescue her from the enforced silence and the maddening little itches that were now beginning to crawl like thistles from one portion of her body to another.

Ah, some action finally. Brian must really be a ring-tailed marvel at building leopard blinds, she thought, for here comes a whole fleet of unsuspecting guinea fowl. They were feeding straight into the blind, working up from the rushes at the rim of the river where they'd undoubtedly been resting out of the heat. Strange, obscene, naked-headed brutes they were, although the way old Aly boiled them and then served them cold in thick coarse-cut slices, with tomatoes and sliced sweet onions and crisp lettuce from the icebox, was wonderful, and they were wonderful too in soups and stews and, when you shot them young enough, broiled on the grill after being hung a couple of days.

Her dietary habits had certainly changed, Katie thought, in the last month. She had never enjoyed game of any sort, but game was the only fresh meat you got out here, and somehow now it didn't taste full of old gunpowder. Also it didn't conjure up vivid ideas of shot and blood-draggled feathers and limp dead necks. But it was just as well they didn't serve the guineas head and all, as they served pheasant in England sometimes, she thought, as one old yellow-helmeted cock minced up to the blind and fixed her wickedly with a rheumy red eye, twisting his scaly naked neck. They were pretty at a distance but as filthily horrid face to face as a turkey or a buzzard. Her lips formed the word "shoo," soundlessly, and after scratching industriously for a moment, her friend fed off with the rest of the flock, which was making big oval purple splashes on the billiard-table baize of the pasture.

In a moment, the guineas were replaced by the grousy-looking yellow-necked francolin, almost as large as hen pheasants, pleasantly plumed in decent brown and yellow and black, and miraculously, lovingly built entirely of white meat by some epicurean Almighty. Katie had shot a lot of francolin; in fact, guinea and francolin and sandgrouse were the only things she *would* shoot. Her conscience pricked her not at all when she saw Muema scoop up a fluttering, wounded bird and twist its neck. They looked slow in the air, but were quite sporty when the boys chased them up and made them fly high, like driven pheasant, and they certainly made a delicious cold lunch or a fine chunky chicken à la king.

Now Katie felt a sneeze mounting. Oh God don't let me sneeze don't let me sneeze don't let me sneeze. Don't let me wreck Bro's leopard don't let me sneeze and make Brian think of me as one more nuisance like all the other women that come on safari and wave their hips and flutter their lashes at him. I will not sneeze will not sneeze will *not* sneeze and I didn't either. It's gone away and will stay away because I willed it that way. I am very proud of me for not sneezing.

Wonder what Brian thinks of when he's sitting in a leopard blind for the thousandth time? He can't be thinking about the leopard. It will come and when it does he'll make Paul do whatever Paul has to do and then we will all go home and they will have drinks and talk all night about the leopard. But Brian must be thinking something.

Maybe he doesn't mind waiting. Maybe he likes to wait. Maybe he just lets his mind go blank and his spirit roves free all over the world, getting into delicious trouble that doesn't bother Brian at all. Maybe Brian's spirit doesn't even tell Brian what it's been up to while Brian sits in a thorn haystack waiting for a spotted cat to show up to chew on a dead pig.

I wonder what would happen if I did sneeze? I wonder what would happen if I coughed? I wonder what would happen if I did what ladies never do and let go an enormous blast of wind?

Katie grinned inwardly. A nice girl certainly had peculiar thoughts sitting in leopard blinds on hot African afternoons listening to birds go *clang-tonk* and *ooo-hooo—ooooh-hoooo—* HOOO! and watching that little *ghekko* lizard running along the grass just behind the blind and the big black ants in that tiny hill that Brian forgot to scrape over with the *panga* when he made the blind and those guinea fowl feeding outside as if there was no human within hundreds of miles.

"Oh, God damn it!" The oath rolled thunderously.

There was Brian, breaking the rules. Katie was appalled. The curse burst out of him loud and shockingly, shatteringly angry.

It wouldn't be an accident, because he was saying it again. Her brother flinched as if a snake had struck him.

"God damn it to hell! Come on, we might as well go on out! I might have known!" Brian's voice blasted the silence apart as if someone had fired a gun in a cathedral.

Now Brian was scrambling out of the blind, offering cigarettes as they stood up and rubbed the cramps out of their legs. He pointed with a toss of head and angry lift of chin over his shoulder. A black-and-white cow was just poking her wall-eyed head from behind a scrubby copse of low creeping thorn at the rise of the gentle hill down which they always drove. A couple of mournful lowings came behind her, and the *clang-tonk* was a cowbell. Both Katie and her brother stared, bewildered.

"Fire the gun," Brian said to Paul Drake. "See if you can hit your bloody pig! Go on, shoot!"

Tranced, Paul Drake raised his rifle and they could hear the *tunk* as the bullet struck the hanging warthog.

"That'll fetch Muema with the car," Brian said disgustedly. "You might as well have sneezed, Katie, the way things turned out. I saw you—you made a very noble effort to no point. All's wrecked; the thrice-bloody ever-blasted Masai have come to call, with a couple hundred head of cattle. I might have known this new grass was too short and green and lovely for the bastards to resist—too handy to water and the big swamp. Oh, well," he shrugged. "*Kwaheri chui. Jambo Masai.* Maybe next year. That's a gone cat, for all our purposes."

The cattle were cropping out now, muzzling eagerly at the tender grass. They were skinny, rack-hipped, white and black and red and piebald. Most had high, wobbly humps, and their horns had been docked or broken when they were calves to allow unusual regrowth to establish the owner's brand. A few had the enormous, trophy-sized long horns she had seen in pictures of old Egyptian cattle, the kind of horns Brian had told her were common to the Ankole herds in Uganda.

They watched the encroaching Masai. This was a family project—one gray old man with a shortened spear-blade, three

women of varying ages, and two small boys. The youngest
woman carried a sucking child. They paid no attention to the
white people—and little attention to the Land Rover when it
came clanking up with Muema disgusted at the sight of the cattle. Kidogo was sitting in the front seat with him. Without stopping to say anything to Brian they drove through the cattle
herd, bumping curious heifers aside with the car, and occasionally blowing the horn to move a calf which stood braced obsti-
nately in the vehicle's pathway. Muema stopped the Land Rover
directly under the tree and Kidogo jumped out to run up
the trunk. Muema stood watching as the old 'Ndrobo hacked at
the ropes which bound the pig, and in a moment it fell to the
ground with a squishy thump. Its quarter-eaten, stinking carcass
was immediately sweatered by the persistent little flies that
clouded over the cattle and the tiny mousy donkeys which carried the mountainous packs of Masai household effects.

"Well," Brian said. "We might as well go back to camp. It's
too late to sit in the other blind—be near dark when we got
there and straggled down the hill. We're lucky to know where's
another big leopard. We'll just kiss this chap here good-by. Why
the hell these people couldn't have gone some place else with
their bloody *ngombe*—well. . . ." He shrugged again. "Their
country, I suppose. Nothing to be done about it. Where the cattle come, the game ain't."

Katie found herself suddenly feeling terribly sorry for Brian
—sorrier for Brian who had probably seen five hundred leopards shot than she was disappointed for her brother, who had
been whetted to a wire edge for his first leopard. Poor little
Brian, she thought; made all his plans and plots and showed off
all his knowledges and skills and then a bunch of flyblown dairy
farmers tore down his playhouse.

Impulsively she kissed Brian's cheek.

"There, there, little boy," she said. "There'll be lots more
leopards for you to play with. Let's go back to camp and
Mama'll make some nice martinis and we can start all over again
playing pussy cat tomorrow."

Paul Drake smiled appreciatively at his sister.

"I felt like I was going to miss this one, anyhow," he said.

They went next day to the other blind where they had seen the big leopard in the tree. The bait had not been touched, so far as Brian could determine with his glasses. They stumbled half a mile down the hill and carefully stalked the last three hundred yards to the blind, painfully bent over, awkwardly trying to melt from rock to brush heap to tree to anthill, Katie striving desperately to avoid stepping on dry twigs or kicking loose stones. She was redfaced and puffing when they finally crawled the last fifty yards, stone-bruising her hands and skinning her knees, until they flopped sweating in the blind. There had been no bugs in the last blind; this one, close-hugging the thick bush of the watercourse, had no cheerful green expanse of grassland between blind and bait to firebreak the insects. The partially chewed bedraggled impala hung sadly in the tree. The frayed edges of his gnawed-out stomach were oxidized black against the tarnishing old-gold of his hide. Katie sat as sadly in the blind, and the mosquitoes fed eagerly on her hands and face and ankles. She had been encouraged to bravado by the buglessness of the other blind, and had neglected to smear herself with insect repellent.

They sat for two and a half hours until black dark, listening to the swamp noises. At seven it was beginning to turn cold and she had never dreamed of such cramps as seized her legs, or such a bruising ache as centered in her seat. She could have cried with relief as Brian said, sighing:

"Well, that's that, chaps. *Hapana chui*," and offered her a cigarette. "No leopard in this tree today—no sign of him along the river. We'd better give him one more day and if he doesn't come we'll see what's doing with the Number Three. But that was a damned big leopard we saw here yesterday."

They were all cold and tired and bone-sore when they got to camp and they bathed swiftly and picked at their food. Brian stayed up to listen to the safari broadcast; she and her brother went silently off to bed.

Use Enough Gun

The next day was a repetition, except that this time Katie had doused herself with greasy lotion and while the bugs buzzed annoyingly, veiling round her head, they didn't bite her afresh. Only her wounds of yesterday itched and smarted, and she drew a glare from her brother as she fidgeted. She no longer let her thoughts roam; they centered fiercely on her bored discomfort while sitting in a blind full of bugs with two dedicated hunters waiting for something that wouldn't come out to be killed. At least you could *see* elephant; even lion were not so hard to come by.

As they left the blind that night a great swollen drop of rain hit her almost painfully in the right eye. It was followed by a brief but violent shower, and they were all soaked by the time they reached the clear ground where the Rover waited to take them back to camp and a fire. This night was the first night of safari on which Katie thought she would give an arm for just one, big, fat snort of anything that was a hundred proof.

"I don't like the feel of this second leopard," Brian said, as they had their drinks round the fire, Katie nibbling without enthusiasm at her tomato juice. "I think this gentleman's upstaked and hightailed it. One night away from the kill, yes—maybe he found something nice and succulent a couple miles away, or got mixed up in love-making, or something. But it's not leopardlike for him to desert that kill after he was so cocky about it first day we saw him. He was happy in that tree if I ever saw a well-adjusted leopard."

"I think we're bewitched," Katie said. "You better have one of your witch doctors tailormake us a curse."

"That's been taken care of," Brian said, and Katie looked up in surprise.

"You're not serious?"

Brian nodded.

"Certainly I'm serious. Kidogo is a *mundumugu* of sorts, especially where it concerns animals. He's already done something with the magic bag."

"And what did the magic bag say?"

"I don't know. I never ask him," Brian said. "I wouldn't want to know in advance if it was dead negative."

Brian let his binoculars fall and reached for a cigarette. It was another bright clear morning, but the clouds were already beginning to mass low and ugly along the hills. Katie and Paul looked at him expectantly.

"Aha," Brian nodded his head with satisfaction. "We're in luck. It's been fed on, and fed on well. Too well, I should say. It could be a lioness if the tree weren't so straight up and down—either a lioness or a simply ee-normous leopard. But I think there's too much meat gone for just *one* leopard. Very probably a pair."

"I thought they didn't let other leopards into their trees much?" Paul said. He was beginning to look a little pinched around the nostrils.

"Sometimes. Not very often. Once in a while the old boy goes soft on his girl friend and lets her have an early whack—or sometimes a late one. Where there's a bitch you'll usually find the dog. If the lady spots the kill first, she uses it quite often as a sort of clip joint to pick up her men friends. I swear, I know one old gal in Tanganyika that I've personally widowed half a dozen times, but it hasn't shaken her faith in that one particular tree. She always shows up with a new boy friend—generally large. She likes big men."

"I think all your shootable leopards live in Tanganyika," Katie said. "I don't think there are any more leopards in Kenya now that the first one's gone. He started a vogue. Exodus."

The sky was much darker, the clouds sagging much lower on the horizon, when the boys roused them from siesta at four. The sun shone eerily from time to time, peeping bloodily round the edges of the blackening clouds, casting strange purple lights on the hills, slanting obliquely on the pillars of far-distant rains. Each day now it darkened earlier in the afternoon, and always the solid shafts of rain seemed closer.

Use Enough Gun

They had been in the blind only half an hour, staring intently at the evil wall of black-green brush. This thorn-armored rampart was backed by towering trees roped heavy with lianas and with accumulated windrows of brush which eventually became so tightly packed as to be nearly impassable except through the slick-worn game trails.

This last was not a happy blind. It might have been cheerful enough in the sunshine; in the gloom of the cloudy afternoon the bush looked sinisterly black and very, very forbidding. It was located near where they forded the stream, where the leaf-dyed waters hurried dark over the smooth white rocks, rushing noisily past the slick-lichened boulders, and where the tangled underbrush came right down to the edge of the river and hung, steam-tugged, whiskering over the banks. It was absolutely black to the eye a few feet away from the water's edge—no needle of sunlight pricked through the mat of leaves and twisted vines and broken fallen boles of creeper-tangled trees. There was a strong stench of baboons and moldy wet leaves about the place. The bait-branch on which the leopard would feed was much lower than the others, and the tree a different kind, considerably more oak-looking. It stood in the midst of a positive jungle of tangled thorn, and was embraced jealously on both sides by arms of the swamp.

A tremendous crack of thunder ripped the clouds and a jagged streak of lightning tore the sky. Purple clouds tumbled over each other and, colliding, clashed like enormous cymbals. The sky blackened almost to twilight, although it was only five o'clock, and a blinding shutter-sheet of gray, warm rain crashed down with such force that the drops bounced in the dust. There was no top to the blind; in two minutes time Katie was drenched. Moving her soaked head slightly, she could see that both her brother and Brian were equally drowned. Paul was wiping slowly and prayerfully at the scope of his rifle with a soggy handkerchief; too late, he took off his soft cap and placed it round the rear lens of the telescope. Rain ran down his eye-glasses as if they were windscreens; his thin hair clung to his white skull in skinny fingers. She looked at Brian whose tumbled thick hair was hammered into a thick mop by the rain. He jerked his chin at the leopard-tree and formed with his lips: *Do you want to leave?* She saw her brother nod slightly but emphatically. No. Brian moved his shoulders slightly in the familiar shrug, and, raising his hand slowly, wiped water out of his eyes.

The rain slacked then, and stopped. But the sun stayed behind the enormous banks of clouds, and the forest ahead looked even more dismal, as Katie could hear the steady thudding drumbeats of the rain from the leaves and branches of the trees. She squinted through the peephole. The chewed-up bait seemed sadder than ever in its rain-blackened mussy package of tattered hide. A light wind rose, and now Katie began to shiver as the clammy shirt clung to her shrinking skin and the wet wool of her socks bristled cold against her ankles.

Now the rain was starting again, not slashing, not pounding down like the other, striking so hard it actually hurt the skin, but seeping, sliding, sneaking down, lying along and actively pressing on the skin instead of bouncing off it. It ran constantly, annoyingly into her eyes. Remembering to move slowly, she raised her wrist to her forehead and when she did she saw it first.

It was slim and beautiful in the first fork, slim and blurred and smoky in the rain. It was yellow no more. Only a gray wraith, blending so perfectly against the dark background that she might never have seen it come but for the white flick of its tail-tip, a tail which dropped now with most of the curl gone. Like my hair now, Katie thought wildly, and slowly reached over to squeeze her brother's thigh. She lifted her chin slowly in the direction of the tree and as her brother's hand went toward the rifle the leopard disappeared, appearing again like a drift of sulphuric fog on the feeding branch. It was almost exactly the color of the dead impala, and the rain had darkened its hide so her naked eye couldn't distinctly pick out the spots. The two animals merged, one dead, one living, and with the wind in their direction Katie could clearly hear the sound of teeth crunching at flesh. The living thing had come soundless;

no raucous shout of baboon, no hysteric scream of monkey, no squawk of bird had heralded the coming.

Her brother never fired. Brian Dermott's hand had come over slowly and moved across her brother's vision to his trigger hand. She saw Brian's mouth make the silent words: *No.* With a tiny negative shake of head, his lips moved again. F-E-M-A-L-E they spelled out slowly. Wait.

In a moment, off to their right, there was a fantastic sudden explosion of savage sound. Baboons abruptly convened a chorus of profanely guttural barking. Small monkeys screamed as if being tortured, and the branches of trees whipped violently, crashingly, as bodies hurled themselves from limb to limb. Birds detonated from treetops and fled shrieking, screaming alarm. A steady *huh-huh-huh* was heard now, and then an indescribable spitting snarl ending in a growl that was followed by a different fleshy bubbling scream from a baboon, as if the sound had been torn from his throat.

At the interruption, the feeding female lifted her head from the belly cavity of the dead animal, turned it with a lofty elegance toward the noise, and disappeared once more, like a plume of smoke, to vanish from the tree. Katie turned her head toward Brian, who was smiling happily, and forming the word: *Now,* with his soundless smiling lips.

There was another roar and a crash in the bush almost at the foot of the tree, another explosion of monkeys in the treetops and another long giant firecracker trail of angry shouting as the baboons, still cursing, plunged through the thick bush. Then there was another asthmatic, throat-caught *huh-huh-huh* under the tree, followed by a rasping scrutching sound, and suddenly the most evil yellow eyes she had ever dreamed of stared straight into Katie's face. The leopard was huge; he filled the fork; his eyes were everywhere at once.

Her brother moved involuntarily, but Brian's restraining hand clasped his arm. The leopard turned his head slowly, his topaz gaze appearing to strike into Katie's soul, and then the Devil disappeared. He did not move: he vanished. As he disappeared there was a slight motion in the blind as Brian released her brother's arm and she heard a tiny noise as Paul slid his rifle up into the crotch of the forked stick and bent to the eyepiece of the telescope. For a second now Katie could see the leopard again; he was standing tall and straight and proud, broad on, head raised slightly by the angle of the branch as he tore hungrily into the rain-sogged meat of the dead impala.

She heard one microsecond of grinding fang on bone before the rifle went off like the explosion of an ammunition dump, rocking the walls of the thorn-thatched blind. The cordite smell hung acridly pleasant in the air, but Katie was stunned and almost blinded for a second by the concussion.

When she could see again, Brian was leaping out of the blind and charging toward the foot of the tree with his shotgun; she saw her brother still sitting stupidly, stunned, his face dead white, his mouth hanging foolishly open. There was a gash over one eye where the scope had reared back and kicked him. The rain was washing the blood down his face and diluting it into little pink trickles.

He scrambled awkwardly out of the blind and stood foolishly, still pale, still gape-mouthed, still holding the gun as if he had never seen a gun before.

"I—I shot too quick," he said to himself. "I got excited and I shot too quick. All the waiting and the rain and the other leopard and I shot too *quick*. I was getting the gun on him when it just went off. I suppose I pulled the trigger but I shot too *quick*."

"Maybe you hit it," Katie said falsely. She reached in her soaking pocket for cigarettes and managed to find some dry ones in the back of the packet. She lit two with a Zippo and handed one to her brother. "You probably hit it. Brian took off with that shotgun and disappeared in the bush there. He'll be back in a minute. Maybe it's dead under the tree."

"No," her brother said, appearing about to weep. "Brian won't find it dead under any tree. I shot too quick. I got excited and I did everything I swore I wouldn't do. I just threw the gun up and jerked. After all this—this perfection and to spoil it like a damned amateur, like some damned schoolgirl frightened by a rabbit."

"Well, just don't commit a hara-kiri until you know," Katie said. "You've done everything else very well. It's probably dead there in the bush. You'll find you've shot it very well."

"No," her brother said miserably. "I won't find I've shot it very well. This is one thing I haven't done very well at all."

They stood lonely in the rain, smoking wet cigarettes, waiting for the hunting car to breast through the gray surf of thorn behind them. Brian and the car arrived at about the same time.

Kidogo and Muema leaped out of the car, and Kidogo was already snapping another shotgun together. Brian said something in Swahili, and Katie could see a wave wash swiftly over the faces of the Africans, wiping out the prints of their eager expressions and almost changing the arrangement of their features. Now they looked grayer, sadder, and much, much older.

"Hakuna damu," Brian was saying to the boys. He held up a thin strip of something white and wiggly-looking like a big tapeworm. *"Mafuta tu."* He turned to Paul, and his face was older, too; he was very serious now.

"You gutshot it," he said flatly. "I'm sorry. I hoped you'd missed it entirely. I thought you had, because it wasn't knocked from the tree. It jumped. But I found this." He held up the white wormy looking strip.

"Gut. Belly lining. And there's no blood." He shook his head, and looked at his watch. "Almost five-thirty. That gives us maybe forty-five minutes of light, in this weather, to dig it out of there."

He went over to the blind and got his rain-soaked old gray sweater, and knotted it round his neck like a thick muffler. He forestalled Katie's question.

"For giving the leopard something to chew on instead of throat until Muema can scrape him off me—or with luck, shoot him off me before he digs in for the long rains." His voice was coldly businesslike, with no hint of levity. "Muema's very good at shooting leopards off me. Had any amount of practice."

Paul was stammering. His face was gradually regaining color.

"I'm dreadfully sorry, Brian. I really don't know what happened. The gun just seemed to go off as if somebody else pulled the trigger. I wouldn't have shot if I hadn't been sure of killing it—not with all this. . . ." He waved helplessly at the dripping gloom of the thick swamp ahead.

Brian smiled slightly, now, tightly.

"Don't take it too much to heart. You're not the first to blow his stack over a leopard. I told you a little of how it would be. Well, this sort of talk doesn't produce any sick leopards. Come on, you chaps!" He spoke sharply to the Africans. "Muema! Kidogo! *Ha-yuh! Upesi!*"

"You two stay with the Rover," he told Paul and Katie. "I'll be out of *that* in a little while." He gestured toward the broading tangle of wet bush.

"Couldn't you—couldn't you just leave it and come back in the morning when it's lighter? Bring some more boys?" Katie knew she was saying the wrong thing, but all this seemed so . . . seemed so shockingly abrupt and coldly final.

"It's sick and hurt and angry in there," Brian said. "It'll suffer until it's eaten alive by hyenas. And there's always the off chance it's not hurt so very bad and will recover enough to either collect the first Wog that bumbles along or, worse, be crippled enough to turn permanent mankiller. And apart from any humanitarian aspects, the Game Department take a very poor view of our leaving wounded dangerous animals strewn about. Well," Brian said sharply to his gunbearers, "what are you waiting for? Let's get cracking!"

"I want to go too, Brian," Paul Drake said. "I wounded it. It was my fault. It's only right I go along and help you with it. I won't be in the way, I promise."

Brian shook his head irritably.

"If you don't mind, I'd rather you didn't, Paul. I've enough on my plate, trying to watch for the leopard and keep an eye on the boys tracking in front of me. Leopards are tricky. They double back, like as not, and then light on your neck when you've passed. Or wait until you're quite on top of them before they spring. They come so fast they're just a blur. It's why I use the shotgun." He held up the weapon in one hand. "Rifle's not fast enough—not enough shock. No, you stay with Katie."

"But can't you *see*. . . . All right. I'll do what you say." Paul turned away. "I'll stay with Katie safely in the car." His voice was bitter. "Women and children first."

"It's not that. It's just that—" Brian stopped when he saw Katie Crane's eyes pleading with him. *Take him with you, please, Brian. It's the only chance he's got to be happy for the rest of his life. Don't take it away from him, Brian. Please.*

"Muema!" Brian's voice halted the gunbearer as he entered the bush. "Give the *Bwana* your shotgun!" He turned to Paul. He spoke crisply, all friendship gone. "Now look here. Stay off to my left and well behind me. Don't shoot me and don't shoot the boys. Don't shoot unless it's directly in front of you, and if it knocks me over, for Christ's sake leave the close-separation work to Muema and Kidogo. I don't want my head blown off out of any hurry-up helpfulness with that bloody shotgun. Understood?"

"Understood," Paul Drake's voice was firm again as he broke the shotgun and checked the loads. He clicked the breech shut. "You won't have to worry about me. And, Brian?"

"Yes?" Brian turned as he started walking toward the leopard tree. His face was irritable and drawn, wet-shining in the rain.

"Thanks," Paul Drake said. "Thanks very much."

"Nothing," Brian said curtly. "One more thing. If it jumps you and is on you, throw your gun crossways in front of your throat and let him chew on the barrel until we peel him off you."

Katie had been forgotten. She printed their pictures on her mind as they left her without good-by and plunged into the dripping bush. The two Africans had fanned out, spooring in front of Brian, and her brother walked two steps behind Brian and well to the left. He held the shotgun diagonally across his chest, ready to jump it to his shoulder, and his back looked straight and his head was held proudly.

"Thank God Brian took him," Katie breathed, as the soaked gray bush closed behind them and silence fell like an enormous stopping blanket on the black forest ahead. She got into the Rover and sat on the wet seat and let the rain hit her in the face. They might at least have put the top on again, she said irritably to herself, rummaging in the dash compartment for a dry pack of cigarettes.

An insane desire to scream for joy filled Paul Drake. He had not believed the sea-change that faced danger could bring to a coward. He had been moved only by expected awe and then regret when he killed the elephant; he had been only vaguely excited by the lion, and that largely because it was all so new and strange.

But never, never had he thought himself capable of feeling as he felt now, as they inched through spiked bush like dirty-nailed fingers, gray, dripping, hateful bush that clutched at your ankles and cut viciously at your face, bush that dragged spitefully at your clothes and looped around your legs. Trees, living and dead, were woven together in combat nets by the tough ropy lianas and the accumulated mass of thorn. If you took your eyes off the man ahead of you he disappeared, even though you could hear him floundering no more than half a dozen yards ahead of you. Once, some animal jumped from its bed snorting and Paul Drake's shotgun was up to his face before the beast's frantic plunge took it crashing away with a clack of horn on bush.

The gunbearers ranged, tracking carefully on each side and just ahead of Brian. Paul could not imagine what they saw to follow; there was no blood. The animal was lying somewhere behind or ahead, sick, furious, hurting horribly now from the fiery blast that had torn its guts away and left them dripping tangled from the wound that would not bleed. The boys carried only the long bush *pangas,* with which they occasionally chopped away a barrier branch or used to point at some slight disarrangement of terrain that only they—and Brian—could recognize and diagnose.

Their circles meshed, and Brian seemed always to act as the communications cross-check; each time the circles locked they would form three intersecting rings with Brian in the middle like one of those Chinese puzzles the magicians slipped on and off. Three times they disputed the possible course of the leopard, and each time Kidogo's opinion held. Each time the opinion was verified as either Brian or Muema came on fresh spoor, if nothing more than a tiny smeared absence of raindrop from an otherwise rain-pimpled leaf. Paul Drake's mouth was dry but he felt a soaring happiness; he hoped, he prayed that when the leopard leaped it would leap straight at him and he would blast it as it sprang with its claws widespread and hooked to seize him.

Once, in his eagerness, he pressed a step too far forward, and Brian warned him back with a curt jerk of the gun and a glare. There were no more society hunter's tricks here; no gratuitous posturing and peeking round bushes and climbing up of trees, saying that you could have climbed one of the creeper-strangled giants of which only the gnarled roots were visible. Brian was a man fully concentrated on a job of killing something that threatened to kill them—kill him, Paul, kill Brian himself, and those unbelievably brave black men tracking half-crouched ahead, half-naked and defenseless except for a bush knife and an implicit trust in Brian Dermott.

Paul hoped he would be able to explain all this to Katie someday: he felt he had learned more about the interdependence of black man and white man from this twenty minutes in a baboon-stinking morass of trees and thorns and fronds and great hummocks of interwoven dead branches and grass than he would ever learn if all the African experts combined to explain it to him in the full light of dry day.

It was appalling, this gloom, darker than twilight as they plunged more and more deeply into the Kali-armed embrace of the bush. Light showed through the laced canopy of trees only in minute splashes and holes. Sodden leaves squished underfoot, slippery, and twice he fell with a tooth-jarring defenseless jolt into hidden pig holes—pitching on his face in the wet underbrush, once losing his grasp on the clammy wet shotgun. The rain did not fall inside this leafy cavern; it struck the treetops and oozed through in maddening big gouts that had accumulated on branch tips, or else gushed in sudden harsh cascades as a released branch flung a shower or a fleeing monkey sluiced a bucketful through the lower branches of his tree.

They came finally to the end. The end was an enormous hummock, a city block long and infinitely wide, looming as high as a house. Brian stopped in a little cleared place in front of this monstrous long house of the melted-down and molded, laced and weather-hammered, impenetrable mass of vegetation, rocks, fallen trees, and possibly ancient anthills, compacted as hard as stone.

Brian kicked at the outer edges of the mound, and his foot made a solid sound, as if he had kicked granite. He grimaced, and lit a cigarette. Then he looked at his gunbearers, sodden, thorn-torn, deadly serious. Simultaneously they all shrugged.

"*Eeeeh*," Brian said.

"*Eeee—eeeh*," they answered.

"He's in *there*," Brian said. "In *that*."

Paul groped for a cigarette and lit it before he spoke. He was panting, and his mouth was still very dry. A backwhipped branch had struck him on the cut that the kicking scope had opened when he fired at the leopard, and it was oozing blood again.

"What do we do now, *Bwana?*" he asked, and grinned, relaxed and still curiously happy. "Crawl in and insult him into action or what?"

"I believe you're actually enjoying the idea of having a hundred and fifty pounds of disenchanted leopard in your lap," Brian said, and smiled unenthusiastically back. "This is really a terrible business. There's no possibility of going in after him, even if we had a bulldozer. Too thick, much too thick."

He turned and spoke rapidly to the Africans.

Use Enough Gun

"All we can do is chuck sticks and stones in there and hope to goose him into a charge. It works—sometimes. You stand over there, and *only* shoot if he comes straight at you or on your left. *Only* to your left, mind. I'll handle the other side here. Okay, *ha-yah!*" He turned again to the boys. "Let's see some work with the rocks!" He stooped and picked up a chunk of stone which he flung into the bulk of clotted bush. The Africans followed, hurling sticks and stones and screaming at the top of their lungs.

Suddenly the old Kidogo held up his hand.

"*Ngruma,*" he said. "Growl."

From the bush, alarmingly close, to the left and just ahead of Paul, there came an unmistakable, throaty growl which ended in a long harsh purr and a sudden rattling, sobbing sigh.

"*Kufa,*" Kidogo said. "*Hi chui nakufa kabisa.*"

"He says that's the leopard's last gasp." Brian said. "The dying growl. This I want to see personally before I take his word for it. It could be—it could be any other variation on sick-leopard sounds. What now, *m'zee?*" he asked the old man.

"*Ngoja kidogo,*" Kidogo said. "*Mupa mimi sigara moja.*"

"He says we'd better wait a minute and smoke a cigarette," Brian said, offering Paul the pack and then handing it to the Africans. He picked up another stone and heaved it in the direction of the last roar. Silence followed the clump of the rock.

They threw more rocks, and finished their cigarettes.

"He's either dead, like the old man says, or he's pushed off with a sigh of relief, and in any case we've had him. There'll be no more than another ten minutes of light, and this is one leopard who's not going to catch me prowling around on my hands and knees with a Coleman lamp as I've been known to do in my silly youth," Brian said. "What else, old man?"

Kidogo aimed a rapid stream of something in Brian's direction. Brian grinned but rather weakly.

"He says it's a very good leopard, a big leopard, and he wouldn't rest easy tonight if he thought the hyenas were tearing it to shreds. He's going to find it for you and drag it out by the tail."

"Can't you stop him?" Paul Drake asked. "I don't want the damned thing that bad. I don't want the old boy hurt."

"I wouldn't try to stop him," Brian said. "Reflection on his reputation, judgment, bushcraft—the lot. Professional standing at stake here. I bow to superior knowledge."

The old man took his *panga* and started to chop his way into the bush. He suddenly stooped and plunged into a hitherto-unseen animal tunnel. Brian got down on his hands and knees and started to crawl after him.

"You actually going in there, in that, with him?" Paul Drake said to Brian's disappearing rump.

"Of course," a mirthless chuckle came back from the game path. "Won't be the first time. Can't let him do it alone. Care to come along for the ride? Mind, don't shoot me in the pants with that bloody shotgun if something jumps at you."

Cursing under his breath, Paul Drake, banker, stockbroker, Harvard '30, Racquet and River clubs, found himself in a greasy animal-smelly, mud-mucky game trail, pushing a shotgun ahead of him in what was almost complete darkness. Thorns bit at his hands and tore at his face. Invisible sharp rocks chewed at his knees. All he could see ahead of him was Brian Dermott's crêpe shoe-soles. Behind him he could hear the breathing of the man Muema who crawled behind him. They crawled for what seemed hours, and for a distance which possibly covered a hundred yards, when Brian's heel suddenly stopped moving. Kidogo was calling back over his shoulder.

"*Iko hapa Bwana chui nakufa kabisa,*" he was saying. "*Hi chui Nakuisha kufa chini.*"

Brian's heels darted like animals.

"He's found the cat dead," he said. "It's got into some sort of hole."

Paul Drake's knees fairly skimmed along the game trail until he saw Brian's heels turn down and the back of Brian's legs, standing now, in front of him. He scrambled to his feet, and saw that they were in a little clearing which looked familiar. They had come full circle in the bush and there, to his right now, was the leopard. Its fur was soaked.

Use Enough Gun

It was dead in the stumphole where it had crawled, hauling itself along with its belly shot clean out by the .300 magnum bullet which had taken it low and unzipped the stomach. It had dragged itself until *it* had been stalking *them*. The spread, extended claws were sunk deep in the dirt on the side of the stumphole. It had been bracing itself to spring when it died.

Brian stood at the edge of the little crater, looking at the wet dead leopard with suddenly disinterested eyes.

He half nodded and waved his hand casually.

"There's your leopard," he said. "Jolly good effort on the old man's part. He knew it was dead, all right. Only one error. It wasn't all the way dead. Hate to think of the action in that game path if he'd been too much wrong. Well, Paul, Katie's got her spotted rug for the long winter nights. Come on, lend a hand, we'll each take a paw. Even without his gut in him he's a damned big cat to be dead in a hole."

Two men stood on each side of the hole, stooping and seized one of the thick-muscled wet-furred legs. They heaved and the leopard surged out of the hole. Brian knelt and tugged at his head, nodding at Muema to straighten out his hindquarters and tail. He measured him swiftly in handspans, leapfrogging his fingers from nose to tail-tip.

"Reasonable *chui*," Brian said, looking up. "Just on eight feet."

"*Hi m'zuri tu*," both of the Africans said, working up a little obviously spurious cheer. Muema fingered the emptied stomach. He said something, and Brian laughed shortly.

Paul stood silent for a moment, looking at the thick yellow fur, the tremendously long curved sharp teeth still bared in a death-snarl, noticing the unbelievable strength in the broad, talon-shod paws. He looked at the white belly-fur where his bullet had ripped, spilling the guts and finally the life out of the cat which had not bled.

"I wish to Christ I'd never shot it at all," he said bitterly. "Anyhow, thanks for letting me come along for the ride, Brian. It was quite an experience, I must say. I don't think I'd want to do it again."

Brian laid a hand on Paul's shoulder.

"I imagine you feel cheated because it didn't charge and let you prove something," he said quietly. "*Don't*. Don't let it bother you. You came along for whatever it was going to do, and what counts really is the fact that you wanted to. That's good enough, Paul. I don't take many people into bush with me after wounded leopards, believe me. You're only the second, if that makes you feel any better."

"Thanks," Paul said. "Let's lug this thing out of here. Katie'll be thinking it ate us all." Each man picked up a leg, and the four men fought their way back out of the bush, the leopard's spine curving down as it sagged between the porters, its tail dragging along the underbrush. Its head had sagged to one side, but its dead yellow eyes were startlingly open, and the long needle teeth were still bared under the stiff whiskers.

PART FIVE

MOSTLY AFRICA

I F Y O U *have learned nothing else from hunting, you have learned patience and stubborness and concentration on what you really want at the expense of what is there to shoot. You have learned that man can as easily be debased as ennobled by a sport, and that optimism is the most vital ingredient of any sort of chase, from girls to greater kudu. Boy does not always get girl, but there is satisfaction in the college try—satisfaction surpassing the easy conquest, the freakish accident that provides reward without work."*

The following pieces, some from magazines, some from syndicated columns, describe Ruark's experiences on safari in Africa and India. They were written over a peripatetic twelve years, from 1951 to 1963.

"One thing I have learned from hunting: how to cuss. This I can do competently in eight languages, and I'm working on the ninth."

THE AFRICAN native, no matter what his tribe, is generally a grave citizen, seldom given to personal jokes and even less frequently stirred to laughter by the life around him. The one never-failing source of mirth, however, is the hyena—*Fisi*—a ridiculous animal that could be called a dirty joke on the entire animal kingdom.

Anything a hyena does is funny to a native. Great humor is found in the fact that *Fisi*, fatally shot, will eat himself before he is dead. He will snap and snarl at his own festooned intestines, or chew greedily on his own feet. His voice is always a subject for great native merriment, whether he be giggling hysterically in homosexual whoops, chuckling, grunting, groaning, howling, moaning, or snarling. *Fisi* has more sounds in his voicebox than a stampeding calliope.

Fisi is stupid, and *Fisi* is smart. When he is smart, he arouses almost frantic laughter. When he is dumb—for instance, when some wild dogs make off with a chunk of *Fisi*'s dinner, and *Fisi* knocks himself stiff by charging into a tree—the Africans clutch their sides and scream with laughter, imitating *Fisi* at his worst and noisiest. *Fisi* is so low on the totempole of life that even the scraggliest aboriginal, fleabitten, diseased, and scrawny, can lose sight of his own misery when he comes upon the hyena.

I discovered pretty early where the sardonic humor lay. You will meet natives with a portion of their faces chewed away, with horrid scars and welts healed over into grotesque masks. You ask them how come, and the answer is always *Simba*—lion. It is seldom true. The truthful answer is *Fisi*—hyena. There is an ingrained fear of *Fisi* that is founded in all the dark hours of a savage existence. *Fisi* means death—meant it more formerly than now, but is still held as a symbol of the dark destroyer.

Many African tribes have such an overweening fear of the spirits which attend death that they will not live in a hut or a kraal in which death has occurred. A day's journey in Kenya or Tanganyika will always point up a handful of ramshackle, deserted huts, with the cactus boma gone to seed and the cane rafters sagging under disheveled thatch. Death has struck here; the survivors have moved to avoid the hovering ghosts of the deceased.

So practical prudence, in past, asserted itself, and when an aged and dying member of the family appeared to be on his last legs he was lifted from his couch of pain and taken out into the bush. He was left there, alive, to be attended by *Fisi*. The hyena became a walking symbol of the cemetery in the native mind. Many a mortally ill native was eaten alive by hyenas well before natural death came to claim him. Not a small percentage had the animal rip a savage chop from his face and was cured, except for the terrible wound, of whatever illness beset him—cured by fright alone. The native who laughs at *Fisi* is laughing uneasily at the angel of death; he is giggling in the graveyard, because the ingrown knowledge is ever present that one day *Fisi* will have the last laugh on him.

The tremendous temerity of this cowardly creature is such that many a man has not needed to be critically ill to suffer a snap of the most powerful jaws in the animal kingdom. *Fisi*, grown blood-bold, is the most arrogant of all African animals.

Not only will he come into your camp, but he will come and sit by your fire, or stride into your tent. And if the mood strikes him, he will bite off half your face.

The African makes a tremendously potent beer, a thin, gruel-like liquor that is only half fermented at time of intake. It continues to ferment inside the drinker, so that a native on a binge eventually accumulates a fantastic load. Instead of sobering, he gets drunker as the beer continues to work in his innards. The jag is only abated by prolonged and deathlike sleep, during some phases of which it is impossible to rouse the sleeper. Here again is where the hyena is apt to bite off your profile. A young native with hyena scars must have a record of occasional drunkenness in his background—*Fisi* ripped a steak off him as he slept in stupor before a dying fire.

Of course, the hyena is a ridiculous beast. God's mind was absent the day he built *Fisi*. He gave him a dog's face and a lion's ears and the burly body of a bear. He permanently crippled his hindquarters, so that his running motion is a slope-spined, humping shuffle. He gave *Fisi* the most powerful jaws of any carnivore, and then made him so slow and so ungainly that the living meat which *Fisi* craves easily outruns him. With the potentiality of killing almost any creature with his enormous, steel-trap jaws, the hyena has been forced to kill the sick and the crippled and the very young. He himself reeks like the corrupt meat he eats. The final joke is that the hyena is frequently hermaphroditic—a blend of both sexes with the secondary manifestations of both. Carr Hartley, a wild-animal collector, once penned together two female hyenas that could not possibly have been impregnated with young at the time he turned them loose together. Both delivered a litter of pups. The hermaphrodism seems to be the last quirk of a grim joke on a pathetic beast.

The sad humor about the hyena is that he's so tragically, terribly awful that he inspires the kind of mirth that unfeeling youngsters derive from the presence of idiocy or malformation. *Fisi* is such a terrible beast that he almost isn't true. If you own a farm, you will hate him when one of your cows is found dying, hamstrung or with an udder ripped off by one snap of those frightful jaws. You will despise him as you see him on the outskirts of a game herd, waiting for a sick or lame animal to lag behind. You will loathe him during calving season, when he attacks the female animals in the midst of their birth pangs and makes off with the fresh-dropped babies. *Fisi* is an arrant coward, nearly always, and anything whole and brave can chase him. Even a little jackal will drive him from a lion's kill. But he will kill the lion if *Simba* is sick.

His persistence is the persistence of Uriah Heep. Shuffling apologetically, he will return after repeated rebuffs. And of nights he sometimes acquires an arrogance that is frightening in its very dumbness. That is when you fear *Fisi*—he might be just dumb enough to shuffle into the tent and have a go at you.

I have seen the hyena become so bold that he raced through the camp like a tame dog, hollering and whooping and stumbling over the tent ropes. Hyenas have been in the tents and eaten shoes and hats and camera covers—anything with leather on it. They have sat by the dozens, a few feet away from the campfire, staring fixedly with wicked, redly gleaming eyes. We seldom shot *Fisi* until one night, when the white hunter woke up and saw a big old hyena sitting at his cot side, looking reflectively through the mosquito netting at his face.

"Damned cheeky," Harry Selby said, and got up. He took a light rifle and a flashlight and dispatched seven, shooting at the eyes. The corpses were still there next morning. *Fisi* is so dreadful that he seldom eats his brother. Can't stand the taste.

But in a peculiar fashion this unwieldy, unhappy ghoul is such a vital part of African life that you would miss him greatly if he disappeared. Very few hunters shoot *Fisi*, although he is classed as vermin, except when he becomes so bold that he gets to be a dangerous nuisance around camp. For one thing, he is the head man in the sanitation corps. He will eat almost anything. He will even eat a dead vulture, although sometimes the nonfinicky buzzard won't eat a dead *Fisi*, figuring that a deceased hyena is even beneath a buzzard's dignity. However, between the hyena, the vulture, the marabou stork, and the ants, the great rolling plains of Africa seldom smell of carrion. Today's kill is clean bleached bone by tomorrow, a sanitation program that is part of the endless cycle of life-and-death of Africa.

It is uncanny how swiftly the legions of the clean-up corps appear. You will shoot a zebra for his hide and tallow, and almost before you have rolled the strips of yellow fat into the still dripping skin a few round-eared, dogfaced, shambling hyenas will be sitting, tongues lolling, a few rods away while the vultures are beginning to volplane down before you have quit the carcass. The vultures and the hyenas snap and snarl at each other, but seem to work together pretty well. More active competition occurs when a fleet of wild dogs come onto the scene, and the fight for carrion becomes a personal issue between *Fisi* and his slinking cousin, the big-eared dog.

In addition to his value as a walking incinerator, the hyena is fairly handy to the hunter. He follows the game concentrations and, more important to the hunter, he follows the carnivores to dine off their leavings. A large incidence of *Fisi* generally means lions about. I have noticed that his abundance also bespeaks cheetah, the hunting leopard that is nearly extinct today. The cheetah kills freshly, and feeds but once from his kill. I saw three cheetah on my last trip to Africa, and always their kills were signposted by hyenas and vultures.

Fisi has his uses as a decoy, too. If you are trying to toll the most timid lion out of the bush with a kill, he will come like a shot when he gets a whiff of a hyena hobbling up to that nice fresh topi or zebra you have thoughtfully supplied for *Simba's* lunch. If you are working overnight on lions with a kill, a concentrated, dedicated corps of hyenas screaming frightfully as they attempt to rip off a protective covering of thorns from the lion kill is almost guaranteed to attract the most reclusive *Simba* in the area. The lion hates *Fisi* because, like the native, the lion knows that the hyena will eventually get him. It is cynically humorous that, one way or another, the king of beasts always finds his tomb inside the knave. It is the crowning indignity to a regal life that the aged and weakened lion is pulled down and consumed, while still alive, by a stinking, snarling, cowardly outcast that is neither true male nor female, but an awful amalgam of both.

But without *Fisi*'s admirable voice range and his ever-present attendance at camp, Africa would never pack the nocturnal wallop that makes night noises, a stiff drink, and a flickering campfire so wonderful. There is no way accurately to describe a dozen hyenas without the camp—the virtuosity of voices is too great. There is a bone-chilling insane giggle—the *heeheeheehee* of a madwoman—and there are enough roars and whoops and screams and growls to fill an album. Eventually you come to miss *Fisi* if he is seldom in the area. He has become a part of your life, like the moon and the bugs and the baboons and the scorpions.

I finally got fond of *Fisi,* and very sorry for him. He is such a dreadful fellow, hated by every living creature, loathed by all, shunned by all, laughed at by all, that I kind of adopted him. No living creature, I thought, should have so much bad luck and live so shamefully, so ignobly. All the other African animals have a dignity that endures until *Fisi,* the undignified, enjoys the last hysterical giggle over their cracked and crunching bones.

And then one day my friend *Fisi* betrayed my good-will by eating up half my portable library, wrecking the booze supply out of sheer vandalism, and chewing up a perfectly good hat. He also made off with the skull and headskin of a greater kudu bull —as he once ate up a fine leopard a friend killed, leaving one wisp of tail to mark his passing. That is when you get all out of sorts with *Fisi,* remembering that next time, no matter how sorry you are for this monster, he may decide to dine on your face.

Use Enough Gun

WELL, let us press on," said Mr. Selby after we had finished lunch and had sighted in a couple of guns. "We need some meat for the camp, and maybe we'll be able to clobber a Grant or a gerenuk on the way to camp. I got a hunch that there are a couple of dry riverbeds an old Turkana tracker showed me where there ought to be an army of elephants and rhino and stuff, all elbowing each other away from the water holes and chewing up the scenery. Off and away!"

While Selby and I rode the jeep, he explained something of the lugger (dry river) country to me. A lugger, or *raga*, or *luga*, is the path in the dry season of what is a mighty river in the wet season. It is studded with stones and the carcasses of wrecked trees. Beneath the sand is water—the only water available. The elephants and rhinos and native cattle and goats and jackasses stumble over each other, digging frantically for water. All life for thousands of square miles concentrates on the luggers, to browse the greenery that rims the beds and to claw up foul, reeking water from the damp sands.

You hunt elephant and rhino by riding painfully up and down the luggers in a British jeep, looking for sign, and when a track shows big enough you dismount the jeep and walk. A really ambitious elephant hunter can spend six weeks walking twenty miles a day in soft sand and bitter desert heat, trailing some old bull that always turns out to be a one-tusker. Outside the lugger rims there is no food, but a rhino will willingly travel twenty miles to water and twenty miles back in a given day over the sere, twisted, stunted thorn of the plains.

As we drove along Harry looked around him and grunted. He

did not look pleased. "It's too green," he said presently. "There are too many animals on the plains. Look at those Grant here. They should be on the luggers. I heard there was rain at Marsabit, too, from the Game Department bloke in Isiolo. It never rains here at this time of the year. It didn't even rain in the rainy season last fall. Weather's been bloody peculiar of late. Rains where it shouldn't, and doesn't rain where it should. We'll see."

A little later on he stopped the jeep and pointed. A lady rhino and calf were browsing smack in the middle of the plain.

"No business to be there," Selby muttered. "I don't like it. Got a hunch that, instead of being clustered around the luggers where a bloke can take his pick, you'll find them scattered all to hell and gone over ten thousand square miles of dreary bush.

Harry popped a shot into the ground in front of the old lady. Muttering, she stopped, collected the calf, and went off. We headed for camp. It was latish afternoon now, with the sun a big red ball in the bitter alkali dust. The huge, rugged mountains looked angry against the sky. The shabby trail through the plains was scarred and rutted with rhino tracks. In a minute we came up on a mob of Grant gazelle, with two or three oryx bulls scattered in the herd and a couple of Grevy zebra as well.

"That's rather a decent bull, that oryx there at the left," Harry said. "Don't see many very good oryx about any more. I've a hunch the natives have been hunting them with dogs. Damn fool, the oryx. Put a dog on him, and he'll run a hundred yards and then stick his tail in a bush and turn around to fight the dog with those long, straight stickers he wears on his head. Any local can come up to him and shoot him with an arrow. I think an awful lot have been killed off. We might as well take one more, because he's as good as you'll see, and he's big enough to keep the whole camp fed for the next three days. We can wallop a gerenuk for ourselves later on. They're as tasty and tender as Tommies. I like 'em better myself. Get out and stalk over behind that bush and when the herd feeds past wallop that big fellow."

Use Enough Gun

I hadn't fired a rifle in eighteen months, not since the last safari to Tanganyika. But the little old .30-06 felt easy and familiar in my hands. I noticed my breath was coming in jerks, as it always does when one starts a safari. I squatted down behind a bush, and shortly the herd moved past. The big oryx bull was inside a hundred yards, a rather close shot for oryx, which are hard to come up on and which mostly get shot over two hundred yards. The bull ambled past, and I squeezed on him and heard the bullet hit and away he went. Where I hit him I couldn't have said, but I was willing to bet me a beer that it was either too far back or too low or both.

Selby drove up in the jeep. "He went thataway," he said. "I couldn't hear the bullet. You hit him?"

"Some place," I said. "Don't know where or how hard, and nobody knows better than you how much they'll take. We put seven in that one at Mto-wa-Mbu last year, remember, and he was still trying to git up and gallop. Let's go look for him."

We made a fast swing around in the jeep, but couldn't see the high, straight horns in the grass anywhere. So we headed back to track him from where he'd jumped. The bull was under a tree, down, with his horns laid back. He hadn't run more than sixty yards from where I'd shot him and had suddenly stopped to lie down, an oryx trick.

We walked up on him and he lurched up. This time I busted him good, through the shoulder and heart, and down he went, permanently. Metheke, the Mohammedan, came up and performed the koshering ceremony with the knife, and we had meat for the camp. I was wrong about where I had hit him the first time. It was too high and too far back to put him down. He could have run a week if he'd chosen. We horsed the oryx up on the back of the high-piled truck and set off for the first camp. It was about an hour until dark.

"Funny thing, hunting," Selby mused as we drove along. "Remember last safari? We hunted oryx until our teeth dropped out, and never got one until the next-to-last day of the trip. We hunted rhino a month in a rhino heaven and never fired a shot. We chased kudu up and down mountains for three weeks and got cheated time and time again just by breaks. And when you did shoot one, it was a sad mistake, that immature bull with the one curl.

"Now, here we are out one afternoon from Isiolo, haven't made camp yet, and already you've shot an oryx and we've seen two rhino and a ton of sign. Maybe our luck's due to change this trip."

We made the first camp in an oasis off the Kinya lugger, where Harry had had abnormally fine luck before. In the safari ahead of mine, he'd taken out a man and his son and, working under heavy pressure, had gotten them two fine elephant, two fine lions, two fine buffalo, two fine rhino, two fine oryx, two fine eland, two fine waterbuck, and all the common game and had them home-bound at the airport thirty days from their arrival date—something of a feat even for Selby.

There was enough light left for a walk down to the dry riverbed, and as far as the eye could see there was nothing but elephant and rhino sign. The bed was cobbled with droppings and deeply waffled with heavy tracks. But the dung was dry, a good three or four days old, and the tracks were shallow and indistinct in the sand.

"There must have been a thousand elephants in this place in the last week and rhino unnumbered," Harry said, "but nothing for the last few days. That unseasonable rain has taken them all back out to the plains again. Tough luck! I was really counting on this place, because I know of some very good bulls here. To-morrow we move on up to another lugger about five miles away —Seralippe—and hunt the plains out from there."

We had a cold supper and went to bed. It is nice at night in the Northern Frontier District, not hot, but balmy and very dry. The moon is bigger and the stars closer on the desert than any other place I know. A couple of lonesome hyenas said hello to their old friends. Dead tired, I went to sleep. We slept late, because we were all beat from the week's festivities.

About 9:30 we got up and had some breakfast that we didn't

much want, still feeling tired and used up. We sighted in a few more guns, and they made a horrid noise. Then we told the boys to saddle up and move on to the next campsite, and hopped into the jeeps for what Selby calls a rekky-run—a look-see about the country before you start to hunt it closely. We never figure to shoot anything for the first few days, until we've got the land pretty well sized.

We rekky-ran for about seven miles on a pretty good road, and about two miles past our next campsite and a Samburu village I heard Metheke's horny black hand hit Selby on the neck and he jammed the brakes.

"*Ndofu*" Metheke, the gunbearer, said. "*Tatu. Doumi.*"

"Oh, no," moaned Master Selby. "Not elephant this morning! Not three bull elephants this morning, of all mornings. We haven't even got here yet. Gimme the glasses."

He looked for a bit and then handed the binoculars to me. I looked. There were three elephants. One was a big bull with what looked like big teeth. The other two were smaller—the *askari* bulls that accompany the old fellow when he is driven from the herd, in order to learn all the old man knows before they go back to take on the new herd bull some fifteen or twenty years later.

I looked at Selby. He looked at me. We both shuddered. Finally I said: "We might as well face it. What color were those elephants?"

"You say first," Selby hedged.

"What I saw looked like three bright pink elephants—in an old Samburu garden surrounded by a herd of goats. That's what I thought I saw."

"That's what I thought I saw too," Selby said. "Gimme the glasses again. I cannot stand the idea of three pink elephants the day after New Year's." He looked some more. "Yep, three pink elephants! That's a damned good bull, though, pink or not. From here, he'll go an easy 80 pounds. Maybe 90. Anything over 60 pounds per tusk is shootable these days, and nobody sneers at 75. Anything over that is exceptional. Tell you what," suggested

Mr. Selby, "let us go shoot the biggest pink elephant and maybe the other two will go away."

"Where do you shoot a pink elephant?" I asked him. "I'm so new at this. Draw me a picture."

Kneeling in the clay, he scratched a picture of an elephant with a stick. He showed me where the heart was and what I would have to do to hit the brain if the elephant was coming at me, and I decided that nobody is good enough to figure out where you shoot a charging elephant in the lower trunk to get up between the tusks and into a brain aperture that's about nine inches long by three inches wide and is entirely surrounded by a coral-like bone structure that soaks lead as a sponge takes water.

"Shoot him in the heart. Aim for behind the point of shoulder, about in his middle section, and you're all right," said Mr. Selby. "Let's go get this over with, hey?"

We took off at a swinging trot, with Selby smoking furiously to test the wind, which kept swirling and changing. Every five minutes it would change and we would run hell-for-leather to try to get around ahead of it. Selby was up and down trees like the baboon who is his cousin, keeping an eye on the progress of the three bulls as they stormed through the scrub. You could hear them tearing down the trees and the rumble of their bellies. From the last tree he swarmed down and said: "Bloody wind has settled for a second. We'll just have to gamble. They're going to come out over there." He pointed. "We'll run a couple of hundred yards and wait behind those bushes. If the wind doesn't veer, they'll come out in our laps. Don't shoot until I say, like always."

We ran. As we ran it started to rain. The rain came in sheets, in buckets, in torrents. We were soaked to the skin when we achieved Selby's bush, soaked and out of breath, but the wind held and we could hear the bulls talking to each other, tearing down this tree and uprooting that one. Selby and I were out ahead, alone. The gunbearers were about twenty feet behind us.

The first bull burst out of a patch of bush. He was small in size, but he had one very decent tusk. The other was broken off short. "I know this chap," Selby whispered. "Old buddy of mine."

Next came the other small bull, with tusks no bigger than baseball bats. And then came my boy. His tusks were logs; they were as big as telephone poles. They were as big around as oil-drums and not quite as long as a football field. Or so they seemed right then. I noticed a strange thing. The elephants were no longer pink. They were blue!

Later, the reason was obvious. They had been rolling in wet ocher clay, and so had appeared pink. When the driving, slashing shower began, it washed off the mud and made their gray-black hides appear blue in the rain. But at the time it seemed unfair of Selby to make me shoot a bull elephant on the day after New Year's in the rain, when the elephants kept changing their color from pink to blue.

The little bull with the tiny tusks wandered off into the bush to the left. The lead bull turned back and merged with the big bull, and then one of them went away. We had switched to another bush. Whichever elephant was up ahead of us was broadside on. It continued to rain, and the safety of my big double .470 was so slippery that I couldn't pull it back on safe. Suddenly Selby ducked back on his tracks to another bush.

"Can't shoot until he comes out in the clear," Harry muttered through very grimly clenched teeth. "Tragic to shoot and find you'd clobbered that one-tusker. Got to wait to see which is which."

Now the bull had switched his engine and was coming into a patch of clear. It was our boy, all right, and we could have done him so easily if we'd only been sure. His tusks were now as big as a couple of obelisks. Then the wind changed.

As the wind changed his head went up, his trunk reached out, his vast tents of tattered ears flanged forward, and he let out a screech fit to wake the dead. He had our scent now, and since he was only about sixty yards away he had us with his eyes and ears as well. He was a mean old rogue with a sore foot and a sore tooth and a hatred of rain, I suspect, and he didn't like people, either.

He came—like a train. His trunk was straight out ahead of him, his tusks upraised, his ears back, and his feet high like a pacing horse. It's funny, but all I could think of was those huge feet, with their nails bigger than dinner plates, coming through the bush, the nails washed clean and white by the rain—a blue elephant coming through black bush, and my eyes full of water and the gun cold and slippery in my hand. And no place to shoot, because he was charging straight on, head on.

I had one brief thought that this was one hell of a poor way to start the new year. There were sounds behind us as some of our followers departed, which was intelligent of them, but there wasn't any place for Mr. Selby and me to go. We stood spraddled and waited out the bull. We waited out the bull and we waited out the bull, and it took ten thousand years. He was about twenty-five yards away, Selby said later—I wouldn't know—when he hit a rock or something and swerved. He didn't swerve much, but he swerved enough to give me a bit of shoulder to shoot at. Remembering to shoot the left-hand trigger first (the gun had a tricky sear and a bad habit of loosing off both barrels if you fired the right trigger first), I touched off two at the corner of his elbow and heard both bullets hit, and he was away into the bush. Then I sat down on the ground and breathed hard through my mouth. My hands were wet, but not from rain. My mouth was dry, but not from sun. I was pale of face, but not from illness. I was never so scared in my life! All I could see still was feet, wider across than my gun barrels, and great tusks as big as pipelines.

"I would like a cigarette, please," I said. "but you light it. I've got the shakes."

We heard the crashing stop, and then we heard the belly rumble and a kind of anguished moan. That was that. The bull was down and dead about a hundred yards away. One tusk was deeply embedded in the ground. He had evidently died in flight.

Use Enough Gun

Cautious as always, Selby said: "We'll sneak around here, and you wallop him in the back of the neck. He looks dead, but maybe he ain't. Dead elephants get up and trample you."

We sneaked around, and I sat down on my hams and wedged my elbows on my knees and pointed at the base of his brain and pulled. I turned a complete flip and wound up, stunned, in a thornbush. The icy-nerved *Bwana* had done it again, even as with the buffalo. Old Cold Steel Ruark, the stanch stander-in-the-way of charging elephants, who always remembered to pull the back trigger first, now shoots a dead elephant and pulls the front trigger first. Both barrels go off, and old Horatio-at-the Bridge Ruark takes a magnificent tail-over-tip and winds up with a fanny full of thorns. The elephant didn't care. He was already dead.

We could tell he was dead from the first shots when I came to and we went up to him. Elephant hunters will tell you that they never knew a heart-shot bull to fall on his unwounded side. Climbing atop him, you could see my bullet holes. One had taken him at the bottom of the top half of his heart. The other had taken him at the top part of the bottom half of his heart. They must have wrecked everything—all the main arteries and pumps and stuff—and he hemorrhaged and died in stride.

Selby walked up a stiff leg and touched the holes. "Jolly nice shooting, *Bwana*," he said, and I believe he meant it.

"Jolly nice nuts," I said, and I meant it. "Thanks for the compliment, but don't compliment me. Send a flower to my reflexes."

We were back in camp at 11:30. We tooted the horn, the formal sound of triumph, and the boys came out, waiting for a joke, because we had been gone but two hours.

"*Nini?*" the head boy said.

"*Ndofu, Tembo*," Metheke, the gunbearer, said. "*M'kubwa sana.*"

"Phooey," said Juma in the Swahili equivalent. "None of you worthless people shoot elephants in the first two hours on the first day out."

"Like I said," Metheke repeated. "Elephant. A big one."

Africans get excited about two animals, and two animals only. If you shoot a lion or an elephant, they succumb to hysteria that is not planned for the clients, and they literally tear you apart. They tore me apart. They hauled me out of the jeep and passed me from hand to hand, and finally threw me breathless onto my cot. It was quite a morning.

Most of the camp went back that afternoon to see the old boy while Katunga, the chief skinner, and his assistants went at the arduous chore of chopping out the tusks. They were quite some tusks, bigger and thicker than any of us first estimated. Selby said they'd go 90 to 95. Being a pessimist, I said 80. Old Katunga said 110.

Katunga was right. One hundred and ten pounds each they were, perfectly symmetrical, not worn down from right- or left-handed rooting, but wonderfully thick and beautifully curved tusks. I believe that Mr. Selby has been party to only three or four sets of tusks over 100, and I know one of the best professional hunters in Africa who has never bagged, in more than twenty years, a set that topped the 100 mark. Maybe eight or ten 100-pluses have been legally shot since the war, if memory holds, but I could be wrong.

This isn't intended to be braggadocio. It is simply a recital of dumb luck. This old bull had been living on a reserve for the last of his hundred years, since they compute elephant age at roughly one pound of ivory per year, and had wandered down off the reserve into legal shooting territory, tempted by the unseasonable rains that greened the prairie. We had stumbled across his path on the first morning out.

All the celebration was over now. The tusks had been hewed from the great beast's head, the nerves removed, the ends plugged with grass, and the weighing accomplished. Because of remarkably small nerves, the old boy went a good ten pounds higher than our brightest expectations, and when you pass 75 pounds every ounce is important. We toasted him right nobly over lunch, and then went out to polish off a few guinea-fowl and francolin on the Seralippe lugger at which we were camped.

Use Enough Gun

The lugger—the dry riverbed—was really in business. There was a Samburu-Rendille *manyatta* (camp) just up the road a piece, close onto where we had first encountered Jumbo, and they seemed to own all the livestock from Isiolo to Addis Ababa. They drove their flocks of goats and sheep and high-humped red, black, and white cattle and their vast herds of Somali donkeys right through the side of the camp down to where they had dug the deep wells in the moist sands of the Seralippe riverbed. They were being jostled by what seemed an alarming number of elephants and rhino that trampled in the wells and otherwise made their presence known. The Samburu-Rendille, a pleasant bloke who is actually a displaced Masai and a great nomad, is handsome to look at but accumulates millions of flies.

We didn't bother to get up very early that second day, having been up late to celebrate the elephant. Mostly we sat around the fire and talked about luck—the kind of luck we hadn't had on the first safari, where we hunted our legs off for rhino and kudu and even oryx for week after dreary week, for nothing but thorn scars and stone bruises. And here I'd already shot a very decent oryx for camp meat, an hour out of Isiolo, and the very next morning the toughest of all to get, a really good elephant, in less than two hours.

"Let's see how the luck holds with rhino," Selby said after breakfast. "Must be a few thousand of them around here. They don't come really high in the horn, like the forest rhino on the side of Mt. Kenya, but they're actually a better and more representative beast. They are bigger and much more rugged in the horn, but they don't go to those slim and freakish lengths that the mountain ones tend to."

We piled into the jeeps, and meandered down the dry riverbed slowly, looking for rhino sign. There was plenty of it—strawy, kicked-up dung and a flock of tracks leading across the lugger into the bush. We'd not gone more than a mile when Harry killed the jeep. It was a good track, a bull's track, and very fresh. The still-damp sand from the early-morning dew was crumbly at the top of the track.

"Very nice, I think," Selby said, "Good bull, from the size of his hoof. Couldn't say about the horn, of course, but worth a little work. Let's go and investigate this gentleman."

I say we were tracking. We weren't, really. I have tracked with Selby when you had to depend on disarranged dew on a blade of grass, a holly berry of blood every five hundred yards, a slightly scuffed stone in rock-hard, bone-dry country. That is tracking, and I can't do it. This was not tracking. This was following the spoor of a Sherman tank through fresh snow on Park Avenue.

We just walked, at route step. Through that rain-soft earth and on that dewy grass our man *Faro* left a spoor that a blind beggar could have followed with his cane. We came to another stack of kicked-up dung, and it was hot and steaming in the morning air. Then all of a sudden things got complicated. Another set of tracks joined his and led into a patch of myrrh bush.

"O-ho," said Mr. Selby. "Love in bloom. He has matched himself up with a *manamouki*. He is in that bush with a cow. This is breeding time, and I imagine he'll not like it if we disturb him in his tryst." Selby actually talks like that.

"Disturb him in his tryst, yet," I said. "How delicate can you get in this business?"

Selby snickered and pointed.

A horn poked out of the bush and pointed inquiringly in our direction. It wasn't very much of a horn, but there was three tons of cow rhino under it. She backed into the bush. These things are funny. The cow had made no threat, although we weren't more than twenty to thirty yards away. But with that queer detachment you get, I noticed that we all suddenly had double rifles cocked at a 45-degree angle across our chests and that all safeties were off. This operation happened without anybody being conscious of it, which is why you hire gunbearers in the first place. A good gunbearer is never more than a yard from you when he is carrying the gun, and when he is tracking ahead *you* are toting the artillery.

We circled around the bush, and then Mr. Selby did a thing that I consider very brave in calculated bravery, not bravado. At least I wouldn't do it. Not to a bush which had in it one rhino you knew about and another you didn't know about. Mr. Selby duck-walked right up to the edge of that bush and parted a branch with his gun barrel and looked in. The whole patch of bush couldn't have been more than twenty-five feet thick; so in effect Mr. Selby was within a minimum ten feet of one, maybe two, large, evilly disposed, nasty-tempered rhino in love.

He looked and looked, then duck-waddled backward and stood up. Motioning us off to the right, he spoke in a low voice. "Nothing in there but the cow. *Doumi's* beggared off someplace. Must've got our scent when we first saw the cow, from the other side. Let's go quietly away and leave the old girl to her tender memories."

We went quietly away, but the wind skirled around again and the lady caught our scent and departed the bush with a whoosh. So we gave the weapons back to the bearers and headed out for the scant few hundred yards in the direction of the jeeps.

"Hey!" Harry said. He pointed over to a small meadow in the bush.

There was the bull. He was a damned fine bull, too, with a very good horn and a second horn nearly as good as the first, and he was standing just outside the bush no more than forty yards away. Black hands gave guns to white hands in something under one-hundredth of a second. You knew those guns were loaded. You didn't have to look to see if they were loaded. We froze.

"I say," Selby said, putting his mental calipers to work. "That's a jolly nice horn, very well proportioned. Nothing stupendous, mind you, but I like a good representative trophy better than the freaks. He'll go twenty-two inches anyhow, and I never saw anything larger up here in recent years. I'd suggest we take him. You want him?"

While I was saying "Yes" my mind was whipping back to another safari, in Tanganyika, where Selby and I got up at 5 A.M. and tortured ourselves until as late as 10 P.M. over miserable roads, crawling through marsh, climbing mountains, baking our brains out in the sun, and running from big, evil-tempered calves and big, evil-tempered shorthorned bulls. Twenty-eight rhino we ran from. Trees we climbed. Shoot we did not.

"You are damned well right I want to shoot him," I said. "I earned him last year."

"Bust him, then."

I looked at the big bull, which was beginning to work out of the meadow, edging off into the bush.

"Now," Harry said. "He's leaving, and I don't want him in that bush."

He was a touch far for safety, but I held on his shoulder and pulled. He turned completely over, a most impressive sight if you have never seen a rhino bowled completely over. I had never seen a rhino bowled completely over.

"*Piga. Kufa. M'uzuri sana,*" all the black boys were saying, and I was acquiring that feverish glow you get when they like the way you do it. Then the bull got up. He was *piga-ed, m'uzuri,* but he wasn't *kufa sana,* which is to say I had busted him real good, but he wasn't very dead yet. He was on his feet, three-quarters on, and I let him have the other half. *Wallop.* Over he went again. The boys went through the *piga-kufa* routine again. Bull didn't understand it. He got up, lowered his horn and started at us.

The dependable Metheke had by this time shoved a fresh clump of .470s into my fist and the tricky Westley Richards was fueled and I clobbered this thing again. Down. *Piga. Kufa.* Up he got again, groggy but gutty, still headed our way. *Boom.* Down again. Then he began to roar and screech and shake his horn high in the air, whirling round and round and raising the roof. He paused for a second, and I gave him the other one. Down. Up. One more. Down. Up—and headed our way.

This seemed to go on for quite a time. I knew where I was hitting and what I was hitting him with, because the rhino is the one big animal I'm not frightened of and don't get excited about. This seemed to be the most durable beast I had met, save one buffalo.

When he got up, he came like a shot, straight onto the lot of us. I let him come and when his head went down there was an awful lot of neck showing with spine under it, and I pointed the gun down and broke his back more or less in our laps. He didn't need the finisher that I told Harry to give him in the head. The reason I told Harry to finish him was that my middle finger was split open from knuckle to nail like an overcooked hot dog. All guns kick me because I hold them wrong, and I had fired this cannon exactly eleven times since yesterday morning, and it wasn't even 10 A.M. today. One of the explosions had been double, when both triggers touched off on the elephant, and 150 grains of cordite is hard on a finger.

Everything that I had put into this beast, except the back-buster, was a killing shot. Everything was in the heart, smack on the shoulders. There is no trick to shooting a rhino in the heart. You more or less aim for where he's biggest. But, bowled over all those times, he still came and was still coming and would have continued to come some more if I had not ruptured his motive machinery. There is no living man who can explain why some come and some don't—as witness the fact that a month later I killed a Cape buffalo stone dead with a .30-06, whereas others have been known to take up to sixteen .470s through the front and still come on.

He is a dreadful-looking beast, the rhino, but this seemed to be a good one. His horn measured out at twenty-three inches and a bit and was as big around the base as it was long. It had green moss on it. He was not covered with ticks, and it occurred to me that this was the only rhino I ever saw that wasn't infested with ticks and covered with tick-birds. I tied a handkerchief around my bleeding finger.

"Why didn't he stay down?" I asked Selby. "Look at those holes. Five hundred grains of solid .470 smack through the shoulders every time, only one a little low, and up he gets and lands in our arms. I thought you said these things are easy to kill!"

"They're supposed to be," Harry said. "Except I've noticed one thing. If they know you're there and are charging and you wallop them right, they'll go over and stay down. But if you shoot them unsuspectingly and they go down, apt as not it's from shock, like hitting a man in the chin when he isn't looking. There's no counter-resistance to make the bullet's impact greater. I don't know, really. He's dead, and we'll skin him out for a couple of *kibokos*—quirts, you call them—and take the head-skin and then we'll go back to camp for a little lunch."

In all formal treatises on Africa, the hero waits until the last page to tell you how he slew the kudu. The greater kudu, known as *tendalla* in Swahili, constitutes the Holy Grail of the African hunter. Not, of course, for the serious collector, who spends nine years crawling through wild-grape thickets after bongo, or the perfectionist who must have a Mrs. Gray's lechwe in order to die happy. But the ordinary *bwana wa safari* who pays his money and spends three months in the bush has just got to kill that kudu for the final page of his memoirs.

The kudu is an elusive critter, and he is certainly a fine trophy. He is possibly the most beautiful of the big African antelopes, with his back-twisting horns, his thick heavily maned neck, his chevroned nose and his white-barred body. He is as big as a racehorse, and he dies pretty easy. There isn't much excuse for missing a kudu if you ever get a shot at one, but a great many hunters seem to fire into the air when they face this dainty hank of Golden Fleece. I know of at least one gentleman who missed four times at point-blank range and then threw his gun at the bull, which was still regarding him with some puzzlement.

Compulsion comes upon the African writer to leave his kudu for the longest last.

One thing about kudu writers is that they make you share all the work. They haul you over all the mountains and make you wait interminable hours at the saltlicks. They scratch you with their thorns and afflict you with their stone bruises and drag you through swamps and make you a free gift of their personal despair. But all the time you know it's going to come out fine. On page 99 of a 100-page manuscript the hero is a cinch to swim two rivers, crawl ten miles, and finally shoot his kudu with the last bullet in the last hour of the last day of the last hunt. Oddly, the very second the kudu is down and the Mohammedan gun-bearer sticks him in the neck, the rains come. It is against the law not to kill a kudu for the wow ending. As a matter of fact, it is against the outdoor writer's union rules not to kill whatever he is after just ten minutes before black desperation sets in and poisons the hunter.

That is where this piece is going to be different. It is only fair to warn you that I will not kill a kudu on the last page. The only kudu I ever shot I will kill right now. Shot him three days after the hunt started. What I aimed at was the biggest kudu bull ever slain by hand of man. I walloped him smack through the heart with a .375 magnum, and he went over like a toppled oak. For thirty seconds I was master of at least a 61-inch kudu bull. When we ran up to gloat, I found that I had murdered an immature male with just one twist to his horns, and consequently worthless as a trophy.

In my time I have had some high-ups-and-low-downs. This was the downest-down I ever experienced. With his head thrown back, against a blood-red rising sun, with only the broad frontal sweep and the first massive curl showing, this was momentarily the grandfather of all kudus. When we ran up to the carcass, there was only a defunct youngster that would have been a magnificent bull in two years, but right then he had only one lousy spiral. We cut off his head and saved the skin and the meat. I may not have wept, but I felt like it. I felt like a butcher.

We may inspect the greater kudu as a lesson in humility. After a brief week when half the best heads in Tanganyika walked into camp and pleaded for immediate taxidermy, I had begun to suspect that this African business was vastly over press-agented as to difficulty. The skinners were working round the clock, and hinting broadly for overtime. We had to brush the leopards out of the path with brooms, drive around the lion prides, and slay record-breaking antelopes only in self-defense.

So we spent the next five weeks after rhino and kudu. *Hapana faro. Hapana tendalla.* In Swahili *hapana* means everything that's negative. Just nothin'. I stalked rhino until horns grew out of my nose. I pursued kudu until my ears developed a double curl, and I was known as the only hunter in Tanganyika with ivory-tipped eyebrows. *Hapana.*

They spun me the old wives' tale of the rich gentlemen who hunted kudu for painful weeks at Kondoa Arangi, and on the last day suddenly came upon a blood spoor accompanied by kudu tracks. They followed the blood for four hours, and finally pulled up to a handsome bull that was groggy on his feet.

He had not been shot or horned by another bull. He had knocked his lovely rack against a stone or a tree and had ruptured a blood-vessel. The six-mile stalk in the heat had weakened him so that he would have collapsed from loss of blood in another mile or so. They shot him, and a beautiful trophy he made. This, of course, was the last day of the safari. Just before the rains came.

And they told me about my friend Bob Maytag, who spent weeks striding mountains until the last day of his hunt. Then he went out while the boys broke camp and jumped a big bull that walked down the hill toward Maytag, took a miss and a hit and then ran across Bob's bow, instead of away into the bush as any intelligent kudu should have done. Maytag plastered him and was back in camp with his gorgeous *tendalla* before his fair Harriet had her underthings packed.

Oh, and they told me all about the bulls that ran together in herds of two and four and up to sixteen in a certain spot, and about the 59-incher that Frank Bowman's last expedition hauled out of this certain spot, and how the kudu hung around the riverbanks as tame as topi. When we got there we saw so many cows and immature bulls, so tame on the first day, that the white hunter said quite seriously: "It's only a matter of picking your bull and then improving on him, and it's a pity, too. We'll be gone so soon."

So the second day we flushed a big bull with the jeep, driving from one camp to the other. I fell out of the car and the bull almost stopped in easy range, but decided not to after all, and when I banged at him as he boiled out from behind a bush he took off like a goosed cheetah, in a giant jump that spoke plainly, *piga*. But if I *piga*-ed him he tied his own tourniquet, because he disappeared into a thorn thicket that would have repelled a tank, with divil a speck of blood to mark his passage.

That afternoon we climbed a steep butte of rock and spotted a huge fellow with a harem, and then lost him in the twilight. And the next day we came on Junior, stock-still and huge-seeming across a broad *donga*, with that great head back-tossed. We looked at him with the nakeds, and we looked at him through the glasses, and we looked at him some more without the glasses. The more we looked the bigger he got, even to the experts. So I whacked him pretty, and down he went, and I said thank-God-that's-over-northern-frontier-here-I-come. But I already told you. One stinkin' curl to the horns.

The hope never died. Each day we saw kudu—cows by the double-score, young bulls by the score, and big-bull sign as thick as cattle tracks in a stockyard. We stalked a big one over two hills—hell, mountains—and by all the rights of hunting he was nailed to the wall. The wind was right, the stalk was quiet, and his retinue of cows and youngsters stared right into the sights at fifty yards. But Father, through some perverse whim, had elected to wander off for the kudu equivalent of a stag party. Not spooked, not going anywhere in particular, just moseying along. We watched the bum jump a thousand yards away. We tracked him the rest of the morning, until he finally winded us or heard us and departed for Rhodesia.

But we saw them by the road and we saw them in the hills. Every day we saw them and jumped them and something happened. Driving along a pretty fair road to a nearby village, we put two young bulls out of the bush, and they crossed back and forth twice ahead of us. I could have stunned either with a stick. And then we knocked up the biggest kudu bull anybody ever saw. My gunbearer, Kidogo, had been in on the death of a 59-incher some months before. Kidogo swore later that this chap had two or three inches on the late 59-er.

This character gallumped down the side of the road, his head laid back and his horns reaching clean back to his tail. He walked away from the road and stood. The hunter braked the jeep and we snuck down the road. The big bull was no more than thirty-five feet away from us—but he had chosen the only baobob tree in the neighborhood to stand behind. This particular baobob was about the size of the houses they sell G.I.'s. There was nothing to do but round it, and just before we cleared the tree the kudu sauntered—not jumped—to a patch of thorn and stood. I got one glimmer of sun off that fantastic head when he barked and leaped. *Hapana.*

So we drove two miles, then left the jeep and walked over a couple more mountains to cut him off on a ridge he had to travel, and we sent the two gunbearers and the carboy behind him to whoop and holler and drive. The odds on him were about eight to one, our way. But Grandfather said nay. He turned on his big splay feet and ran right through the boys, and is now a taxpayer in Indo-China, for all I know. We never saw him again.

We had just about ten days of this. We hunted the hills, and we hunted the river. We hunted the plains, and we hunted the licks. We acquired local gentlemen who had just seen *mingi sana doumi m'kuba tendalla*—job lots of big bulls—that very morning. We jumped kudu bulls out of abandoned native gardens. We heard them bark and crash in the thicks. We shooed the cows out of camp. One big bull literally ran through camp when we were off some ten miles away, crawling after his cousins. Toward the end I didn't care who shot what. Master Harry Selby is the kind of white hunter who shoots nothing unless you command him. I armed Selby. I also armed Kidogo. I commanded.

"Look," I said. "I have earned me a kudu. We have all earned a kudu. Every time we come back to camp, kudu-less, all the boys run and hide in the bush to avoid being beaten to death by *Bwana.* I do not care who shoots a kudu. But a principle is at stake.

"Furthermore," I said with suitable profanity, "with the exception of that spike buck, I have not fired a shot in anger in two

weeks. The guinea-fowl are about to take the canned goods away
from us, but nobody will let me shoot the shotty-gun because it
will frighten the kudu. We are starving to death while the impala jump over the jeep and the buffalo and eland sidle up with
autograph pads, begging for a pencil. The elephants are stomp-
ing back and forth through the camp, but nobody can shoot because it will scare the so-and-so *tendalla*. I have walked slightly
under a thousand miles. We have built roads, bridges, and swum
rivers. Dammit, somebody has to shoot a kudu!"

Master Selby is a fair hand with a rifle, which is to say he can
take the eye out of a downwind gnat at two hundred yards. So
the next day a .50-incher stands nice in a bush, with his head and
breast showing, and Master Selby takes a belt at him. The kudu
lurched—the boys said—and we went to pick him up. No kudu.
No blood. No tracks. *Hapana. Hapana tendalla.*

More days. Another big one. Another baobab tree. *Pfhht!* He
went thataway. Nobody shot.

Finally all the time ran out. In the interests of preserving san-
ity, we broke the camp and shoved off for the long trek back to
Nairobi. We stopped some hours away in a little Tanganyika
city to have a drink of the first scotch we had seen for weeks and
to investigate the mysteries of flush toilets and running water.
And also to wait for the lorry which was traveling slowly behind
us.

When the lorry finally showed up, the boys who were clinging
to the top of the load were jabbering like demented monkeys.
The gist was that due to some *shauri-mungu*—everything from a
dose of diarrhea to sand in the soup is an act of God in Tanganyika—three kudu bulls had jumped and stood by the road, staring fixedly at the truck as she labored along behind us. And one
of the bulls, *Bwana,* was *M'kubwa sana,* with at least 120-inch
horns!

That is the day we all got drunk in Iringa. To further celebrate futility, we also burnt out two jeep bearings.

The entire kudu family, greater and lesser, were my sworn
enemies on this safari. We were devoting about one hundred
and fifty rump-sore miles a day to rhino in the vicinity of the

Lake Manyara–Kiteti Swamp area of Tanganyika, and we turned
up three fine lesser kudu bulls unexpectedly over a period of two
weeks-plus. One lovely bull—the lesser kudu is even more beautiful than his horse-high cousin, since he duplicates him in every
respect save size—stuck his snout into a bush in fairly easy range
and I held fire, since all I had was a clear shot at his fanny, and I
don't like shooting blind into bushes. He melted off into a patch
of bush that was easily beatable. It was a thin and scabby sanctu-
ary at best. I went to the correct end, everything from the kudu's
eventual destination to windage figured. He went the other way.
Ran right over one of the beaters.

If you are choosing up the simplest of all African dangerous
game to find and shoot, the rhino is far and away the easiest.
Easiest, that is, for most people but not for Buster. All you do to
kill a rhino in Tanganyika is go to a big alkali lake called Manyara, under the beetling brow of the huge crater of Ngoro-
Ngoro. You get into the hunting car and you drive along the
lake shore. Feeding out from the bush, to snatch a drink and
absorb a little sunshine, are always ten or a dozen *faro*. You put
the mental calipers on the horn, and then you get out of the car
and stalk a thousand yards or so. At about twenty-five or thirty
yards you hold the old double rifle on the sore spot under his
neck, or about eighteen inches up on his shoulder. You pull the
trigger twice. You pose for pictures sitting on his back, while the
boys take the head-skin, and then you push off for more difficult
game. But this does not happen to me. It does not even happen
to my seester.

When the lake is down, it is easy to ride up from your camp
on the little river known aptly as Mto-Wa-Mbu, or Mosquito
Crick. From Mto-Wa-Mbu up to Majimoto is only forty-five
minutes drive, and the place is populous with assorted buffalo
and rhino, mostly rhino. When the lake is up, the drive of eighteen little miles is three solid hours, each way, of toothrattling
anguish, with your liver driven up into your tonsils. The tsetse
flies and mosquitos attack in squadrons. No less than five treacherous streams must be crossed.

Use Enough Gun

Up toward Kiteti, from Mto-Wa-Mbu, it is about thirty miles each way, through lava dust so thick and fine that your lips crack wide open, your hair assumes a Congo curl, and the filth is an inch deep on your face. You cough like the combined consumptives of the world. The Rift valley peters out there around Kiteti, but the hills are high and the thorns are scratchy. Eight-foot grasses threaten your eyesight with flying seeds, and grasshoppers as big as bars of soap hurtle through the air and knock you silly.

Down by the lake, you run out of passable ground for vehicles, and then you walk around the point in stinking ooze and tripping marsh. Rounding the ultimate point, you struggle through sword grass that rips and tears like knives. You flounder through watery ooze up to your waist, and you get back by an ancient elephant trail through reeds so high and thick that the man ahead is lost to sight.

On the first day by the lake we saw eight rhino, and did not shoot because they weren't so much in the horn department. The only shootable *faro* was a member of a trio that Selby came across on the only scouting sally that I neglected to make in two months. I was resting my weary bones with a detective story in the jeep, three miles away.

Then the gods of hunting came and took all the rhino away from Manyara, although we made the six-hour run daily, leaving at five in the dark and returning to camp, wet, mean and miserable, at 8:30 or 9 P.M. We spent the midday in boredom, enlivened only by the tsetses, which drilled through three layers of clothes and a film of insecticide with no appreciable effort. Day after day after dreary, bloody day.

We spotted a vast armored tank of a bull up toward Kiteti, and made the pilgrimage faithfully to his shrine. The gods of hunting took him away too, leaving only tracks as big as ashcan covers. After a week of trying all the tricks in the business we finally gave up on Grandpa. Most rhinos are dumb—Grandpa was the Einstein of his breed.

"From the looks of his sign and his rolling-baths," Selby said, "this old boy has been here many a year. He is a creature of habit. We will learn his habits. Then we will collect him. It is merely a matter of time."

We worked on him, and then went off on the abortive kudu expedition. On the way back to Nairobi we stopped off and gave him another week.

"It is still only a matter of time," Selby said as we broke camp finally, "but I haven't got twenty-five years to devote to learning his habits. Good-by, *m'zee*," he said. *M'zee* means old man, venerable sir. "You should live another hundred years."

We looked at twenty-eight rhinos all told, not counting two half-grown *faro* at Kioma, which were nearly as tame as puppies, and a pregnant cow we ran into on the Serengeti Plains, where you can't shoot anymore. The last bloke we saw was a stupid young buck at Kiteti. His horn was about the size of a banana. We shooed him off and wished him ill. *Hapana faro. . .*

On the safari following, a man who was not interested in rhino literally tripped over a big bull, a big cow, and a big calf as he headed back to camp. The camp was in a place where nobody in his right mind would ever think to hunt rhino. These three had wandered in from somewhere, the Lord only knows where. The bull was a good twenty-one inches, a very decent rhino. The cow was a miracle for those parts. She had a non-freakish 26-inch horn that was thicker and more symmetrical than the bull's. More in sorrow than in excitement, the sport reluctantly shot the cow. He didn't want the whole head-skin. He just wanted to hack off the horn!

This one is almost in keeping with the latest bongo story. A bongo antelope, in case you don't know about him, is so rare and so hard to come by that killing a mature bull without using dogs is regarded as next to impossible. There are maybe only fifty or sixty good bulls in Kenya. They live high in the rain forests, in impenetrable vines at from ten to twelve thousand feet. Hunting them is a horror of constant wet and clammy cold. You stalk them to within twenty-five or thirty feet, taking utmost precaution against their radar noses and sonar ears. Then they crash

Use Enough Gun

away, and you never see what you've courted pneumonia to hunt.

The best bongo of the last two decades was killed in the following manner: A local farmer was sitting in a blind by a salt-lick, waiting for a bushbuck or anything else with meat on it. He was carrying a buckshot-loaded scatter-gun. The bushbuck came down to drink. The farmer blazed away, and missed. Before he reloaded, two bongo cows came to drink. They were followed by a young bull. The young bull was followed by an old bull. The farmer aimed his shotgun at the old boy's neck and dropped him dead with the left-hand barrel.

The yokel crawled out of his ambush. He cut off the head—sacrilege—and threw it in the bush. He cut off a leg, shouldered it and went away. When somebody told him what he had killed, they returned for the head. It wore the next best horns to the all-time record! There are serious bongo hunters who go mad and gnaw tentpoles when they hear the story.

Which is why I said earlier that you learn humility from hunting fruitlessly. I would rather own the kudus I did not shoot, than to own a shotgun-slain bongo or a two-foot rhino that I killed semi-accidentally. None of it is any good unless you work for it, and if the work is hard enough you do not really have to possess the trophy to own it. If that is Pollyanna talk, I'm sorry, but any hunter, any angler, makes his first-chop fetish out of the one that got away.

There was a Russian school of acting which once maintained stoutly that a good tragic actor had to suffer. The same must be true of all hunters, and most fishermen. The free lunch is taste-less on the tongue. The value of a trophy is computed directly in terms of personal investment in its acquisition.

O N E of the things I never clearly understood before was about the Southern Masai of today. The Southern Masai area is out from Nairobi. You must get Game Department permission to enter it. You have to pass through a piece of it on your way to Tanganyika if you are headed for the Serengeti and a town called Loliondo. Its Game Warden is a Major Lynn Temple-Borum, a massive bloke with fierce mustaches who dislikes society hunters, by and large, and loves lions. He likes his lions alive.

Major Temple-Borum knows that license fees which hunters pay for the privilege of shooting things in Kenya provide his salary and allow him to develop the land he loves, which is the vast reservation fanning out from Narok, where the most colorful, least civilized, and haughtiest of the Central Africans—the Masai—rove with their herds of cattle and goats and sheep and donkeys. The Masai is almost definitely not a pure Negroid type, although there is a Bantu strain in him.

He is slim and proud and very haughty. When he throws a spear, his two fingers propel the haft so that the spear spins in flight, whistles like a bullet, and flies truly to a mark at more than one hundred yards. He is a classic killer of lions, which he kills with spears and knives, and he wears a lion's mane as a headdress and carries scars on his body to prove he killed the headdress himself. His buffalo-hide shields are works of art, bearing the proud heraldic emblem of his clan.

The Southern Masai region is cut into two parts—the fly area and the nonfly area. The fly is tsetse, the awl-billed demon that lives in bush and bites like a small tiger shark. This particular brand of tsetse is not a carrier of sleeping sickness to humans but is fatal to cattle. An African axiom has it that wild animals do not flourish close to human habitation; so where you have extensive cattle ranging, the game is likely to be pretty short. Conversely, game flourishes in the bush which breeds the tsetse and in which cattle cannot live very long.

So the African Game Department of Kenya, a rather thoughtful organization, chops its Masai into two parts. In the fly area, one is not permitted to shoot lions or leopards. You may hunt buffalo and common game and elephants if you wish, but the Masai elephants are known for a shortness of temper that is matched only by the shortness of their tusks, and they are not deemed worth the trouble. But some of the best Cape buffaloes in the world live in the fly area of the Southern Masai, and its rolling green plains, just after the wet season, are miracles of scenic beauty and migrating game.

There were only about four shootable lions left in the fly area when it was closed by Temple-Borum and Co. to cat shooting a few years ago. Now the place is loaded with lions, nearly as tame as dogs. They have bred up again, and some prides, such as the Jagatiak pride, will touch better than twenty members. If you wish to photograph lions, you can go to a specific spot and see as many as sixty in a given day. You can approach them to six feet. And they come ripping out of the bush when a gun goes off. Gunfire means dinner to the Masai lions, which will leap into the back of a lorry if the correct bait is displayed. They associate man only with the provision of food.

Outside the fly area you can shoot lions and leopards if you like, and have the license of course. The foothills up from the Loita plains, close to the border of the fly area, always have a fringe population of *simbas*. And if you know about hanging baits in the right trees, you can shoot nearly as many leopards as you'd like along the riversides where the impala and Thomson's gazelles come to drink. If you have the licenses.

So it is that the first-time safari comes out from Narok about twenty-five miles and camps at a likely spot by the river among

the yellow-mottled fever trees—less than a day's drive from Nairobi—and spends a couple of weeks on lions and leopards and
common game in the most beautiful of all the shooting places,
unless the wind's blowing strongly off the Loita plains. Then, if
the hunter is a determined man with a mouth fixed for real
hunting, he moves up from Oldonya Rash to around Talek and
the Mara River, in the fly area, up around Lolorok and Jagatiak,
where the great, big, beautiful buffaloes live, and forgets cats.

We have a camp up there in the hills of the fly area, close to a
place I won't tell you the name of because of just being selfish,
but it's near a mountain and by a brook and on a meadow and is
possibly the place I would like to go to die in and be buried in,
and if I ever came back as a reed-buck or a lion in the other
reincarnation I would like to live there and die there all over
again. This was where, on a second safari, and knowing a little
bit more about what was what, we went for the explicit purpose
of doing nothing but hunt buffaloes. Buffaloes, from the last ex-
periment, had become a mania. It didn't seem possible that a
man could continue to be as frightened of any one thing as I was
frightened of buffaloes—and also I'd been frustrated plenty in-
sofar as shooting a really good one was concerned. I wanted to
bury myself in buffaloes.

Many of you will know that the Cape buffalo is no buffalo at
all, but a true wild ox and first cousin to both the Asian gaur, or
sladang, and the Spanish fighting bull. He'll weigh better than a
ton, and for absolute cold ferocity when hurt—for canny venge-
fulness—there's nothing in my book to equal him. You can kill
him dead with one shot, but if you wound him he'll take all you
can give him and still come on remorselessly. His hide is a
couple of inches thick in spots, and he has a cabled crisscross of
muscles that would repel a rocket. I can sum him up: One I shot
went three hours for three miles shot through the heart.

The thing about buffaloes, however, is not the shooting but
the selective hunting. And one of the great things about the
selective hunting of buffaloes is the chances you can take with
this monster and still live, meanwhile accumulating more

bloodcurdling thrills than Russian roulette ever gave a man. You must hunt buff a lot, and foolishly, before you reach past the basic fright and into the calculated madness in which you handle the buffalo as a good Spanish vaquero handles cattle. I do believe Harry Selby invented a special technique with them, which I now know enough about to talk about.

We had on this trip a photographer and a wife and a guest. We shipped them off from the camp every day to go play with lions and look at the scenery. Selby and I went buffalo hunting. We almost, I might say, enjoyed a chunk of preclimax, as we had had with the elephant and the rhino. Just casing the joint, first afternoon out, with Mama along, we came upon three old bulls, and one of them must have been a 50. A good buff is 45 inches in span of horns. People shoot them at 39 and hang them on the walls. A fantastically good buff is anything over 45. A record buff is 47 or 48. A 50-incher is an opium eater's dream. I believe Andy Holmberg has the record, something around 56, and that could only be called a freak, because the conformation isn't right and it isn't a representative trophy. What I'm saying is that you can spend two months looking at twenty thousand buffaloes and not see anything past 43 inches—and if his boss, the casque of horn that covers his skull, isn't hard horn and a complete helmet he's no good as a type, either.

This old possibly-50 bull was jogtrotting along with two bachelor friends when we jammed the brakes on the power wagon and checked him with the glasses. As he went away you could see the heavy swing of his horns outside the bulging barrel of his belly. It's one way to tell how big they are. A buff's ears'll go about 33 inches from tip to tip; so the horn beyond that is computable. This one was enormous.

"This is a dish of tea," Selby said. "A piece of cake. But over yonder is one bloody great band of wildebeest, and I will tell you right now that if we can stalk that long mile to behind those trees, without spooking those wildebeest, which will in turn spook the buffalo, that you and I will go diamond hunting in Tanganyika and be millionaires by next Christmas. Because we'll have that much luck, chum. I don't like to be a pessimist, but I am betting no gun gets fired today."

Mr. Selby's reputation for acumen did not suffer. We walked and crawled the necessary mile. At precisely the right moment the wildebeest spooked and took off like a herd of insane clowns in a circus fire. The buffaloes, being sensitive types, went over the horizon. We cast disconsolately around to see if we could locate them, and couldn't. They were pointed more or less at Tanganyika. I was glad. The elephant on the first day and the rhino on the second had cured me of trying to say it all in the first paragraph.

So then we started to hunt. Hunting buffaloes means up before dawn and bumping along in the jeep to where you can see a lot of miles. Then you park the jeep on the crag and get out the glasses and start sweeping the miles and miles of bloody Africa, and mostly you will not see herds of buffaloes, although you know the herd should be where you're looking. Then you bump along with the tsetses chewing merrily on your pelt and find another high point and sweep the horizon some more, and then you find the herd. The herd will be exactly seven miles away. Two of those miles you ride, and then Selby will get nervous and say: "Best not take the car any farther. Too much noise. And anyhow there's the river, and we can't get the car across it."

So you walk. You walk four miles, carrying your big double rifle by the barrels, plus a spare gun with scope if the grass is short and you might have to take a long shot if you can't crawl any farther. By crawl I mean crawl. You will find your herd of buff feeding out from a mountainside in a little green glade, looking like cattle in the Swiss mountains when the plane dips low at Zurich, little black bugs on a panel of pale green. There will be a windy-twisty riverbed somewhere along the way, and to cross it you must squirm along old rhino-and-elephant trails, overgrown and full of fresh sign, and hope you don't meet any local citizens while you are crawling through their private tunnels in the thick, lush greenery.

Use Enough Gun

The last mile is always in these overgrown tunnels. Then you come up to the buff, which are scattered around for all the world like happy Holsteins. Some are sleeping. Some are standing. Some are grazing. If the wind changes on you and your scent reaches them, they stampede. If they stampede, they will probably stampede away from your scent. Probably. If the wind changes again, they will stampede back again. In this case it is nice if there is a hill or a tree to hide behind. Or even a bush.

Now the task is simple. Without giving away your presence, you must take the glasses and sweep a herd of anywhere from two hundred to one thousand buffaloes looking for a bull that is worth shooting, in a forest of horns that shifts constantly. To do this you climb trees, perhaps, or wiggle a little closer on your belly, and try to spot the boss man, which very often is off in the hills, maybe shooting craps with some bachelor friends.

Always, then, something happens. The wind changes. Your good friends, three miles away, gun the motor of their jeep or shoot a Tommy for the pot, and off go the buff. The animals just get nervous and take off. Or one of your outriding gunbearers, whom you've sent to scout the flank of the herd, steps on a surly old gentleman rhino and the ensuing noise starts the herd to panic. Then the day's over and you crawl the one mile and walk the fifty—because now the five has become fifty—and I notice that while it is always downhill coming after buffaloes, it is always uphill, going back from buffaloes you haven't got. Also, when you get back to the jeep, the carboy has drunk all the water. There are never any matches, and you have run out of cigarettes. Since we have a rule never to carry any booze in the hunting car, it is a long way home in the cold.

That is a typical day, starting at 5 A.M., ending at camp at 8. There will be elephants in the track on the way back, and you have to wait for them to cross. At least one more rhino will snort, puff, and charge as you creep through the bush. This is also the time when you have tire punctures, or the gas pump quits, or the fanbelt breaks. Or you run over a rock and bust the sump. Anything to delay that return trek to cold water to drink

(265)

and hot water to wash in and cigarettes to smoke and clean clothes to put on and whisky to drink and a fire to sit in front of and food to eat and, finally, a bed to fall into so that you can get up and do the whole damned thing over again next day.

And then there are the special days. One of the special days gave us all the routine with some special trimmings. We did the stalk, and we were sitting behind some low bushes waiting for the buffs to separate themselves so that we could see who was what, when something spooked them. Five hundred buffaloes, weighing two thousand pounds apiece, charged blindly at our little corpse of bushes, in which there was no tree thicker than your finger. And we happened to be sitting in a buffalo trail at the time—a well-used highway to thicker bush.

I must say Mr. Selby is an inventive man. On the spot he conceived the idea of charging the buffaloes right back, as there was very little point in running away from them, and they were boiling merrily along toward our skimpy patch of bush.

"Come on!" squawked Mr. Selby, lurching to his feet. I followed. Chalo, the gunbearer, followed. We charged the herd, whooping and waving our hats. The herd stopped cold, looking in bovine amazement at the visitation of idiots.

"Shoot that one there," Selby said quickly, pointing at the lead bull.

All I had was the little common-game gun, the .30-06. I obeyed the master. I shot the lead bull and his knees buckled. From somewhere out of the blue Chalo arrived with the big ugly double, and as the buff started away I got one of the .470s into his shoulder and stopped him where he was. The other buffaloes went away. I was just about to brag when Selby yelled again.

Another herd, just as large, which we didn't know about, was charging over the brow of a hill behind us. So we stampeded again, and the buff turned back at, I swear, no more than fifty yards. This time we had been on completely open plain.

We went up to the dead buff and took his head-skin and his tongue and his scrotum and feet and marrow, and the boy hacked out a rib section. Then we sweated the huge, heavy head-skin and the other stuff back to the jeep. By now it was 3:30 and we were headed home when Chalo, from the back of the jeep said the word I now hated to hear: *"Mbogo."*

These buffs were on another hill. Harry used the glasses and said, "Hey, Junior, there's one up there looks like a fifty or better. You want to work some more?"

That was the day we toiled up the hill for another two miles and then had to back around two rhinos and walk another mile so as not to disturb them. There wasn't any way, really, to get up to look at the buffaloes, closely; so Harry sent Chalo around to let his scent drift down gently and drive them past us. Chalo fell headlong into the *other* half of the herd, which stampeded mildly away from us and stopped on another mountain. We sent him around behind that one and waited for his scent to drive them down so that we could sort them out and see the big fellow Selby had spotted. Then, I believe, we saw something that Selby had never seen before, and the good Lord knows I've never seen before. Nor want to see again.

With Chalo's scent in their nostrils, the buffs came—not galloping, but moving as steadily as cattle. We were sitting behind a very small stump. Five hundred buffaloes passed within ten yards of us on one side. Five hundred buffaloes passed within ten yards of us on the other side. The big bull turned out to be an abnormally well-developed cow.

They looked at us curiously as they filed past. We were sitting absolutely motionless. They couldn't smell us and we weren't moving, so that we might as well have been an adjunct to the stump. They went a mile past us, and then there was a snort as they picked up our scent, downwind. They turned and charged back to us, fleeing our scent and returning to the safety of our actual persons! They filed past us again, half on one side, half on the other, and fed peacefully over the hill. . . .

Even Selby was stunned. To say what I was is impossible, because I don't know. Nuts, I guess.

A little later on we were looking over the Mara River for possibilities, and Metheke said that awful ugly word again. There they were, a short mile from the track, and the wind right so that they hadn't heard the vehicle. Off we went and into a patch of bush, and Metheke grabbed me by the arm and pulled me down and everybody else sank onto the sward. We were four—Chalo, Metheke, Selby, and me. And we were right in the middle of a herd of buffs. There was a little green glade, and we were in the middle of it. There were buffs on both sides and ahead and behind.There was not one weed higher than six inches to hide behind. So we sat. Like 8-balls on a pool table.

We sat for fifteen of the longest minutes I have ever spent in my life. Flies crawled over my eyeballs and into my nostrils and over my lips and into my ears, and I never batted an eyelash. One of the reasons I never batted an eyelash was that there was an old cow with a very young calf six feet away from me, regarding me with something beyond curiosity. What I can remember was Selby's thumb gently edging over the safety of his .416, and the whites of the eyes of the tickbird that was standing upside down on the old cow's nose, pecking bugs out of her nostrils, which were slightly flared as she looked, at four immovable humans, two white, two black, and wondered what possible menace there might be there for her baby.

After six or seven thousand years she snorted and moved off. So, gently, did the other two hundred characters that surrounded us. The bull came last. He came out of a mud wallow with a rush and almost stepped in our laps as he passed. *He wouldn't go more than 43 or 44, I said to myself, even if I had the strength to raise the gun and miss him.*

That was a day. Another day was the one we sent Chalo around again on the other herd, and they stampeded past a small hill we figured was protection, since maybe the buffaloes were lazy and wouldn't care to run *over* a six-foot nubbin of hill when they could run *around* it. We were sitting hopefully on the top of it, since Mr. Selby's judgment dictated that a stalk of grass wasn't a real deterrent to a stampede. They tore past, and there, finally, was the *good* bull. There was the 50-incher. He was no more than twenty yards away as he went past. He was easy a 50-incher. I could have shot him with a bow and arrow.

Use Enough Gun

"No," said my chaperon. "He's too young. Let him grow up for somebody else."

The reason he was too young was that his boss—the casque over his skull—was soft and widespread at the dividing line in the middle. His enormous horns were not heavy enough and had not yet reached their full down-curve and up-curve; they more or less stuck out straight and angled backward, like a cow's. Off they went, 50-incher and all, kicking up a cloud of dust and leaving a moist smell of cattle behind in the acrid air.

"My oath," Selby murmured reverently, *"what* a bull he will be two years from now if some trigger-happy idiot doesn't murder him before those horns develop and his skullcap hardens."

So we walked the four miles and crawled the one to get back to the car.

Nobody was speaking to anybody in camp by now, as is customary. The *memsaab* was afraid to stay in camp because of the Mau Mau, which weren't there, and afraid to go buffalo hunting with us because she couldn't do the crawling and was afraid to stay in the car because of the elephants.

We hunted buffaloes, and let the unhappy ones get unhappier. Every day was a repetition of the last—walk, crawl, run, stampede, look, nothing.

And then we gave it the old Sunday finish. We quit buffalo hunting. We had one morning left before we were leaving the area on the long, mean drive to Uganda. Mama, two boys, and I in a borrowed power wagon, and John Sutton in John's jeep. We were to look for lions and rendezvous at 11 A.M.

Mama was telling me some marvelous piece of gossip as we rode along in the fine fresh morning, involving a vicious character assault on a best friend, when four or five bulls—lone bulls, buffalo bulls—burst from a patch of bush ahead of us.

Selby didn't say, "That's a good one," or "Lookit the horns on him." He said, "Oh, yessss," in the tones of a Mohammedan who has crawled over broken bottles to get to Mecca and who sees the Kaaba for the first time. There was only one place the buffs could go to get where they were heading, and we both knew it. We beat them there, and I fell out of the car, and the car went far away and killed its motor and I waited for the buffs to come. And I didn't need Mr. Selby to tell me which one was the boss man, because I can see horns, too, and this boy was equipped to protect himself.

The bulls came along and my buff was on my side of the bunch. I hauled up the old .470 and as they passed at full gallop I led the outrider as you would lead a mallard and squeezed off on what I thought was his shoulder. I over-led him.

I broke his neck. In full stride he turned tail-over-tip, two-tons-plus somersaulting in full stride, one of the most amazing sights I shall ever see. I looked stupidly around. Away off, the power wagon was coming up and the boys were yelling and kissing the *memsaab,* and there was hand clapping and screaming going on. I thought of a very brilliant thing to say as the car came up. I had hunted buffalo before, and couldn't believe what I had seen.

"He musta tripped," I said.

"Go finish him," Selby said. "You broke his neck but he isn't dead yet."

I walked up to the buff, which had more horn on his head than any animal needs. I aimed carefully at him. From a range of I should say not more than ten yards. Two-thousand-plus pounds of buffalo, helpless on the ground with a broken neck. I missed him clean. I wouldn't say I was nervous or wrought up or anything like that, would you?

He was as good a buff as I ever want to see. I had, in two safaris, invested nearly three months of hard hunting to see a buff like this. He was 48 1/2 inches on the horns, very massive, and his boss was 18 1/2 inches, which is quite a measurement for the top of the head. This was all the buff I'd ever want, need or look for, and he came at the last hour of the last morning of the last day after three straight weeks of dedicated hunting. "This time," I said, "we finally did it right, hey?"

Use Enough Gun

A DEAD tiger is the biggest thing I have ever seen in my life, and I have shot an elephant. A live tiger is the most exciting thing I have ever seen in my life, and I have shot a lion. A tiger in a hurry is the fastest thing I have ever seen in my life, and I have shot a leopard. A wild tiger is the most frightening thing I have ever seen in my life, and I have shot a Cape buffalo. But for the sport involved, today I would rather shoot quail than shoot another tiger.

I am not discounting the fact that if you wait for a driven tiger on the ground or in a pit, or in a tree at night there is a certain tendency to choke on your heart. Nor do I ignore the trophy value of the tiger, because spread flat on the floor or draped on a wall he will dominate any room. It is just that I would not walk from here to the corner to shoot another tiger. It's too easy.

The longer you hunt the more attention you pay to skill, and the more difficulty involved in the hunting the sweeter the ultimate triumph. A gift-wrapped tiger is just that. A gift. Wrapped. And I don't know any other way to hunt him, practically. It seems a pity, because he is truly royal game.

Recently I shot three tigers in India. Two I collected, and one got away after he was dead, but that is another story. One I shot the hard way, which was easy, if you fancy yourself a wing-shot. The second might have been collected by a young friend of mine named Susie, who is not yet six. The third—well . . .

Anybody can shoot a tiger today in perfect safety if he can afford the price of a round trip to India and about a thousand dollars to pay to a firm called Allwyn Cooper Limited of Nagpur, India. A young Brahman named Vidhya Shukla runs the firm, and he will guarantee you a tiger shown within shooting distance, or he will refund a portion of your money. He has never had to refund any money.

The tigers are there, there in the Madhya Pradesh, or Central Provinces. Shukla rents from the government the shooting blocks where the tigers roam. His *shikaris* (hunters) know their business about tigers. This constitutes small wonder, because if you will pay me a small fee I will guarantee you a tiger, too, provided I can rent a shooting block of about ten square miles in that area. It is simple, too simple, if you want to compare it to finding a really good African buffalo or a prime leopard, and I am not even mentioning African elephant with tusks weighing more than 75 pounds each.

To fully understand tiger shooting, there should be a sort of primer about his habits. One fact is that he must be baited or driven. That is a rule of thumb in tiger hunting. The exceptions are accidental. You might see one sitting by the side of a road, and shoot him. You might stumble across one accidentally, and shoot him. You might find one on your back porch, and shoot him. But to hunt him you have to bait him or beat him.

You will rarely find him in the open, because he hates it, but he will stride a road at night, leaving huge pugmarks in the dust. But when he turns off that track, he heads for country so thick that you can't spoor him unless he's wounded and leaving a blood-trail. He is not a creature of habit; so you can't play on his fondness for a certain spot. He does not associate with his family; so you can't depend on any father-love to anchor him. As a matter of fact, he eats his male cubs unless the tigress hides them. He will kill in one area briefly and then depart for the next range. He is a great rover. Unless he is accidentally a man-eater, due to age, or to an old wound that renders him slow and infirm, he has no food problem. There are all the oxen and tame buffalo he needs in India's thickly populated countryside. He will eat his way happily over a couple of hundred square miles. When he leaves an area, he's long gone. He will generally return to a kill only once, and then he gits up and goes.

Use Enough Gun

You can kill an awful lot of accidental tigers if you just ride around country roads at night or in the early morn. But to hunt one, you come right back to the basics: beat him or bait him. And that way, it's money for jam.

It doesn't make any difference what form the beat-or-bait takes. In beats, you can shoot him from a *machan* (platform in a tree) or from the back of an elephant, or just squatting behind a bush on the ground. On baits, you can ambush him from a pit, as they do in Assam, or you can sit in a tree and wait for him to come to a staked-out buffalo calf, or you can perch over a fresh-killed animal off which he's been shooed, and wait for him to return to finish his dinner. But it's really all the same. Either you hire threescore natives to drive him to you, or you bet on his appetite. In either case all you've got to do is shoot him.

How anybody misses a tiger I cannot say. He is as big as a Shetland pony. Unless you see him under fifty yards, you won't see him at all. Shoot him in the neck or head or shoulder, and he's a dead cat. Cats die real easy if they're shot right, because they are tenderboned and thin-skinned. Only when they are badly shot and non-grievously wounded do they bring the other eight lives into play. If it's an axiom you're seeking, if you have to shoot a tiger more than once, you will spend a power of bullets before you quiet him permanently. This also applies to lions and leopards.

Just for the record, I shot two tigers from *machans*, neither more than seven feet off the ground, by daylight. This *machan* shooting was neither from fear nor caution. A ten-foot tiger leaps about three times his length; so a seven-foot *machan* provides no haven, since tigers have been known to leap into a *machan* and pull the shooter out. It was just that in the case of these two tigers the bush was thick and high and you couldn't see the animal unless you had an elevation from which to shoot.

I waited for, and did not shoot, another tiger sitting flat on the ground on a bare hillside. The tiger came to within fifty yards, roared horribly, turned and whipped back through the beaters. The beaters were drunk and careless. The tiger had been beaten before, and slightly wounded, in some other year.

I got more kick out of that one tiger's close roar than out of the others that I saw and shot.

The third tiger I shot from a high *machan* at night, over a slain buffalo, using a spotlight. There was no danger involved except from walking a mile through a cobra-ridden jungle at night, and walking a mile back through a jungle that now contained a wounded tiger.

A modern tiger shoot today works about like this: Your *shikari* will stake out a few baits—live bullocks or buffalo, bought from a native village. They are staked in areas where tigers, or their footmarks, have been seen, or where they have been heard calling or fighting at night. This information is brought to your head *shikari* by various game scouts from the little villages. They are men who tend flocks or cut wood and live in the forests. They can tell you exactly how many tigers are using the neighborhood, what their sex is, how old they are, what they'll weigh and how long they'll measure from tip to tip. They know all this from the pugmarks.

The tiger will do one of two things: he'll kill the bait and drag it off, or he'll ignore it and go rambling off to clobber a free bullock on his own. If he kills the bait, you beat him. If he makes a natural kill, you drive him off, build a sketchy *machan*, and sit over the kill at night. For some reason or other, he'll come back to a natural kill, whereas he often won't come back to a planted bait, once he's been disturbed.

When the tiger takes a bait, he'll drag it off to a deep thicket or to a rocky den. Since he kills at night, he will eat himself out of shape and then flop down to sleep it off. He will get thirsty in the early midday and go off to drink some water. Then he will come back to finish off the meal. At about 3 P.M. he's through with the carcass and is of a mind to stroll. So you will shoot him before 3 P.M., if you intend to shoot him at all, that day, over that area.

It's very easy to know the tiger's exact location. When he's on the kill, the vultures and carrion-kites and ravens are in the air, slipping, swirling, and cursing. When he leaves the kill, the birds slide swiftly down and dive into what's left of his dinner. This is easy; the tiger always attacks his dinner hind-end-to, going in through the anus and soft abdomen into the guts. If the kill is thickly haired, he shaves the eating area as cleanly as a surgeon's barber prepares an area for an operation. This shaving is done with the front incisors, not the canines. The birds just dive head first into the hole that the tiger has made.

A good *shikari*, such as Khan Sahib Jamshed Butt, the fierce-whiskered Mohammedan who took me in tow, knows his terrain. He knows where the tiger is likely to drag his kill; so he arranges his beat around it. First Khan Sahib has a talk with the *mukia-dom*, or headman, of the nearest village, and all the young bucks, beardless boys, and wizened ancients turn out like a small army. They get a rupee each for the beating job. That's about thirty cents.

The beat is shaped like a horseshoe. The beaters are on the closed end. The "stoppers" are on the two long sides. You sit at the open end. The beaters move in on the tiger's kill. The stoppers, perched in trees, are supposed to keep the tiger within the corridor. The beaters bang drums, whack trees with their axes, and make a sound that is indescribable. It sounds like Ohooooo-OHOOOOOOooooooHO!! and is mingled with hoots, whistles, screeches, and barks. The stoppers remain silent, unless the tiger tries to break through the side lines. Then they clap hands, not loudly, but like a polite audience at a theater. This deters the tiger, or is supposed to, from busting out and heading for the high hill-country.

If all goes well, your tiger will move about two hundred yards ahead of the beaters, stepping lightly and cautiously, moving only a few feet at a time, and stopping to turn his head and case the countryside with his huge, wide, clear yellow eyes. As the beaters draw near, he will move on again, not frightened, merely disturbed. Before you see the tiger you will always hear a small rustle as minor life rushes on ahead of him—a bevy of monkeys, leaping and chattering, a cheetal deer, a barking deer, or a wildcat. The beaters will be practically in your lap before you see your tiger, before you hear his sinuous rustle through the bush.

Now, *Shere*, or *Bagh*, as the old double-striped murderer is called, possesses a common defect of the cat family. He possibly can smell blood, but mostly his sniffing apparatus is about as effective as that of a heavy smoker who also suffers from sinus trouble. Some people say he can't smell at all. He hears magnificently, though, and he has a buzzard's eyesight.

His lack of smell is what brings him directly under your gun —that and the avenue of stoppers. You will have put up your *machan* that morning, a simple task, since it merely means roping a few small logs to the crotch of the tree and making them fast with a leathery liana that grows profusely in the jungle and grips with the strength and tenacity of wet rawhide left in the sun. You will be sitting up on your perch—or squatting on the ground, according to the thickness of the underbrush and the shape of the terrain—and you will be very quiet indeed. You will be very still, because a flicker of motion, a sigh, or a cough is enough to turn the tiger. But you could be a skunk sitting on an asafetida pillow, and a full wind in the tiger's face wouldn't turn him. He will keep coming, and pass within easy gunshot, if only you freeze.

The noise of the beaters comes closer, and then you will hear a polite clap-clap, and then a tippy-toed sound, and then the most awful roar you ever heard in your life if the tiger is going to boil out of the open end of the horn. But if he's just moving, it'll be a little swish-swish and he will suddenly melt onto the scene, as if he were part of the stage-set.

To shoot him, you hope he'll be sideways or quarter on, and not facing you. You shoot a tiger in the chest, and he'll land in your lap, because he jumps the way he's headed. Cats are peculiar that way. A chest shot will kill them, but not then. By no means then. But a slug through the shoulders or on the point of the shoulders will drop them flat. So, of course, will one through the neck, and a he-tiger's 48-inch neck is all the target you need at thirty or forty yards. If he's looking straight at you, the thing to do is point at his nose and get him in the brain. Tigers have a tricky skull structure and a low forehead, and the bullet is apt to glance if you hold too high or a little bit to one side.

For a money bet I will shoot a tiger and kill him with a .22 Hornet if I am high in a tree. For practical purposes a .30-06 is plenty. For my personal purposes, on anything that can kick me, bite me, claw me, or trample me, I use a Westley-Richards .470 double-barreled express rifle. I notice that most pros use too much gun, and what's good enough for pros is good enough for amateurs.

Well, now it's a bright day in the Supkhar Range of the Madhya Pradesh of central India, equidistant from Bombay and Calcutta. The wind is stirring in the sal trees, and the sun is warm, and you have toiled about a half mile through the jungle. Your *mem-sahib* has crawled up in the tree ahead of you and is sitting uncomfortably on the slim logs that form the little nest. The beaters are beating, and the stoppers are in trees. Khan Sahib is sitting with a .375 magnum—which he uses when he is in a tree—at your left.

Both of your feet are asleep, and a fly is crawling in one nostril and another is investigating your lips. A couple of barking-deer does have jumped out of the bushes, scaring you to death, and a huge male peacock, his breast brilliant blue, his tail as long as a log, has squawked and flown right over your head. You are quivering gently inside and sweating at the palms, and if you've checked the safety on the .470 once you've checked it a hundred times. You now know everything there is to know about tigers.

All of a swift sudden you hear a roar that makes a lion's best effort sound like a canary with the croup. You hear the hurried clap-clap of the stoppers, and you are looking for a big tiger— proud, slow, arrogant, cautious—to walk out to you and under you so that you can shoot him in the back of the neck the way Charlie Vorm did the other day, off on his beat down the road.

And what you get is a teal. A blue-winged teal, coming downwind. Except this teal is nine feet eleven inches long, is striped black on a golden hide, has teeth as long as railroad spikes, has a ruff that stands out from his face like a misdirected white halo, has an old wound on his left hind leg, is making jumps of better than twenty feet, and is roaring as if somebody scalded him. I was unprepared for this activity. They told me tigers always come quietly.

Well, a duck hunter is a duck hunter, a quail shot is a quail shot, and, while I don't know much about rifles, a double is a double, and a flying bird is a flying bird. I wing-shot this teal—this tiger—in the middle of a jump that carried him higher than the *machan*. I led him four feet and busted his shoulder, and down he came like a four-motored aircraft and spun on his tail as if it was a Maypole. I walloped him again in the somewhere, and he quit, about eight feet from the tree in which the *machan* was tied. I looked at Mama, and you could have scraped her eyes off with spoons. I tried to light a cigarette and couldn't. My hands were shaking like a maraca player's in a Cuban dance band.

"God Almighty," I said, and I wasn't swearing. In the language of my youth, I never seen nothing like that in my whole put-together. I was accepting congratulations when the tiger let out a roar and started to crawl off, spinebusted but still trying. It took two more .470s in the back of the neck to convert him into a rug.

Khan Sahib is writing his memoirs of forty-five years of jungling, and he has just sent me an excerpt, in his handhewn prose, of this particular tiger:

"It appeared the tiger did not walk; it was moving on air. It appeared as though a cloud was coming rolling in the air and thundering and thundering again and again. When I saw the speed of the tiger, I was convinced Mr. Ruark would be unable to shoot the tiger, especially when he had no experience of shooting a tiger in his life and had not heard the roar of the king of the jungle. . . . I was about to tell Mr. Ruark not to shoot this animal and let it go, because if it was not hurt at a vital part and ran amuck it would cause untold injury and finish off many beaters.

"I was about to tell all this when the tiger came like a bolt from the blue just in front of us and I heard two gunshot sounds and saw the tiger lying on the ground. I became so happy looking at all this, and my joy knew no bounds, because a new man like Mr. Ruark, who had never before seen a tiger, could shoot at it, especially when it was moving like lightning . . ."

Mr. Ruark's joy knew no bounds either. Mr. Ruark had heard about Flying Tigers in the war, but he had never seen one fly past his roost. There's nothing like quail shooting to make a tiger hunter.

This was a pretty good pussy-cat, lying there dead and huge in the yellow, tiger-tawny grasses. He had a nasty old but badly healed wound in the underpart of his leg, but he was an inch off ten feet and in fine condition. He was enough tiger for one day and, all spraddled out, he looked bigger than any horse. The boys sweated him out and dumped him in the trailer. He filled it and hung over the sides. A lion shrinks when he's dead, but a tiger seems to grow larger.

Three days later we beat another tiger off a natural kill on which he was lying. He was huge, 10 feet 1, and beautifully ruffed. He came like they said, stepping quietly, stopping to pose broadside on, no more than twenty yards away. I busted him in the neck, and he never moved out of his tracks. He just slumped and spread and stayed there. He was a much better tiger than the other—older, primer, unscarred by shot and shell, mine or anybody else's. But he sure was anticlimax—a Royal Bengal tiger that never learned to fly.

This is going to be the story of a mistake. I suppose everybody has made a big one, but I reckon nobody ever made a sillier one than the one I made. You might say it is unique in the history of hunting mistakes. There never was a hunter or a fisherman who didn't have one great big silly to hang on his wall, but this silly of mine is the all-time world's record. This is a silly with pearl handles, and a built-in moral. I may as well tell you about it, because it has already made me foolishly famous from Calcutta to Nairobi, and was last seen headed for New York.

If some of the first part of this sounds like bragging, it is meant to, because I was bragging to myself, and that is what caused me to make the mistake. If I hadn't been bragging I wouldn't have made the mistake. Pride goeth *after* a fall.

It was like this:

The Madhya Pradesh of India was beautiful last spring, cool and crisp at night, bright and breezy-warm by day. Mama and I were hunting out of a hill camp near a place called Gondia, a few hours out of Nagpur. We were hunting tigers and wild bison, or gaur, and sambur stags and cheetal deer. We were living very comfortably in a *dâk*-bungalow which the Indian forest service owned, and it was like living in a country club. There was a big, kerosene-fed refrigerator, and two cooks, and a *dhobi* to wash your clothes, and a couple of personal servants to wait on you. There was Swedish beer and Gordon's gin and Coca-Cola and more fancy canned goods than you can buy on Madison Avenue. The food, from curry to corn flakes, was elegant.

The hunting was so easy, it was pathetic. We hunted along good country roads, out of jeeps. There were about a thousand wild aboriginals—Gonds and Baigas—in the immediate neighborhood, so we had more game scouts and beaters and bearers than we needed. The countryside was lovely. They call it *jungal*, but it is about as jungly as Westchester County in the fall, full of evergreen trees and bright scarlet trees and tall green sort-of-poplar trees. The thickest part of this *jungal* wasn't half as tough as the quail country in Carolina.

Down the road a piece, a couple of friends named Jack Roach and Charlie Vorm were shooting out on another block. Jack comes from Houston, Texas, and Charlie is an Indiana man. They are both old hands at tigers and at the large African stuff. Nice neighbors to have around, but not people you would like to make a damned fool out of yourself in front of.

Use Enough Gun

Charlie shot himself a very good old cattle-lifting tiger within three hours after arrival at his block. The tiger came slowly and easily and walked right under Charlie's *machan*, his roost in the tree. Charlie is an old, cool customer, and he let him come on until he was directly underneath, and then he shot him in the back of the neck. He gave him the other barrel, although the tiger didn't need it at all. A couple of days later he shot another tiger, and he was all ready to go home.

Jack was having bad luck. They'd been hunting all spring, in Assam and here, but hadn't shot anything until now. And Jack couldn't seem to see a tiger. But it wasn't troubling him much, because back home in Houston, in his automobile agency, he has a full mount of a snarling ten-foot four-incher that may be the best trophy the Jonas boys ever handled. Apart from a certain impatience on Jack's part, we were a relaxed community. Because this place was loaded with tigers.

Tigers are peculiar. They have an awful lot of house cat in them. They love human habitation. They are at ease and very daring about contact with humans. They will live in country that otherwise would not produce a rabbit, in the way of game, because while they will kill for fun, they do not hunt for fun. They like to kill it easy and eat it close by. And since every little village of Gond or Baiga has its work buffaloes, milch cows, and spans of oxen, for a tiger this is heaven on earth. He doesn't have to run his legs off chasing sambur. He just saunters down the road and clobbers the first tender-looking bullock he comes across. And if he's really feeling in a high, joyous mood, he may kill half a dozen just to watch 'em fall. In my vicinity, one tiger slew seven buffalo in a matter of minutes, and spectators saw him dancing up and down on the carcasses like a leopard in a henhouse. And in the road exactly in front of my *dâk*-bungalow, one single tiger killed five horses apparently just for fun.

There were thirteen tigers, all big males but one, feeding in my block, which was about ten miles square. The Suphkar block has been famous for as long as men have shot tigers, and has been shot over by two hundred years of maharajas and viceroys.

The day I got there, two tigers had killed and were feeding, but both consumed their kills and left the area. My *shikari,* a big, mustachioed Moslem from the Punjabi, name Khan Sahib Jamshed Butt, was blithe.

"My dear," he said, "in one, two days we must shoot a tiger. In a week we must shoot two tiger. In ten days we must shoot three tiger."

For five days we beat, and sat up at night over kills, before I shot my first tiger. Three days later I shot my second. It seemed to me I had the tiger situation solved. The good Lord knows they are easy to beat, if your *shikari* knows his business, and how anybody could ever miss one I don't know, because you shoot them at under fifty yards and they offer as much target as Jersey bull. Tigers? Phooey. Nothing to it.

I started hunting some other things, including a big panther that was as large as a small tigress and was killing the buffaloes we had staked out for their baits. I never saw this panther. He didn't get that old and that big by being stupid. We sat up for him night after night, using his most recent kills as bait, and a little, brave black goat named Babu Sahib to baa and lure the cat, but we never saw a hair of him. He'd just slink down the road a bit and kill another buffalo.

The other hunting was pretty good. We shot some peacocks and jungle fowl and doves. We shot some pigs. I shot two sambur stags, neither one very good in the horns, and I shot them both running and broke both necks. I shot a very good cheetal buck and busted *his* neck, too. I was collecting peacocks at a couple hundred yards with a scoped Hornet, and was feeling very fine about the whole business and pleased with myself.

One day Khan Sahib and I were away the hellangone off trying to shoot a blackbuck and a bear, without any luck, and I got something in my eye and ordered the little expedition back home to the *dâk*-bungalow, where Mama and the beer lived. When we got back, there was Brother Vorm come to call, to tell us about *his* two tigers, and there was also the Game Ranger, in a high state of excitement over a very big, very old rooster tiger that had killed a tame buffalo that morning and had been driven from the kill without having had a chance to feed off it. The Game Ranger had built a *machan* on the scene and was hoping we would come home in time to get to the platform before dusk. He said he was sure the tiger would return. I welcomed Brother Vorm, made myself a sandwich, and we took off. My eye had suddenly quit hurting.

The kill wasn't far away, about a mile in the jeep, with about another mile to walk. The jungle there was very thin, but you had to ford a small river to get to where the tiger had killed the buffalo. The buff was lying in the middle of an open field, and had not been fed on. The cat had broken his neck and there were talon marks on his flanks, but he was untasted. On the far side of the field there was a rising ridge of thicker bush and a spring of water. The tiger was almost certain to be nearby.

The Game Ranger had built his *machan* just at the edge of the field. Khan Sahib and I went through the usual business of crawling up on a shaky ladder, and receiving the guns and blanket and the canteen and the flash-lamp apparatus. It was almost night when we got settled down for the longest wait in the world. The day had cooled and the peafowl were beginning their nightfall cries, which are as harsh as any sound in the world. The male says "Meeoww," like a human imitating a cat badly, and the females answer "Halp!" like an old maid in a melodrama.

I was no newcomer to jungle nights in trees by now. We had sat up five nights waiting for the panther. We had sat up two nights over other tiger kills. We had sat up a very short time in the late afternoon waiting for a bull gaur to come down to water from the top of a mountain he lived on, and on him we had been very lucky. Before I began to fidget I heard the stones being dislodged as he came slowly down the mountainside, and in a very short time I could see his plumed tail switching against the flies, and his dainty, oddly delicate little white-stockinged feet as he picked his way down the hill. I let his mountainous body come good and close and walloped him twice with my .470, just where the neck joins the shoulder. He turned tail over tip, rolled down the trail, and came to a halt, very dead, right at the bottom of the tree in which we were roosting. That had been painless, because it takes luck to shoot this huge wild ox, and we had spent less than half an hour in the process.

But apart from that I was hating nightwork. For one thing I have never liked the idea of night shooting. You can't see the animal clearly and the light distorts him. Unless you kill him dead in his tracks he's off, wounded, and you dare not go after him until dawn, which gives him an entire night to suffer in unless he is very badly hit. And sitting in any sort of night blind is the toughest work in the world.

I am a chain smoker, and you can't smoke. I am a fidgeter, and you dare not fidget. You can't cough, sneeze, clear your throat, scratch, or belch. If you move one limb, the rasping of the trouser cloth is louder than a kid running a stick along a paling fence. Your feet go to sleep and your legs cramp. Ants crawl up the tree and bite you. Mosquitoes chew you.

I believe there is nothing quite like a jungle at night to refresh your memory on what a short distance man has come from ape.

There you sit in a tree, like a monkey, in a night full of fear and awful noise. The ravens just at dusk are ghoulish enough, with their grave robber's chuckle and maniac's laugh. The peacocks are unbelievably loud. The monkeys chatter and grunt and bark.

Just when night comes black around you, there is absolute silence, and then the little noises start. A bird hits a six-note soliloquy like a Swiss bellringer. The last dove up gives a suicidal moan and goes to sleep. Then the crickets start, and a lot of night birds you'll never see or know chime in. Then there are pops and grunts and groans and crashes. Over there a sambur stag bells, a cheetah barks, and is answered by a barking deer. Monkeys scream. A tree falls, and it sounds like a cannon shot. A mile away, on a road, some frightened, probably drunken, Gonds are singing their way home in the dark. Then there are little pitters and patters and slithering sounds in the bush all round you. And in your tree you sit, your nerves sharp-whetted.

You do not know if the tiger will come. He has never come before. You have never shot at a tiger at night, because only the Indians would think of classifying this truly noble beast as vermin, shootable at any hour with any means in any numbers. In Africa they won't even let you go after a wounded leopard with a camp lantern when night falls.

But you know that if this tiger does come he will be the biggest and last tiger you will ever shoot, because his pugmarks place him at least ten foot four, and the record for the area is ten four, back through the memory of the oldest *shikari* in the Gond Village. And you are leaving in a couple of days, anyhow, to look for wild water buffalo.

And you wait. You think about heaven and hell and your liver. You think about the money you owe and the sins you've committed and wonder if cigarettes really *do* cause cancer. Not that you wouldn't swap a mild case of cancer for one pull at a cigarette right this minute. You think about the work you ought to do and haven't done. You reflect that you are treading on the toes of forty years of age, and that your life is about two-thirds finished. You think about where you've left things you want to find but can't remember where you put them. While maintaining absolute immobility, your whole nervous system jumps at each new hoot, each giggle from a far-distant hyena, each rustle and crash. A thin sliver of moon edges up and the night gets colder and the mosquitoes knock off. The wind veers and blows the smell of the dead buffalo right at you. After a day in the sun he smells like hell.

Four or five thousand years pass, and you say to yourself, well, I wonder how much longer we'll give this old so-and-so, and then your stomach rumbles with a horrible noise, and you start thinking about a very cold, very dry martini, and a hot Madrasi curry, and tender slabs of cold, boiled peacock with the mustard mayonnaise, and a big cup of coffee with a double-dip of brandy in it, and the fire roaring and the cold, crisp, clean sheets on the bed. Khan Sahib's belly growls louder than yours, louder than a tiger, and you can see that his innards are thinking, too. They are thinking about four or five pounds of mutton and a mountain of rice, a cup of tea and some sweet, sticky cakes. Your feet are completely numb now. There is a dreadful ache in your back. But now you nod, halfway between sleep and daydream. . . .

You do not know how long you've dozed, but suddenly a hand clamps your neck, pressing gently. It is black dark where the dead buffalo lies, black as night and tree shadow can make it. You strain your eyes to the popping point but you can't see anything. You can hear, though. You can hear the awfulest assortment of noises you ever heard. The old *bagh* has come to the kill while you dozed. And he is very busy getting himself stuck all the way into that kill.

First you hear him shaving the rear end of the dead buffalo, biting off the thick hair as close and clean as a barber would shave it. Then you can hear the gurgling *whoosh* as he hauls out a whole section of entrails. Then you can hear him grunt and hear the ripping of teeth into flesh as he tears off huge, 25-pound hunks of flesh, swallowing them without chewing—gurgling and growling and belching as he gobbles.

This is the hardest part of it, the waiting when the cat has come, the waiting when you want to shoot more than you've ever wanted anything, the waiting while the cat gets so deeply interested in his dinner that he is impervious to all life around him. The waiting takes ten minutes. A ten-year stretch in jail would pass more swiftly. *Munch. Crunch. Rip. Tear. Burp. Growl. Gurgle.*

. . . And now Khan Sahib's fingers gradually relax and leave your neck. The icy-cold steel of the big double rifle slides through your hands, and slowly, very, very slowly, you ease the gun from its leaning position on the limber branch, out and over the branch, out toward the tearing, crunching sounds, and the butt is snug against your shoulder, the steel freezing against your face. An arm slides past your back and all of a sudden the black is white as a powerful hand lamp comes alive across your shoulder, and makes a brilliant pathway through the night to where *Shere Khan, Bagh Sahib,* is taking his dinner.

The tiger looks upward into the light. He has eaten a quarter through the rear end of the buffalo. His great clear yellow eyes reflect the yellow tongue of the torch, and seem to strike splinters from the beam. His face is as big as a bushel basket. His huge ruff, his sideburns and old man's whiskers, his long white beard, are clotted with blood. His mouth, with those three-inch fangs, is a bloody smear, through which the teeth gleam when he snarls. He snarls at the light, as at an enemy come to steal his meal. He looks up the tree to me.

Does anybody ever really remember exactly when he shot or where he shot or how he chose the spot to shoot at or the time to do it? All I know is that I put the bead somewhere on his neck behind the ear and squeezed. The big Westley-Richards, which I trusted so much, roared and possibly kicked, but I never felt it.

The tiger never left his crouch over the dead buffalo. He never moved his head. His chin dropped an inch and came to rest on the buffalo's flank. He did not flex his forearms. He did not kick. He was stone-dead on the body of his victim, his eyes closed in the strong light of the torch.

I raised the gun again to give him the other half, the finisher, the tenderizer.

"No, *sahib,*" Khan Sahib said. "Don't shoot again. He is dead. He is as dead as the last one. The neck shot is deadly. Do not spoil the hide. Nobody ever killed a tiger any more dead."

"Great," said I, and the conceit mounted. Khan Sahib shook me by the hand and beat me on the back and danced up and down so that the *machan* shook under his feet. He said I was about the greatest one-shot *sahib* since the invention of gunpowder. I agreed with him freely. I told him that without doubt he was the greatest *shikari* ever to deserve the patronage of such a miraculous *sahib* as I. I lit a cigarette and gave it to him. Then I lit one for myself, and looked at my tiger lying dead in the light,

snugly pillowed on the bloody rump of the dead buffalo. I took
the little flask of emergency ointment and had a long pull at it. I
toasted the tiger. I toasted Khan Sahib. I toasted me.

Old Three-Tiger Ruark. One-shot Bob. Some people miss
'em. Some people wound 'em. Not The Boy Genius. He shoots
them in the neck. Poor Old Charlie Vorm, back in the *dâk*-
bungalow. Only two tigers, one of them little and one of them
female. Wonderful Magnificent Me. Wait'll I tell the boys
around the Norfolk Bar in Nairobi. You know anybody else
shoots three tigers in a week, and always in the neck?

Khan Sahib was hollering for the natives to come and let us
down out of the tree. It would take them half an hour to get
through the black jungle. I gave Khan another cigarette. I lit
one myself and had another small toast to the tiger.

I thought about that house I was going to build some day, the
man's house where a big Cape buffalo, two lions, two leopards, a
rhino, the 110-pound tusks of an African elephant, a champion
waterbuck, and other bric-a-brac like elands and Grant's gazelles
and impalas and gaurs and cheetals and Spanish stags would
blend very nicely with three hand-shot tigers, and always in the
neck. Why shoot 'em twice when you can kill 'em with one bullet? Old Charlie Vorm'll think I missed, and he'll drop dead
when we dump about ten foot four of tiger on the bungalow's
front porch.

I was on the third cigarette and Khan Sahib had turned off
the torch. I had just run for President and had been elected. You
could hear the natives talking as they came to let us down out of
the tree and admire our tiger. I had just been re-elected to a
second term as President and had won the water-boiling contest
at the Campfire Club when I heard an awful roar.

Khan Sahib Jamshed Butt flicked on the light. He flicked it
on just in time to see my dead tiger's tail disappear into some
high, dusty-yellow grasses, and now all we had on the ground
was a quarter-eaten domestic buffalo. That, the Raven said, and
nothing more.

At least fifteen minutes had elapsed from the shooting until the disappearance, but the tiger had got up and gone away. I knew right then I would never see that tiger again, although all common sense told me that this was a death flurry and he would be dead in the bush fifty yards away and we would take the buffaloes and find him in the morning.

The reason I knew we wouldn't see him was because I was remembering my friend, Harry Selby, who in my book is the best professional hunter in the world. I could hear Harry's English schoolboy voice saying: "When it's big and it's dangerous, shoot it once and shoot it twice and then when you're absolutely certain it's dead, shoot it again. It's the dead ones that get up and kill you."

I remembered all the things we'd shot together—the lions and the elephant and the leopards and the rhino and the buff—always the extra pop for precaution. I then remembered that Khan Sahib, too, had always said the rule of thumb on tigers was to kick in the extra bullet. Hell, the extra bullet doesn't cost much, and you can sew up the extra hole it makes. Forty-five years this man has hunted tigers, and he not only breaks his own rule, but *commands* me to help him break it. "Don't shoot, *sahib,*" he says. "Don't spoil the skin."

Gold old One-Bullet Bob. The new president of the jerk factory. The loser in the flapjack-flipping contest in the Campfire Club. All his Abercrombie and Fitch buttons cut off, and his Merit Badges burnt. And now to face Mama and Charlie Vorm.

We explained to the Gonds and the Game Ranger and crawled down out of the tree and walked a mile through pitch-black jungle which now contained, in addition to cobras, a wounded tiger. I didn't care if I got snake-bit. I would have welcomed a charge from the tiger. Nothing happened, of course. And I must say that Mama and Brother Vorm were quite polite. But I didn't sleep much that night, and when I slept I dreamed about a long line of bullets, dancing and laughing at me like the performing cigarettes in the television shows.

The next day we got up very early and took a herd of buffa-

loes to hunt the wounded tiger. That's how you do it, you know.
You use the tiger's mortal enemy as a bird dog. About twenty-
five buffaloes go milling along in the wake of the tiger's blood
spoor. If he's hurt bad he'll find a hidey-hole and lie up, and the
buff smell him and go mad with fear and anger. Then the tiger
charges the buffalo and you shoot the tiger. This is if you don't
get trampled by the fear-crazed buffaloes, each of which weighs
two-thirds of a ton.

We found the bright slashes of blood on the grass and trailed
him a quarter mile to a long grassy ravine with a mountain on
each side of it, and then he quit bleeding. We looked him high
and looked him low for two days, Khan Sahib nearly delirious
with malaria and remorse, and me just sick at heart. No tiger.
There wasn't ever going to be a tiger, because what I had clearly
done was crease him on the spine. The bullet had gone all the
way through the fleshy neck, touching the spine and knocking
him out briefly, but not hitting bone and inflicting no more
damage than a hatpin. He didn't even bleed after that quarter
mile, because the wound closed tight. We wore out the buffaloes
and ourselves, but that tiger was well again and long gone.

Well, there's the shameful story. I don't remember ever hearing of anybody else who had a prize tiger dead on the ground for
fifteen minutes and lost the tiger, and Khan Sahib said that he
never heard of it before, either. It just goes to show you, that
vanity will murder you, and the most horrible mistake a hunter
can make is to start counting his bullets.

I redeemed myself a little bit next week, in a place called
Raipur, when I shot a stampeding wild water buffalo neatly
through the neck and dropped him stone-dead. I am sorry I
can't furnish any pictures of this particular beast, whose horns
probably measured around ninety inches from tip to tip.

You see, when we were looking for the wounded tiger, the boy
who was carrying the cameras fell into the creek and water-
logged both Rolleiflexes, ruining the lens because he was afraid
to confess his accident and we didn't find out about the dunking
until both cameras were wrecked. The next time, I intend to
spend that other bullet. It comes out cheaper in the end.

Use Enough Gun

WE ARE just up from Tabora, a God-blighted section of Tanganyika which is notable for three things—the viciousness of its tsetse flies, the dreariness of its landscape (wet or dry), and the high incidence of its sables.

A sable here is not a candidate for a lady's coat. It is possibly the handsomest of all the African antelopes.

I suppose the two most cherished trophies in African big-game hunting are sable and kudu—take your pick.

The kudu with his enormous ears and a penchant for living in mountains is warier but both sable and kudu can only be hunted in certain places at certain times of the year—generally when it's hot, miserable, and flyblown or icy-cold and miserable.

The kudu is quite a thing. He is as big as a horse but as dainty as a deer. He is gray-blue-fawn with white stripes barring his hide. His enormous horns twist backward in a double-curl like taffy with two twists. They are the color of walnut meats and finish up in a fine ivory point.

A shootable kudu is about 45 inches in horn-length. My friend Charley Vorm once collected a 59-incher and I swear I saw one once that would have gone 62, which is a mess of horn. The kudu's long deer-like legs make him look bigger than he is but in these parts he'll run 700 pounds on an empty stomach.

These particular animals are a big game hunter's cognac with the coffee. You come out bright-eyed and bushy-tailed for the first time and it is all so new and wonderful. You see a million head of zebra and wildebeeste in one day on the Serengeti plains.

You see sixty lions in a day and you see all the antelopes, birds, monkeys, baboons, elephants, leopards, and rhino and you go a little gun-happy. You shoot your license on the common stuff

(291)

and if you're lucky you get a leopard, leopards being rather cagey about coming to a given tree at a given time.

Then you look around in this zoo-in-aspic and there is no kudu. There is no sable. By this time you are a self-taught naturalist. You dream in Swahili and curse in Wakamba Gond Baiga and Kikuyu. These tongues come in very handy when cursing architects and builders.

So you go to a blackened, fly-ridden, dusty, awful place like Tabora on the Ugalla River and hope for the best. You pitch camp about a hundred miles out of town and climb into the jeep and go a-prowl for sable—magnificent crested vicious-horned sable. You are out twenty minutes from camp when you spy a lone sable bull whose horns seem to be pricking his rump.

You hop out of the car, using anthills and trees for camouflage, and stalk this gorgeous brute until you have an easy shot from a steady rest on a thorn tree at fifty yards using the trustiest .30-'06 ever made and miss him cold.

He ambles away and you stalk up to him again and miss him again. Then he ambles a far piece down the pike and you have another bash at him and hear the bullet hit and he is away.

"*Piga*," the boys say. "*Kufa*." Shot and dead. It cannot be because you held on the same spot the other two *pigas* past. But there he is splitting distance from a record, dead as bones and he will look gorgeous on the wall.

All I could think of was that that was the dumbest damn sable I am ever likely to meet and how he ever survived long enough to grow those fantastic horns is a mystery.

Don't let anybody tell you any different, we made it. I know we made it because here we are and I just saw an old friend, a hyena who borrowed a sawbuck off me seven years ago. But how we made it nobody is ever going to know.

We is me, of course, Professor Frank Bowman, and twelve Africans plus one truck and one jeep. Professor Bowman is a scholarly type hunter who looks like General MacArthur in a

Use Enough Gun

Mexican War hat and he is my chaperon in the absence of the mump-ridden Harry Selby. Frank and I just arrived after a harrowing journey from Singida in the other end of Tanganyika and the exodus of the Israelites was free of trouble by comparison.

We have just devoted six days to a journey which a sane man could make in six hours on a modern road. Between mountains and deserts, rain and dust shoe-casting vehicles and digestive upsets, African temperament and acts of God known as *"shauri a mungu"* in these parts, I have some kinship for Moses and Noah.

We started out blithely enough with the horns of a beautiful kudu bull and similar sable antelope in two new vehicles. The boys went ahead in the truck which made around nine miles before a mild forest fire occurred in its innards.

Two and a half days later, involving 200-mile trips for spare parts and some of the fanciest profanity I ever heard from the grease-smeared professor, we departed.

The rains were now arriving. When the rains come in East Africa, you remain where you is at because the terrain is divided equally between black cotton soil like wet concrete—red gumbo clay and lava dust. Half-an-hour's rain is sufficient to reduce it to an absorbency so potent that it will swallow a five-ton truck as easily as you lose a four-ounce sinker in an ocean.

The truck lumbered along, boiling over only occasionally like an overenthusiastic coffee pot, and then the jeep took sick.

The jeep stuck. The truck stuck. We dodged rain squalls with varying success but forgot to duck on one big one and wound up mired like pigs in a bog.

We could not return whence we came because the rains had swept ahead and made a morass of the roads from Singida to Mwanza to Musoma and one section of road—we learned later —was closed.

We were faced with spending the winter where we were or attempting a straight-up ascent of Ngoro-Ngoro, a tidy little peak of seventy-five hundred feet, all wet clay of malted milk consistency with a sheer drop sufficient to hurt you permanently if you skidded.

The angels got us up and over this one and the truck only caught fire once. This time it was an oil leak on the exhaust.

Going down the other side the rain clouds gathered and we missed freedom by ten minutes. The wet got us on a cotton-soil slope so slippery the laden truck would skid completely around and head back up the hill until another skid reversed her. We off-loaded the boys and pushed her down the mountain.

We pushed the truck down onto the plain and so help me a miracle occurred. The rains marched to a certain point as we raced madly away from them, halted, and stopped. The rains ahead quit and by the time we got to their former position the ground had dried. We crossed the desert on two beers and an orange crush and the truck never boiled once.

We finally came to a river which was the final barrier between us and camp and as if by magic it quit its swelling and started to fall in its foam-flecked banks. We swam the vehicles across, made camp, got unloaded, pitched the tents, and the heavens opened again and drowned East Africa.

We were marooned but we were dry, we had food and we were here against all odds. We also had several cases of nerve tonic. Mr. Bowman and I solemnly shook hands.

"Pass the jug," said the good professor. "Everybody thinks we are drowned anyhow so we might as well have a wake. Who'll we drink to?"

"Noah," I said. "I never really appreciated that kid before."

The rain has stopped, the sun is out and I am once again— first time in seven years—in the one spot I love better than any single place on earth. This is the Grummetti River, where first I came to know Africa.

We made a camp we called *"Bahiti"* or "Lucky" in Swahili.

There is no more beautiful spot in heaven or earth than this Eden-like pocket of Tanganyika, freshly greened by the rains and the animals pouring by millions from the reserves of Ngoro-Ngoro, the Serengeti Park, and from the Masai country in Kenya.

When the big migration is on it's easy to see a million zebra and wildebeeste crossing the plains in a day. Frank Bowman reckons he saw four million in one day.

What's nice about this trip is we aren't trying to shoot anything apart from a little camp meat. We aren't even taking many pictures. It's enough just to look and feel eager to arise at dawn twenty years younger, spend a tiring day soaking up all there is to see and hear, eat two men's massive meals, and know how lovely a gin and tonic or a slap of scotch can be at the end of a fourteen-hour day.

Most of my old boys are with me—Juma, a coffee-colored Mickey Rooney, a cheerful rogue who upbraids me because I've brought nothing worth his stealing. There is my second father, old Ali, the cook who can take a buzzard and turn it into a turkey dinner. Metheke, the gunbearer, who has no front teeth and can blow his nose louder than the report of a five-inch gun. Chalo, another gunbearer and skinner. And half-mad old Katunga, who bays at the moon and is the best skinner in the world. He also invented penicillin quite some time before Sir Arthur Fleming heard about it.

I T I S my considered opinion that 90 percent of India's fast vanishing game is shot at night, on the road, by flashlight, from a moving vehicle. This is not counting the famed tigers the maharajas pen up for visiting firemen, such as Prince Philip, at so much a head, to be shot inside a staked enclosure from the lofty back of an elephant.

The visiting American with his dollars has compounded the felony of total lack of sportsmanship on the part of the Indian hunter. The man pays his money and he wants a tiger. The *shikar* firms will guarantee you a tiger or part of your money back.

It is possible to shoot tigers decently on their own terrain here. I collected three some eight years ago, by light of day, and with the tiger having a fair chance at me. But the intervening years plus the Indian greed for the American dollar, have corrupted the hunting firms.

An incident of the shocking cynicism of the well-advertised, high-powered hunter-safari firm in India, such as Tiger Trails of Betul, just recently happened to me. The headman of Tiger Trails is the most famous *shikari* in all India. His name is Khan Sahib Jamshed Butt.

Butt, with whom I hunted eight years ago, has now forgotten how to hunt by daylight. He shoots from the car by flashlight when possible, and attracts his panthers with tethered dogs.

Butt, in defiance of all the efforts of the Indian tourist operation, the ambitious Air India, and the governmental greed for the tourist dollar, has operated spuriously under a government permission he has not yet received, although he has advertised in American publications as a going concern for two years. He will guarantee a tiger or a panther.

In face of my refusal to be a night riding assassin, which, incidentally, is strictly against the law (but there is no law in Betul) Butt decided that I needed a little diversion. After a day's absence from camp—after having taken my best gun without permission—he arrived in camp at 8 P.M. with the news that a leopard was to be shot within half an hour.

I went along with the gag. At a measured distance from camp, Butt jammed on the brakes. His assistant flashed the lamp and my noble guide said:

"There is leopard, *Sahib;* you are shooting quickly. I am shooting behind you, isn't it?"

I have remarkably good eyes for an old and battered boy, but I could not see any leopard nor could I see any movement for a solid five minutes.

"Why are you not shooting leopard?" said Khan Sahib Jamshed Butt.

Use Enough Gun

"I am not shooting bloody leopard, because I am not being able to see bloody leopard, and I am not shooting what I am not seeing, isn't it?" I am saying.

No gun exploded, and back to camp we went, where *Memsahib* Ruark was saying, "Did you give the warehouse leopard a decent burial?"

Sharp on midnight, there was a sound of a jeep leaving the compound. The assistant *shikari* was off on business of his own. Hugh Allen—formerly a director of this firm before his co-directors beat the bejabbers out of him, thereby dissolving the corporation—relieved the assistant of the keys, and backtracked our trail on his own. He progressed about three miles until he came to a neat pile of rocks and the tire signs of a jeep being abruptly halted.

And what, children, do you think he found?

Neatly propped, chin proudly lifted under another pile of rocks, under a teak tree, was quite a reasonable, very dead male leopard, which had been shot by our gallant but no longer employed chief of *shikar* earlier that evening with, to make the insult worse, my own gun.

Only my refusal to shoot had spoiled the plot.

It was not a very large leopard; that is, it wasn't very large afterwards. But for a long century under a sickly moon in the Indian teak forests it appeared to be an enormous leopard and, by all odds, the noisiest one that I have ever seen in all the years I have been looking at leopards.

Nobody has yet written or will ever write just how much ground a wounded leopard can cover, or be able to describe the spitting, growling, roaring, snarling fury that one small cat can distill when its prime aim is your throat for its fangs, your belly for its ripping hind claws.

The fact that we finally choked it to death on my left arm and some shotgun barrels does not describe heroism or fear in the party of the second part. It's just that there is no place to go to get away from a hate-filled beast who seemed to resemble, under that lemon moon, all of the bad magazine covers that I have ever seen—snarling black lips, fangs looking like railroad spikes, and the talons of its forepaws flung wide in a most unwelcome embrace.

The peculiar thing was that it was a dead leopard that got me. It had been well and truly drilled front and center with a soft-nosed bullet from a .30-'06 rifle, and there was a hole in its back as big as a soup plate where the bullet came out.

It had been flat down and dead for five minutes before it got its second wind and then took three close blasts from a buck-shot-loaded shotgun (later examination showed that the faulty Indian ammunition had barely penetrated the skin) without visibly dampening its enthusiasm for me out of a possible selection of four people.

It arose from the dead and came like a blur of evil while I was trying to untangle a jammed rifle (faulty Indian ammunition again), and all I was able to do was to feed it my left arm as a kind of hush puppy while I fought the bolt on a gun that had never failed me in a dozen years of big-game shooting.

The leopard started at the wrist and worked up to the shoulder—a reasonably unpleasant sensation, particularly when you are on the ground and the cat is trying for your tummy with the ripping hooks on its hind feet.

A rather brave English gentleman named Hugh Allen picked up a decent six-inch gash on his own arm while attempting to beat the cat off me with the butt end of Mama's shotgun and eventually succeeded in replacing my arm with the barrels of said gun down the leopard's gullet. It made a strange sight under the feeble moon, but there was nobody to see it as our gallant Indian gunbearers had fled with the lamps.

Bleeding like the proverbial stuck hog, I was finally able to clear the jam in the rifle and managed to blow the head off the pinioned pussy cat without shooting Allen in the process.

All of this nonsense started with a routine nocturnal hunt for a cattle-killing leopard that the Indians called panther and is generally more feared by the locals than its bigger cousin, the tiger. We had been sitting in a blind over the carcass of a dead buffalo, close by a little Gond aboriginal village, listening to the coughing and grunts of the murderer as he circled, coming closer and closer to the reeking corpse of his buffalo.

From our spot under a big mango tree, we saw him, huge and wraithlike, cross some open ground in the moonlight but he would not come back to reclaim his kill.

The answer was reasonably simple. We had tackled a leopard in love, and love has odd effects on leopards, as is customary with most animals, human or otherwise. We gave up on the lovesick Don Juan, who was making the night reasonably horrid with his tomcat protestations of true devotion, and left the blind about 10 o'clock. The moon, God bless that moon, was riding high in the sky and one could see fairly well, since the jungle was not so thick as usual, due to the recent autumn leaf fall.

It was thus we came upon the object of our boy's affection—a rather handsome, largish lady sitting smack in the middle of the road.

In India leopard are accorded to be vermin because of the fact that they kill thousands of people and literally hundreds of thousands of livestock annually. They may be shot by day or night, poisoned, trapped, or otherwise exterminated with no limit. There are considerably more man-eating leopard about than man-eating tiger, since the Indian leopard seems to fancy human companionship and human flesh as a diet.

It was, therefore, with very little compunction that I unslung my battered old Remington and smacked this local Brigitte Bardot front and center, she thereby becoming an immediate rug. Cautious to the bitter end, I traded the jammed rifle for a shotgun before moving up on what appeared to be a dead cat.

It looked to be still breathing, though, so I gave it both barrels at very close range, which is more than enough medicine for a tiger, let alone a leopard. This is where one of our gallant *shikari* chose to fling a large stone at the dead cat, which aroused it into its first reincarnation as a live leopard. The rest of the action has been described above.

(299)

As a hunter of big-toothed stuff, I have often wondered about the sensation of close work with a wounded, angry animal. There are no sensations, not even of fear. It is all reactions—such as automatically handing the cat your left arm to munch on so that your right hand can be free to unfoul a jammed gun, at the same time trying to protect your throat and groin from what appear to be thousands of flashing claws.

There was enough blood around to float a small rowboat, but you didn't notice it. I didn't really start to hurt until I got back to the *dâk*-bungalow about 18 miles away, although the road was horribly rutty and four makeshift tourniquets don't exactly give you confidence when the arm continues to gush your life fluid.

I must say that in some twenty-four years of matrimony I have handed the *memsahib* some unpleasant shocks, but I imagine my emergence from a jeep at midnight in front of a ghost-ridden *dâk*-bungalow on top of a high hill by a lonely Indian railroad junction, gushing blood and with my shirt ripped off my back, might have been a fresh answer to the usual wifely query, "What did you do today, dear?" Nothing seems very real under these circumstances.

I remember that the eyeballs of a dozen dark natives seemed very white and that I was unduly testy with Mama about her slowness in preparing a large quadruple gin, while people were scurrying around looking for something harsh and antiseptic to scour off the damaged area to see how big the holes were.

The damage was fairly extensive when the muck was cleared away, but there was nothing much to do about it in the middle of the night except pour another gin and wait for morning. Next to the bites of man and monkey, the carrion-eating leopard is supposed to be the most infectious of all the animals. The next morning I was wearing a bright red arm the rough size of a respectable teak log.

The Irish luck worked again, though. We were, fortunately, only thirty miles from a Swedish mission where the headman, thanks be to Martin Luther and his followers, also happened to be a qualified medical doctor with a large supply of a word that has come to be prettier to me than any other in the language—penicillin. The only other comparable word I know for sheer beauty is antitetanus. If it is of any concern to the reader, I lived.

PART SIX

THE
LAST
SAFARI

I DON'T KNOW *any other people except bartend-ers, fishermen, and professional hunters."*

It wasn't true, but the remark has a sort of swashbuckling bravado that goes with big game hunting in the second half of the twentieth century, a touch anachronistic but endearing.

These two last pieces are elegies for two very old animals, a lion and an elephant. The first comes from Ruark's last novel, The Honey Badger, *which was published posthumously in 1965, while the second Ruark did for the* Saturday Evening Post *in 1962, commemorating his last safari in Kenya.*

A L E C had come along for the ride, and it seemed to him he had never enjoyed anything quite so much as the sun-bright days in the high cool meadows—you couldn't rightly call them plains—of yellow grasses and the orchardy-looking scrub forests that held so many millions of animals. The Ikoma area joined Kenya's Masai on the one hand and Tanganyika's Serengeti Plains on the other. It was the natural channel for the migration of zebra and wildebeeste, the huge herds which searched for the tender grass that was always edibly short in the Ikoma area. The cats followed the herds, and Alec came to know several score lions on a friendly, personal basis.

There was no desire to kill, although a certain amount of daily shooting was necessary to feed the camp. Sandy Lang traveled with an entourage of half a dozen game scouts, ex-poachers all, dedicated wardens now they had been bailed by their original captor from the Kingi Georgi Hoteli, or jailhouse. Alec and Sandy shot francolin and guinea fowl for their personal table and an occasional big piece of meat for the boys. But mostly they wandered happily, rebuilding a washed-out bridge, performing public-works repair on damaged drifts that crossed dry streams, always keenly checking the area for poacher camps.

The only notable creature Alec had shot on this trip was a lion. They had followed some hyena hysteria, and a slow circling of vulture, and they came upon the lion in a little shady glade. He was starving, that was clear, as he lay fly-clustered under the dappled-yellow fever trees. His hide hung in folds, and his ribs showed like staves under the fang-scarred, thorn-tattered skin. He was ringed round by the hyenas—hyenas squatting, doglike, tongues lolling, as they waited. Occasionally one of the hyenas ventured closer, and the old male would attempt to drag himself by his forepaws toward the hyena. Sandy Lang dropped his thonged binoculars thumping on his chest.

"Poor old bugger," he said. "That'll be Brutus. I wondered why we hadn't seen him. You know the full story on this little tableau?"

"Appears to me his back's broken, and the *fisi* are just sweating him out, waiting for him to become weak enough to warrant a fast finisher."

"You're dead right. I really should have put two and two together when we saw that handsome young chap licking his wounds the other day. It was evidently a hell of a fight. Younger male kicked the old man out of the pride, and broke Papa's back in the process. But he's still king here, though. Look."

Another hyena had edged closer, and the old lion growled feebly, hunching his shoulders in an ineffectual effort to get at the emboldened scavenger. The hyena retreated.

"*Bundouki,*" Sandy Lang snapped over his shoulder to one of the game scouts. "*Bundouki ya Bwana.*" He turned to Alex. "I imagine from the look of him the old boy's been without food of any sort for a week, and has kept himself barely alive from the dew off the grass. He couldn't have crawled to any water. Would you mind finishing him for me, Alec? He's rather an old friend of mine—sentimental of me, I confess, but I've known him a good fifteen years."

"Of course." Alec took the rifle from the gunbearer. They

walked up to the little glade, and as they approached the hyenas gallumped away, their inherently crippled hindquarters making an obscene parody of the old lion with the broken back. Vultures, perched in the thorn trees and sitting on the ground well back from the hyenas, rose with a creaking of wings.

The old lion swung his great maned head as they approached, and turned his sad yellow eyes toward the men.

Sandy Lang made the lion-coughing sound in his throat. "Poor old Brutus, poor old chap," he said, merging the words with the lion-talk. "Poor old fellow. Good-by, old boy. Take him in the ear, Alec," he said and walked away until he heard the flat crack of the rifle. Then he stopped and turned.

"Well done," he said. "We'll leave him to the hyenas and the birds now. No!" he said to one of the game scouts, who was approaching the dead lion with a knife in his hands. "*Hapana kata ndefu!* Leave his whiskers alone!"

"They'd strip him clean if I'd let them," Sandy Lang said. "They'd have his balls off him—broiled lion testicles make you brave. They'd have his whiskers—lion-beard ground up and taken in tea cures impotence, like powdered rhino horn. If he had any fat on him they'd have that, as well—to sell to the Wahindi—because lion fat cures gonorrhea. Off would come the mane to be sold, and the claws and teeth for jewelry. Leave him!" he said again to the game scout. "I'd rather the hyenas and the birds had him entire than let some bloody Indian *duccawallah* buy his spare parts."

They were walking back to the Land Rover now. Over his shoulder Alec saw the hyenas moving in, the vultures beginning to land with a bump behind the hyenas. Sandy Lang stared straight ahead and spoke, almost to himself.

"I don't know," he said. "I really don't know how to explain it. I'm always tremendously saddened when I have to polish off one of my friends, like the old gentleman back there. That's the chief trouble with this wonderful goddam country. There's no such thing as a decent finish, for animal *or* man. The only wild creatures that profit from death are the hyenas and vultures, and they cop it as well, eventually. The hyena even eats himself, poor chap. Makes you wonder about it all."

"I think we'd better open the chopbox and sprinkle a little gin on your friend's memory," Alec said. "Wakes are customary in most portions of the world."

Sandy Lang grinned again.

"I guess I *was* being a touch heavy," he said. "After all, everybody winds up inside the hyenas. One way or the other we lose the balls and the fangs and the claws. Even the whiskers. I say, this *has* been a doleful day. I suggest we take out the shotguns and relieve our feelings with a few murdered sand grouse at the nearest waterhole. Somehow, the sound of a shotgun tends to cheer one up."

T H I S was a very important trip for me. The elephant underlined it—much, I suspect, as Moby Dick had the heavy psychic significance for Melville's Ahab. It was literally, although I didn't know it at the time, the end of the line. Last safari—in Kenya, anyhow, which to me was second home. Nobody had bothered to inform me that in a very short time a certain amount of emerging-African-nationalist displeasure with my work would write me solidly in the books as what they still call, in nineteenth-century civil service cliché, a "prohibited immigrant," and that I was having my last real look at the land I loved most.

The weather economy of the country was topsy-turvied. It even affected the birds. There had always been birds at Maji Moto in the Masai country. Now there were no birds at Maji Moto. The extensive floods had wrecked their laying cycle, or rotted their feed, or something. And the elephants were acting most peculiarly, too, way up here on the Northern Frontier.

After the long rains I had seen the elephant at Ngornit, and on the plains well outside Illaut, making Japanese hats for themself out of bales of hay. It is quite a staggering sight to watch a herd of a couple of hundred African elephants scything great swatches of high grass with their trunks, and clapping the hay on their heads to fend off the smiting sun, tugging and pulling at the straw bonnets for all the world like women primping in front of a mirror.

Elephant, more than any of the African animals, held a special fascination for me. This was the first time I had seen the haberdashery operation. The explanation finally was simple: Occasionally, after rains, a yellow gourdish sort of fruit, the size of a squash, with blunt spikes, grows on rambling green vines over the high lava-rocked plateaus of the Northern Kenya country. The pulpy gourds contain enough moisture to satisfy both food and thirst. An elephant is a mysterious, but intensely practical beast.

Mostly elephant will come daily out of the dry riverbeds, where the water lurks below the surface of the sand, to forage on the plains, returning to the dôm-palm-shaded *lugas* when the heat of midday becomes unbearable. Contrary to common belief, an elephant's skin is quite sensitive to irritation. A fairly common sight is to see a whole congregation of Jumbos tearing off branches, clasping them in the fist of their trunks, and swishing the leafy limbs over their shoulders and backs to drive off the flies. When the bugs are really very bad, and surface water is available, they will coat themselves completely with mud.

But it is a long walk to water—sometimes elephant will graze an area of as much as a hundred miles out from certain water, since they carry a reserve tank in their oddly constructed stomachs. So these Jumbos were merely saving wear and tear on their feet. The yellow gourds were providing the water; all the elephant had to solve was the sun. They solved the sun by making hats. Simple, when you think of it simply.

I had been fascinated for weeks, sitting on a high blue hill in the Samburu country, with powerful telescopes mounted on tripods, scanning the countryside, and looking for a big bull, with bigger tusks than any I'd ever shot before.

I had heard that elephant only breed at night. That isn't so. We saw several instances of breeding in broad daylight, with the bull mounting the cow in the approved barnyard fashion. I knew that cow elephants had their breasts up front, under the forelegs, instead of aft, like most mammals. We saw the tiny calves nursing, butting at their mothers. We also saw a whole fleet of the big beasts sitting on their backsides, in order to slide down a steep hill.

We saw an elephant kindergarten, which is not too rare; one old dry cow babysitting a whole flock of youngsters of assorted sizes, and whacking them irritably with her trunk when the play got too boisterous. We saw, as well, an elephant christening (this for the first time) in which the proud papa stands astride the new heir, shaking hands trunkwise with all the uncles and aunts and godparents and family friends; accepting congratulations freely, and all but handing out cigars. There is much milling about and trumpeting, and father stands athwart the body of his new baby for the most practical of reasons: he doesn't want Junior to get stomped by old Uncle Henry, who might be a little high on palm toddy.

I knew that elephant talked with each other, using a gentle prodding of trunks for emphasis, and speaking a real conversation with a gurgling noise that is commonly mistaken for a belly-rumble. I knew that they would return, sometimes, to a dead relative, and cover his body with brush, the while screeching the heavens down, and that they would do the same thing when they killed a native. I had seen elephant walking along the bottom of a river, using their uptilted trunks as a periscope. And I had heard about this radar communication business. But I hadn't seen it until now.

For two weeks we sat on hills and watched maybe fifteen hundred elephants, covering a space of perhaps fifty miles from

horizon to horizon. We saw the same beasts again and again—
the one-tusker young bull, the cow with the crooked teeth, the
same biggish bulls of perhaps 85-90 pounds per tusk. They slid
like great black slugs through the tall yellowed grasses. There
was no major exodus or ingress of elephant for those two weeks.

But one day a signal spread from Illaut to Ngornit. How it
spread no man can say, because some elephant were as much as
fifty miles from the others. But spread it did, and we had the
unusual sight of seeing a mass logistical movement that would
have shamed a crack army corps. Companies were formed, and
within the companies, platoons. Sergeants fell out to march beside the squads, dropping back to whack a laggard across the
backside with a trunk, used now like a baton. The columns
merged, fell into route step, with the sergeants—always old cows
—cursing and batting at the irregulars in the ranks, and the
older bulls forming companies of their own, to one side and
usually ahead of the procession.

One day we had fifteen-hundred elephant to watch. The next
day we had nothing but drying pyramids of droppings, deep
footprints, and pushed-over trees to indicate that there had ever
been an elephant in the area. Don't ask me how the signal was
made; Harry Selby doesn't know either. And this *was* the first
time Harry had ever seen elephant making straw hats.

Until recently, no white man had ever hunted this Samburu
country, which lies in northwestern Kenya with Mount Marsabit to the east and Lake Rudolph and Ol Kalau westering ahead.

The hunting blocks of the Samburu had just been opened—
and opened only to foot, horse, and camel safaris. The old ivory
killers had never patronized it; it was too tough a country to
make it worth the foot-slogging pain. Your Karamojo Bells and
similar freebooters pillaged the Lado Enclave or the outer lips
of the Congo. That is soft country there, and easy to get the
ivory out of. This Samburu was sheer murder, a vast wasteland
of dry riverbeds and carelessly strewn mountains, as if God had
gotten tired of packing and thrown away his excess baggage.
This was the land of the migrant graziers, the Samburu. These

were the people whose God sat on Mount Kenya—these were the people who spoke names like Ololokwe and Serarua and Seralippi and who frequently crossed a big brown twisty river named Uaso Nyero. These people know the lean, maneless desert lion and the rangy hungry leopards. These people counted their wealth in the only kind of riches worth having in that country—spotted Boran cattle, high-humped and durable, and tawny camels untold—the only wealth that carries itself.

The Samburu are lovely people—Nilotic, Hamitic in origin, with carved hawk noses and gorgeous bodies. The men are more beautiful than the women, but they would sling a spear clean through you if you accused them of being effeminate just because they hold hands when they walk, paint their faces in thick red ocher, and spend more time on their hair-dos than the average affluent female New Yorker. They are happy people, robust on a diet of blood and milk curdled by woodash and cow urine. They are unemerged. The uplifters would not know where to start with them, because they want nothing they do not own—space which includes blurred blue hills and angry red mountains and wicked flood-slashed riverbeds and the odd "Somali canary," the fawn-colored, striped-spined donkey, to carry their meager pots and the hides with which they roof their little wickiups of mud and cow-dung and wattle ribs.

In years before I had been close to this part of the country—by car around its edges, and over it in planes. But this was the first time that what had been called "National Parks" had been opened to hunting. I'd known that the place was going to be legalized for hunting as part of a scheme to plow back some license money to the local tribes—a scheme to attempt to educate the African in game conservation.

So now I was here, one of the first white men to hunt legally in this area since God made the earth. The impact was shocking: every time I did something even as simple as disappearing behind a bush, it was the first time it had ever been done by an *auslander*. Each thornbush and scrubby tree as much mine as if I were Adam; each elephant, each rhino, my own personal pet. The enormity staggered me.

(314)

Use Enough Gun

So did the horses. I am not afraid of elephant, rhino, or lion, but horses frighten me, and all of a sudden I had to hunt wild elephant on horseback; dodge unsophisticated rhino on horse-back—suddenly I investigated involuntary bravery I did not know I had. An example.

We had moved from a camp on a dry riverbed called Keno, moving the whole safari a-foot, a-horse, and a-camel fifteen miles away to another dry riverbed called Ireri. There were supposed to be elephant, *mingi-mingi sana*, elephant on Ireri. *Mingi sana* means "a lot" in Swahili. It turned out that the unpaid game scouts were right. There were a lot of elephant—the wrong sort.

We rode our steeds and trooped our camels over the baked ground in the smiting heat—with me looking picturesque as all hell in an Arab rag headdress—and made camp on the snow white sand of Ireri. The *luga*—dry riverbed—was very narrow, and the bush alongside it was very sinisterly black and thick. The camels trudged placidly along with their shock absorber ankles squishing up and down, and our noble nags managed almost to keep up with the parade. A dozen of our African safari hands walked, while the two white hunters rode these scraggly ponies. All told, we comprised a tragedy going anywhere to happen.

The first day out of camp we were backtracking the *luga* which we had just invaded the day before. Three gunbearer-trackers were spooring out ahead of us on the blinding white sand, sand cobbled by old elephant sign. It happened as swiftly as this, *snap!* There was a trumpeting screech, and where there had only been horses and men there was now a charging elephant, boiling full ahead from some greenery no more than twenty-five yards from our thoroughfare.

Rather fortunately, the elephant went for the pedestrian natives, who managed to scramble straight up the sheer wall of an escarpment almost as swiftly as we got off the horses and dragged them up the other side of the mountain. By the time the screaming elephant had lost a close view of the three Africans, the other visitors had made it up the hill on foot with the gee-gees reluctantly in tow. One thing I learned about horses on this trip is that a horse isn't worth a damn in an emergency. *You* have to carry *him*.

Once we got our breath, and saw that our stanchly fleeing gunbearers had achieved the sheer steep bastion of the other hill, we were confronted with a fresh problem. The noisy elephant had disappeared in dense bush, and it looked like an elephant who might have a couple of unannounced relatives. On the considered advice of Selby, we decided unanimously that we would *not* proceed along the avenue which we had prospected the day before.

Harry was dead right, as usual. We went all the way up to the top of the frowning scarp and swept the bush with glasses. Before long a double dozen elephant appeared like brown anthills in the redundant verdure. And they were mostly cows, with tiny calves—as close a synonym for suicide as anything I ever met in narrow corners. We spent the best part of the day on that mountain. Game Department restrictions allow only one elephant license for the entire party, in the Samburu Area, and it appeared to all of us that a testy sort named Rodney Elliott, warden for the outflung miles, would take unkindly to the idea of a dozen or more dead elephant slain in self-defense.

We had threshed the area relentlessly for weeks—Keno, Ireri, Ngornit, and now we were fine-combing Illaut. When Illaut was finished we were finished.

Lodosoit remained, but there weren't any elephant there, either, because the camel-train had come through there and had noticed no recent elephant sign. There weren't *any* elephant on the eastern side of the Matthews Range.

So when a streakily daubed Samburu warrior sauntered into camp with news of two enormous bull elephants still at the water at Illaut, we struck the camp at Ngornit and whistled up the camels, who complained noisily and bitterly as usual. The Somali ponies just looked dispirited. We merely looked skeptical. Most native game reports are useless.

But there *was* an elephant in the area of Illaut—not two, not ninety, but one. He was a bull and he was old, very old. His fresh big tracks were corrugated by age, and you could tell by the concentration of his waste that he foraged close by the scanty water in the blinding white sands of the *luga*.

So there was this elephant at Illaut, and Selby and I were drinking coffee in our tentless camp in the middle of the *luga* when Areng, the plum-black Turkana horse-wrangler, marched up to the table pushing a scared ten-year-old Samburu-Rendille girl ahead of him.

"This *ndito*, this maiden, says she was off looking for strayed goats this morning and she was charged by a very big elephant with very big teeth," said our one-eyed horse-wrangling genius, Areng. "It sounds like the bull of the loose talk and of the big footprints."

Selby and I grunted. The longer one lives in Africa, the more one grunts. One grunts or one coos or one changes his voice from bass to falsetto to denote shadings of assent, dissent, or skepticism—enthusiasm, despair, disbelief. We grunted skeptical. But you always run out your hits in Africa.

We jogged the nags to a little hill and climbed up it just as the sun began to paint the stern blue mountains and the sere brown stretch of the scorched wasteland. Selby and Metheke had the glasses, and they began to search the terrain.

Metheke is a Wakamba gunbearer, and I have hunted with him for a dozen years. He is possibly the keenest sportsman I know, and, above all, he respects big elephant with big teeth. They scoured the land with the glasses, and suddenly, both Africans—white Selby, black Metheke—began to coo.

They turned, beaming, twinlike despite the disparity of race and color, merged soulfully in true hunters' delight. They handed me the binoculars, and pointed. Something filled the binoculars, and suddenly I began to coo too.

"Ah-ah-ah-ah-ah-ah-AH-EEEEE!" I crooned, and almost fell off the boulder on which, apelike, I was perched in the crisp breeze of an early Kenya morning. Then we all slid down the hill and kicked the horses into a trot. Cap'n Ahab, crudely adapted to camels and Somali ponies, had finally raised Moby Dick.

The old man was terribly, awfully old. He had lived too long

—much too long. Quite possibly he had seen more than one century switch—the eighteenth change over to the nineteenth, the nineteenth to the twentieth. Nobody will ever know accurately just how long a wild elephant lives. In zoos his life-length is an average man's three-score-and-ten span. Twenty-one to grow up; twenty-one to fight and breed; twenty-one to teach his wisdom to the young bulls; and ten or twenty more to brood and die. In Africa you would have to follow him on his multi-thousand miles of aimless meanderings from Ethiopia to Rhodesia to check him; to watch him grow huge and fight and breed and finally become outcaste, and you would still never know if it were the same elephant if you had a hundred years to follow his plod. From the look of him, our old gentleman was at least a hundred and fifty years old.

For many, many years he had been prison-pent. He had lived on this dry-river *luga* named Illaut. As long as the oldest native around the waterhole could remember, he had lived near Illaut. He came to drink daily at the waterhole a few hundred yards away from the only crap game in town—the one-room Somali general store. He was so far gone in ignobility that he no longer minded drinking with goats and donkeys. He did not even try to murder people any more, because people and goats and sheep were really all he had to associate with.

The old bull was possibly fifty years past his last breeding. He was long exiled from the world of other elephants. Likely one of his own sons had kicked him out. In any case his memory of women and palm toddy was dim and possibly exaggerated. The young bulls no longer came to him for counsel, although his accumulated wisdom was vast. He had long since run through his repertoire of jokes, and no longer found listeners for the chest-rumbling, trunk-probing, nostalgic tales of the good old days before the white man came with guns—the quiet days before the iron birds ripped the heavens apart with rude noise on their way to Ethiopia. Somehow the skies had been bluer in those days, and you could count on the seasons. Now the weather, like everything else, had gone bloody well mad. Three straight years of drought, for instance—and then it rained until it fair washed the country away, the Tana pouring red with eroded earth as it swept Kenya's lifeblood forty miles out into the Indian Ocean.

He was more than a little deaf, of course, and certainly his eyesight was clouded by the years. His great ears, which once clapped like giant hands as he shook them irritably at the little hold-me-close flies, or smacked thunderously against his head in harsh anger as he lofted his trunk and screamed in a charge, now hung in pathetic tatters; now his ears swung limp and shredded and flapped only feebly as he waved them. Over his entire back a green-mossy excrescence had grown. He was as barnacly as an old turtle or an ancient salt-water piling. He was wrinkled excessively, and perhaps he had lost three tons of weight from his original seven. He carried his tusks awkwardly, as if they were too ponderous for his head; too heavy to tote in comfort now that all the counterbalancing weight had left his behind. How he'd reached this great age without breaking one or both tusks in this harsh stone-studded country, with the full thirty years of routine fights, was one of God's mysteries. But there they were, great ivory parentheses stretching low and out and upward from his pendulous nether-lip. Age had made him visually ridiculous; he wore a warrior's heavy weapons on his front end, and no single hair survived in his obscenely naked tail.

There would be curious growths in his belly that old elephant frequently have, like the hair-balls one finds in the stomach of a crocodile or big catfish. Ants would have trammeled the length of his trunk; certainly his feet would be cracked and wincingly hurty on the lava rocks of his self-imposed prison. You could tell that from the ridged tracks of his pad-marks that covered ten miles of country outside the water area. Old gentlemen's feet always hurt, and are apt to make the owner tempery.

He swayed from side to side now and grumbled to himself, as old men will, and the burden of his complaint rode clear on the wind as we walked close—carelessly close—leaving the Somali ponies tethered to a thorn tree. The old bull had been a flashy

traveling man in his time—all the way from the high blue hills
of Ethiopia through Tanganyika and then into the Rhodesias,
traversing the miles and miles of bloody Africa as he followed
the dôm-palms whose red nuts he adored—as he occasionally
ravished a maize field, as he whimsically butted over a railway
train or upended a water tank; or, just for the hell of it, swung
his trunk like a rubbery scythe to wreck a native village. Cows
had touched him tentatively with their trunks, in girlish admi-
ration; he had smelled the blood of a close cousin as he took out
his tusks from a gut-spilling belly. Sycophants had swarmed
around him—young *askaris* eager for the knowledge he had
amply to give; stooges to fetch and carry and, always, to heed his
wit and wisdom.

But now he was very much all alone; chained by necessity to
the creaking rocking chair of the limitations of old age. All the
cows and calves and younger bulls were long gone. They had
tolerated his presence in the area, even though he had become a
bore with his stories of old slave caravans and regiments of spear-
hunters. The country had played out. It had rained again on the
other side of the mountain, and everybody had whistled off, following the fresh green that thrust upward under the rim of the
escarpment. Everybody had gone but the old bull. He was too
feeble to trek with them. His head was heavy and his feet hurt.

Now he stood sadly alone, because he could not leave certain
water for an uncertain excursion for food. And he was starving
himself, because he had eaten the country clear. But he would
not travel the usual two-day, two-hundred-mile grazing distance
of a younger bull. He had grazed his land rock-hard, and his
tracks were imprinted atop each other. His dung abraded on itself in piles, and was scattered by the clichéd passage of his own
feet. He had made tracks enough for two hundred elephant, and
they were all his own.

Soon he would die. Unless the rains came almost immediately
to green his prison yards, he would die, of senile decay and lack
of nourishment—and most of all, of purest boredom. The boredom was the worst of all the ills, and he would be glad to see the
finish of it all.

Use Enough Gun

There he stood now, pathetically magnificent on the slope of a sere brown rise, with the morning sun red behind him. There he stood against a cruel blue hill, his enormous curving tusks a monument to himself and to the Africa that was—the Africa that had changed, was changing, would forevermore change until nothing beloved of it was left.

"Poor old begger," the white hunter Selby said. "Poor, poor old boy."

We had come there to shoot an elephant, in an untouched savage land, a land untrod by tires, unseen by tourists. I did not weep when I shot the old bull twice through the heart and he crumpled to his creaking knees. In retrospect, yes, of course I would weep—but only for a testimonial to another age. When the old bull fell with a mighty crash, much of what I loved best of old Africa died with him.

Now Moby Dick lay stiff-legged in the bright morning sun, his age-blackened tusks looming huge in his oddly small dead face. Quite soon the chief skinner, wizened old Katunga, who is as ancient as a man as the bull was as an elephant, would come with his assistants carefully to hack the great teeth from the sunken old head.

Katunga would croon *"eeeeeeeh"* in ecstatic piping falsetto when he saw them, and would take extra care in drawing them from the skull. For Katunga it may have been his thousandth, perhaps his two thousandth, elephant, for he is older than Philip Percival, to whom he first came as 'prentice when both were boys in Africa, and Philip was nudging hard on the eighties.

At eighty Katunga still ran ahead of a camel caravan, singing: he finished a twenty-mile walk in the smiting sun at a gallop, and jeered at his younger colleagues, men half his age, whose tails were dragging at the end. Katunga is a *man*—I heard him once tell a congregation that he was the best man in camp, and that he could defeat them all with words apart from blows.

Katunga is as much a part of the dead elephant as the vultures which are still sliding, circling slowly, on stiffened wings in the freshly laundered Kenya sky—as much a part as the jackals and hyenas which will contest with the vultures for the rights to the monarch's mortal remains. But there is more to it than Katunga. There is now the business of the reward.

The reward of a hundred shillings is always paid to the local native who first brings news of a big elephant, and this is a very big elephant, well over a hundred pounds per tusk. And the reward in this case goes to a little prepubescent Samburu maid, the *ndito* who was off seeking strayed goats in the early dawn when she stumbled on the big elephant, and reported his presence to the camp.

Her name is Lukumai, the local equivalent of Mary, and her little brown face peeps from a huge mound of beads that covers her neck and shoulders like a cape. She goes bare to the waist, over a kirtle of skin, and her legs and arms are tightly wrapped in coils of copper wire. She is shy; she weeps before she smiles when she poses with me and the dead elephant for Selby's camera.

She has earned the reward—more money than she can comprehend if she understands money at all. But just watch the vultures try to take it from her—watch the sophisticated African jackal at work with his still-unemerging savage sister.

First it is Salah, the snidely handsome camel-wrangler, a good man with camels, but like many Somalis, devious about money.

"Her father is in Marsabit," says Salah. "Her father is my brother. She will only waste the money or lose it. The people in the *ducca* will cheat her. Give me the money and I will give it to my brother when I see him after his return from Marsabit."

Selby and I look at Salah. He is pure Somali—a black Aryan, with a face like Errol Flynn. He is a Mohammedan and the chance of his being related to a Samburu maiden's father is roughly the same as Jackie Kennedy tracing her ancestry through Eskimos. I laugh. I summon my best Swahili.

"You *bloody* liar," say I. "Go maltreat the camels. The camels are your brother. Go have congress with the donkeys. The asses are your wives."

Salah doesn't quit easy.

"Well, perhaps the little girl's father is not my *true* brother,"

Use Enough Gun

says he. "Not *mama moja*—not the same mother. But we are such friends that we are *like* brothers. I will mind the money for the little girl until her father, who is like my brother in my love for him, gets back."

Now Selby laughs.

"Your mother was a hyena and your brother was a jackal," says Selby. "Go away from my sight and talk to your mother and your brother."

Salah dies hard.

"Well," he says, "perhaps the little girl's father is not my close friend, but at least *I*" (heavily accented) "at least *I* told her to go and look for the elephant. It was my fault that she found it. I deserve the reward, for she is only a *manamouki*—a she-thing."

Now I snort.

"Shaitan will wrap you in pigskin through eternity for your lies," say I. For I know that we have sent our Wakamba gun-bearer, Metheke, to investigate some more water before dawn—illegal water—on the off-chance the bull is drinking at that hole, and Metheke saw the little goat-seeking girl at dawn. And it was Areng the *syce* who brought her into camp with the news.

"Just go away," Harry says to the con man. "Go and steal from some other Somalis. Go far away. Go all the way to Moga-dishu, if necessary. Go celebrate uhuru in Mogadishu."

Salah retreats now. Enter Big Brother. He is painted like something out of a New Orleans Saturday night. He wears a red skirt and is ostentatiously moody in his handling of his spear.

"I am the *ndito's* true brother," he said. *"Mama moja,* but different father. *I* will guard her money for her."" He smirks, the family honor accounted for, responsibility established.

Then up speaks a member of our own entourage—a sophis-ticated Wakamba safari hand who flaunts a sharp dinner jacket when he is in Nairobi.

"These are *all* thieves, *Bwana*," he says. "Give the money to *us*, who really deserve it. She is only a girl—why, she hasn't even *been circumcized yet*. Much better that the money come to us."

"The money goes to the girl," say I. "And we take a picture of the money being given to the girl. We send the picture to the *Bwana* D.C. And if the *Bwana* D.C. hears about little dreamie here getting a short count in that *ducca,* we are going to have some Somalis for breakfast. Raw. Dig?"

The sophisticate dug. Big Brother didn't.

"Paper money's no good," he said. "We want it in white shillings." (White shillings are silver.)

A Samburu backside makes a tempting target for a foot. But we were weary of Africans helping other Africans by now. It was beginning to resemble the United Nations. It took less than twenty paces for Big Brother to relieve Little Sister of her loot. Selby shrugged.

"That gives you some idea of the political future," he said sourly. "Let's go swindle that Somali *bint* in the *ducca* out of her scales and weigh the tusks."

There is nothing really so conclusive as shooting a big elephant. I made a swift summary: in ten years I had shot three elephant, for a gross weight of six hundred pounds plus, or an average of better than a hundred pounds per tusk. I know one very fine professional hunter who has never fetched in a hundred-pound elephant in thirty-five years of hard hunt. Karamojo Bell's best was 140, and he killed something over two thousand bulls for an average of around forty pounds per tooth. This chap was 108 one side; 106 on the other. He had looked bigger because of his bodily desiccation, but anything over a hundred is a lot of tooth.

We permitted the boys in camp to rough us up a little, out of jubilation and the scent of a tip at the end of safari.

Eventually we became motorized again, and I must say it came as a shock to have wheels under us. You have just carved a new country for yourself out of raw bush. Your first tracks have become roads. You have built bridges and cut passes through steep *dongas.* You have felled trees and moved rocks and the whole outback has become home. And now you have to say good-by to the green-rimmed dry riverbeds, the purpling hills and the great sweep of rolling plain. You sit for hours in front of the last campfire and wonder if you will ever do it again. We did not regret the elephant; the only way to keep him with us always was to shoot him and we had shot him very well in terms of succinctness.

"I guess we've tied the ribbon on it," I said to Selby. "I guess we've wrapped it up."

"Well," he said slowly. "Komm is only a couple of days hard driving out of our way. The Lichtenstein sand grouse still come in fast at evening. The pintails still arrive on schedule in the morning. It's hard to say how long *that'll* last under the new rules."

"You just bought yourself a boy," I said. "And then what?"

"We never did shoot that biggest buffalo in the Masai," Selby said. "And the Masai is kind of on the way home, too."

"I don't particularly want to shoot him," I said. "I just want to see him in the Masai. I've grown accustomed to the country."

"It has a way of growing on one," Harry Selby said. "It's a pity we don't own it any more, isn't it?"

SAFARI GLOSSARY

asante—thanks
askari—police or soldier, also a young elephant

barafu—ice
baridi—cold
bibi—young female, woman
biltong—jerked or sun-dried thin strips of meat
boma—thorn enclosure or formal title of District Commisioner's compound
bongo—large member of bushbuck family, very wild antelope who lives on highest slopes of Kenya mountains
Boran—wild and very savage nomadic tribe of North Frontier
bundouki—gun
bwana—white master, title of respect

chai—tea
chacula—food
colobus—black-and-white monkey

ducca—any general store, mostly run by East Indians

Engai—God Almighty, as opposed to separate gods

fisi—hyena
faro—rhinoceros

gharri—car

hapa—here

iko—is there, or there is, according to inflexion

jambo—hello
ju—up

'Kamba—member of the Wakamba fighting tribe
kanga—guinea fowl
kanzu—long white robe worn by servants, like old-fashioned nightgown
karibu—water bag
kibiriti—matches
kiboko—hippo; or, more popularly, a lash or switch made of either rhino or hippo hide
kidogo—little
kishoto—left
ktsu—knife
kufa—dead
kuisha—finish, through
kuja—come
ku-lala—to sleep
kulia—right
kwaheri—good-by
kwenda—come on, or let's go

lala—a nap
letti—bring
lini—down
Loita—the broad volcanic plains leading to the High Masai country

manamouki—female, either animal or human
manyatta—Masai village

(330)

marabou—carnivorous stork, which lives off carrion

Masai—fierce fighting tribe of Bantu origin which lives in southern Kenya and Tanganyika

maui—rock, stone

mberi—straight

mbile—two

mbogo—Cape buffalo

mbuzi—goat

memsaab—African corruption of *memsahib*, meaning lady; opposite of *bwana*

Meru—members of Bantu race, quite similar to Kikuyu in appearance, tradition, and agricultural background

mingi sana—very many

m'kubwa—big

moran—Masai warrior

moto—hot

mtoto—baby, animal or human

mundumugu—wise man, witch doctor

Mungu— Swahili word for God

musth—male elephant's breeding period, when elephant is rendered mad by excretion from glands in head

mutu—man

m'zee—old man; term of respect

na—and

Nandi—one of Kenya's best-known warrior tribes

ndege—bird; airplane or people who fly airplanes

ndio—yes

ndofu—elephant

'Ndrobo—wild detribalized hunters who can be of any tribal derivation

Ngai—other spelling for God Almighty

nini—who

nugu—monkey

panga—large bush knife, very much like a South American machete

papaya—yellow-fleshed, black-seeded, tree-grown melon

pese—hurry

pie-dog—any masterless cur in the state of semi-starvation
piga—shoot, hit, or commit
pombe—booze
punda—zebra

Rendille—nomadic pastoral tribe, close cousin to Masai, which roves Northern Frontier of Kenya
risase—bullets

safari—journey, a walking out
Samburu—nomadic pastoral tribe, close cousin to Masai, which roves Northern Frontier of Kenya
sana—much, very
sasa—now
semama—stop
shamba—farm or area of cultivation or group of huts
shauri—business, act
shauri gani—how are things going?
shenzis—wild men, shaggy
simba—lion
Somali—dark Aryan pastoral race of Mohammedan faith which inhabits the Northern Frontier of Kenya up through Somaliland
soupi—soup
sundouki—box or suitcase
suria—obscene word for extreme hurry
Swahili—trade language, baby talk used in Central Africa to communicate between different tribes; also formal name of a coastal race of bastard Arab/Negro derivation.

tasama—look for
Telek—river in the Masai country
tembo—elephant
terai—wide double-brimmed hat
thahu—curse
thingira—Kikuyu bachelor hut into which no wife may intrude
tia—put in
tinni-kata—can opener
toa—take out
Tommy—small golden gazelle about the size of small pointer dog; named after famous explorer, Thomson

Use Enough Gun

Turkana—very savage primitive tribe of hunters who inhabit the Northern Frontier of Kenya

tyari—ready

villi-villi—likewise; as well

wa—common Swahili language prefix to most tribal and proper names in Kenya. It means simply "of", so that the 'Kamba tribe is called Wakamba and a Hindu is called Wahindi. A man's full name would be Karanja wa Kariuki, meaning Karanja (son) of Kariuki (father)

Waikoma—savage relative of Masai, found close by the Serengeti desert in Tanganyika

wattle—long thin tree used extensively for tanbark, hut constrution, and as money crop

weka hi—put it here

Kwenda tasama Tommy na letti hi pese pese bloody nugu. Go and look for the Tommy and bring it here in a hurry, you bloody baboon.

Letti ginni kwa Bwana pese pese. Bring the gin for the master in a hurry.

Toa bundouki m'kubwa kwa Bwana Kidogo pese pese na tia risase. Take out the big gun for the little master in a hurry and put in the bullets.

Kata hi ya tumbo. Slit the stomach here.

Martini a maui mbile. Double martini on the rocks.

Letti soupi leo hapana keshu. Bring the soup today, not tomorrow.

Letti hi hapa majimoto kwa memsaab pese pese. Bring the hot water here for the lady in a hurry.

Letti beer-ikwa bwana. Fetch the beer for the master.

Iko hapa chai. Here is the tea.

ABOUT THE AUTHOR

Robert Chester Ruark was born in Wilmington, North Carolina, in 1915, and spent much of his childhood in Southport, a nearby fishing village, where he was brought up by his grandfather, a retired sea captain. At fifteen he entered the University of North Carolina. Enough of his journalism course there rubbed off to get him a job on a small-town weekly, as editor, reporter, advertising manager and subscription seller at ten dollars a week. Subsequently and briefly, he worked as an accountant for the WPA, as a seaman, an office boy, a copy boy, and a sports writer.

A commissioned officer in World War II, he began writing and selling articles about his wartime experiences to various national magazines, and although wounded, he returned to duty as press censor after he recovered. When the Japanese surrendered, he was hired by Scripps-Howard as a reporter.

His rise was meteoric. Travel and writing filled the postwar years in which he became one of the best-known journalists and syndicated columnists in the nation. His first book, *Grenadine Etching,* appeared in 1947. His intimate knowledge of the African scene, the result of his many trips to that country, inspired two tremendously successful books, *Something of Value* and *Uhuru.* After 1952 Mr. Ruark lived abroad, dividing his time between Africa, Spain, and London. In late June, 1965, he was taken ill and flown to London, where he died on July 1, at the age of forty-nine. His last novel, *The Honey Badger,* was published posthumously in 1965.

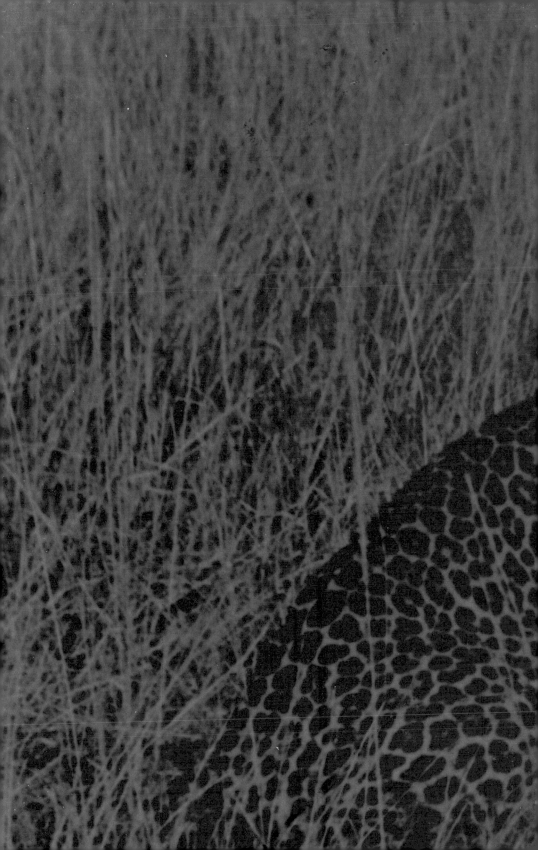